OUT OF ORDER

OUT OF ORDER

Thomas E. Patterson

Fran,
With all best
wishes.
Tom

ALFRED A. KNOPF   NEW YORK
1993

THIS IS A BORZOI BOOK
PUBLISHED BY ALFRED A. KNOPF, INC.

Library of Congress Cataloging-in-Publication Data

Patterson, Thomas E.
Out of order / by Thomas Patterson.—1st ed.
p.   cm.
Includes bibliographical references.
ISBN 0-679-41929-2
1. Presidents—United States—Election. 2. Mass media—Political aspects—United States. I. Title.
JK524.P38   1993
324.973'092—dc20   93-9374
                                                    CIP

Manufactured in the United States of America
First Edition

To Professor Michael J. Robinson,
whose ideas define our questions

CONTENTS

ACKNOWLEDGMENTS

Although I could not possibly have known it at the time, I
started work on this book in 1972, when, with the help of a
grant from the National Science Foundation, I co-directed a
study on television's impact on the presidential selection process. The resulting book, *The Unseeing Eye*, provoked debate in
the press, among political types, and in the academic community. The book reportedly even made it to the Oval Office, but,
judging by the outcome of the 1976 election, a knowledge of its
contents did not help the Ford campaign very much.

This experience led to a book on the 1976 campaign, by
which time I was hooked on the subject of the press and elections. *Out of Order* in some ways represents the concluding statement of this research agenda. It takes a sweeping look at
presidential campaigns to show why a sound electoral system
cannot be organized around the press.

Over the years, I have benefited from the assistance of more
scholars, students, journalists, foundation officers, and political
practitioners than I could possibly list here. I can hope only to
mention those who contributed directly to this book. I will
make an exception, however, in thanking Lloyd Morrisett of
the Markle Foundation. The Foundation did not underwrite
this book, but it was substantially influenced by work supported by an earlier Markle grant. Through its research grants,
conference sponsorship, Commission on Campaign '88, and the
underwriting of a portion of CNN's 1992 election coverage, the
Markle Foundation has made a singular contribution to improving the quality of election news.

This book also owes a substantial debt to the Center for
Media and Public Affairs in Washington, the Freedom Forum
Media Studies Center at Columbia University, the Twentieth
Century Fund in New York City, and the Joan Shorenstein

Barone Center on the Press, Politics and Public Policy at Harvard University. Even a cursory review of the endnotes will reveal a book that could not have been written without the many conference reports and research studies sponsored by these organizations.

My thinking about the press and politics has been influenced by numerous scholars. They include Kathleen Hall Jamieson, Doris Graber, Shanto Iyengar, James David Barber, Russell Neuman, Wolfgang Donsbach, Jay Blumler, Maxwell McCombs, Steven Chaffee, Robert Entman, Larry Bartels, Robert Lichter, and Colin Seymour-Ure. Dog-eared copies of their books and articles on my bookshelves testify to my reliance on their ideas. The writings of the journalist Walter Lippmann have also been a constant source of wisdom.

I owe the greatest debt to Professor Michael Robinson, to whom this book is dedicated. Long before the rest of us, he recognized the key issues in the relationship between the press and presidential candidates. The grace and wit that characterize his writing make it a pleasure to turn time and again to his studies. Those who know Michael Robinson's work will recognize its impact on this book. His contribution to the field has been both substantial and unique.

The book was written in the supportive setting of the Maxwell School at Syracuse University. The Maxwell School's dedication to public service is exemplary, and its congenial atmosphere makes me continually thankful to be on its faculty. My colleague Robert D. McClure got me started on the study of political communication. Professors Jeffrey Stonecash, Linda Fowler, Kristi Andersen, Stuart Thorson, and Arthur LeGacy also share and deepen my interests. John Palmer, Maxwell's dean, encourages scholarship that extends beyond the academy to the real world of politics.

A number of Syracuse University students helped me to put the book together. Joe Montecalvo directed the content analysis; Jessica Sawyer provided regular guidance; Clark Gettinger spent endless hours in library archives; and Patrick Doyle held the project together. No person had a greater impact on the final wording of the manuscript than Lakshmi Srinivasan; her editing skills are unmatched among the many editorial assistants I have had over the years, save perhaps for Robin Toner, who now uses her writing talents toward a purpose higher than the redemption of my labored prose. Also contributing to the book were Brian Gottlieb, Jim Welte, Neal Carter, Robin Fritz, Nataya Nerngchamong, Jude McCartin, Nicole Arslanian, and Mark O'Gorman. Georgette Duncan, Krisan Evenson, and Jacqueline Meyer provided administrative support. Jennifer Barber and Rachel Piorkowski, two Cornell University students, assisted on the project during a productive summer.

Ironically, this book would not have been written had I not deserted the Maxwell School temporarily to assume the position of Visiting Professor in the Lombard Chair at a rival institution, the Kennedy School at Harvard. While at the Joan Shorenstein Barone Center on the Press, Politics and Public Policy, I was able to listen and learn from the seemingly endless flow of visiting journalists, scholars, and politicians. It was somewhere in the middle of a Tuesday brown-bag luncheon talk that the idea for this book took shape. I want to thank Marvin Kalb, Gary Orren, Ellen Hume, Frederick Schauer, and the Barone Center's administrative staff, Edith Holway, Nancy Palmer, Brenda Laribee, and Jennifer Quinlan, for providing a warm welcome and stimulating experience.

Ashbel Green, my editor at Knopf, offered encouragement and sound advice. Ash also selected the book's title, after gently steering me from the one I had proposed. In addition to Ash, Melvin Rosenthal, Peter Andersen, and Jenny McPhee of Knopf all helped with the book and deserve my thanks. A suggestion from Bertrand Lummus, my editor on a previous book for a different publisher, reshaped the book's concluding chapter.

My father and his good friend Dr. H. C. Flynn were an earlier source of guidance. Their love for Minnesota's DFL party, which included hauling me 160 miles each year to the annual Jefferson-Jackson dinner to listen to the likes of Hubert Humphrey and Eugene McCarthy, kindled a youthful interest in politics. Professors Laurel Engberg, J. P. Hendrickson, Frank Sorauf, Charles Backstrom, and William Flanigan turned that interest toward the study of political science.

My newest political mentors are my young children, Alexander and Leigh. I learn fresh lessons from them each day. No scholar or father could be more fortunate.

Thomas E. Patterson
Syracuse, New York
June 1993

OUT OF ORDER

Truth and Falsehood
on the Campaign Trail

Public opinions must be organized for the press if they are
to be sound, not by the press as is the case today.

WALTER LIPPMANN [1]

There was nothing exceptional about the campaign events of
September 25, 1992. Bill Clinton was on the road in Hartford
and Boston, challenging George Bush's leadership on the economy and detailing his own economic plan. Bush gave a radio
interview in the morning before flying to Chicago to speak at a
conference on new technology. Ross Perot was in Texas, meeting with his advisers.

Nor was there anything exceptional about the election coverage of September 25. Election news is normally negative in
tone. So it was this day, as evidenced by this report on the
"CBS Evening News":

VIDEO:	AUDIO:
	Dan Rather: President Bush's economic policies came in for more criticism from
[Dan Rather, face to camera] CAMPAIGN 92	Governor Bill Clinton today. The governor said Mr. Bush is, and I quote, "out of ideas and out of time."

The Bush economic record is Clinton's number-one target. Tonight, CBS News correspondent Eric Engberg matches the Clinton words against the Bush record in a "Campaign 92, Reality Check."

CAMPAIGN 92,
REALITY CHECK

Eric Engberg: The economy is the issue that will win it or lose it for Bill Clinton. And as he dwells on the recession, his exuberance for gloom-and-doom numbers sometimes gets the best of him.

[Clinton in crowd, shaking hands]

Bill Clinton: The President promised us 15 million new jobs. He is over 14 million short.

[Clinton speaking at outdoor rally]

Engberg: True.

Clinton: And get this. This administration, which hates the government, has actually presided over a period when there has been a decline in employment in the private sector.

[Clinton at rally]

JOBS
OMISSION:
PRIVATE SECTOR
MARCH '90
91.7 million
MARCH '91
90 million

Engberg: Yes, but Clinton doesn't mention that it's a decline from the high achieved in March 1990, during the Bush years.

Clinton: And now, for the first time in American history, there are more people going to work in government offices every day than in factories throughout the United States.

[Clinton at rally]

GOVT JOBS
TRUE,
BUT INCLUDES
ALL LOCAL
AND STATE
GOVT WORKERS

Engberg: True, but only if you lump in every cop, meter maid, and bus driver who works for local and state governments, most of them run by Democrats.

[Clinton at rally]

Clinton: A 50-percent increase in the number of people who get up every day and play by the rules, and do their best to raise their children, and they're still living below the poverty line. Eighteen percent of the workforce. Nearly one in five Americans.

POVERTY
DISTORTION:
11% FAMILIES
LIVE IN
POVERTY

Engberg: Here Clinton overstates the case. Census figures show 11 percent of American families live in poverty. Clinton makes it sound twice as bad through statistical chicanery.

[Map of North America]
NO. AMERICAN FREE
TRADE AGREEMENT

On the explosive question of passing a treaty to lower trade barriers with Mexico and Canada, and risk more U.S. job losses, Clinton has sounded all year like he wants it both ways, protectionist and free trade.

[Clinton speaking at outdoor rally]
BATTLE CREEK,
MICHIGAN,
AUGUST 20

Clinton: I don't want to protect anybody who can't compete and win, but I don't want to stand by in the White House and let people who can compete and win get their brains beat out because of unfair practices in other governments, and I won't do it.

Engberg: With unions against the treaty and consumers for, the candidate is in the middle, and stalling.

[Clinton speaking at labor convention]
DETROIT, MICHIGAN,
AUGUST 21

Clinton: I'm reviewing it [the Trade Agreement] carefully, and when I have a definitive opinion, I will say so. It's a very long and complex document; it was negotiated over a long period of time. And I think we have to go through it, and check it all off.

[Engberg on camera]

Engberg: Time out! Clinton has a reputation as a committed policy wonk who soaks up details like a sponge, but on an issue which will likely cost him votes no matter what side he takes, the onetime Rhodes scholar is a conveniently slow learner.[2]

This was not the Republican George Bush calling the Democrat Bill Clinton a huckster. In effect, it was the journalist Eric Engberg doing the labeling.

Engberg's harsh words were typical of 1992 election coverage. A study by the Center for Media and Public Affairs found that Bill Clinton, George Bush, and Ross Perot each received more bad press than good (63 percent, 69 percent, and 54 percent, respectively) on network evening newscasts during the general election. These figures excluded "horse race" judgments; included were references to the candidates' ideas, campaign conduct, personalities, job performance, and the like.[3]

Some of this negative coverage consisted simply in reports of partisan attacks by one side against the other, as when Rather quoted Clinton describing Bush as "out of ideas and out of time." But the remaining content was still more bad news than good. Statements by supposedly nonpartisan sources, including policy experts and voters but mainly reporters themselves, were 60 percent negative.[4]

Statistics can be misleading, but these figures are well founded. There have been several scholarly studies on the tone of election news over the years—including those conducted by Michael Robinson at Georgetown University, C. Richard Hofstetter of San Diego State University,[5] and Marion Just and her colleagues at Harvard's Joan Shorenstein Barone Center[6]— and their findings are consistent: Candidates receive a high level of criticism from the press, and many of them get more bad press than good.

The most revealing of these studies is Robinson's *Over the Wire and on TV*, which examined CBS and UPI coverage of the 1980 election. Robinson and his co-author, Margaret Sheehan, excluded explicit references by journalists to a candidate's chances of winning and focused on whether the other things said about the candidate could be considered favorable or unfavorable. If a news story had three times as much positive as negative information about the principal candidate involved, it was considered "good news." If it had three times as much negative as positive information, it was regarded as "bad news." Events were not labeled good or bad in and of themselves; they were placed in one category or the other depending on whether the conclusions drawn from them were positive or negative for the candidate.[7]

Robinson and Sheehan found that all of the major candidates in 1980—Ronald Reagan, Jimmy Carter, Edward Kennedy, and John Anderson—received more bad coverage than good. Reporters, they concluded, "do seem to want to make the public aware of the frailties and inadequacies of their elected leadership."[8]

In 1984, Robinson extended his analysis to include all three broadcast networks. Once again, bad news dominated the coverage. President Reagan got over five times as much negative as positive news. His running mate, George Bush, received even less favorable coverage. Reporters, as Robinson suggests, seemed to have taken some motherly advice and turned it upside down: "If you don't have anything bad to say about someone, don't say anything at all."[9]

Reporters have a variety of bad-news messages, but none

more prevalent than the suggestion that the candidates cannot be trusted. When candidates speak out on the issues, the press scrutinizes their statements for an ulterior motive. Most bad-press stories criticize candidates for shifting their positions, waffling on tough issues, posturing, or pandering to whichever group they are addressing.[10]

After the 1992 election, I asked several of the nation's top journalists why they portray the candidates as liars. "Because they *are* liars," was the most common response, which was usually followed by an example, such as Bush's 1988 pledge not to raise taxes ("Read my lips") and Clinton's description of his marijuana experience ("I didn't inhale.").[11]

Candidates do lie.[12] But are they hardened, inveterate, cynical liars? Are they habitually prone to lying?

Some campaign falsehoods are not only tolerated but applauded. While on the campaign trail, candidates are expected to say how great it is to be in Dubuque and to praise the people who have come to see them as the best crowd yet. They are supposed to call their host a great American and one of the country's finest public servants. Such lies are part of the hoopla of politics and help enliven it.

Some of the candidates' lies are more rhetorical than real. In the heat of the campaign, candidates can seemingly convince themselves that wild charges about their opponents are true. When George Bush called Democratic vice-presidential nominee Al Gore "the Ozone Man" and said his environmental positions were "crazy, way out, far out, man," he may have been trying to win votes, but it is also likely that he truly believed Gore's views to be "way out," and perhaps they were from Bush's own policy stance—a reluctance to pursue environmental goals that are incompatible with economic growth. Bush's comment, then, was more silly than cynical; it did more to tarnish his credibility than his opponent's.

Candidates at times stretch their will to believe so far that it goes beyond any reasonable standard of truth. Clinton was the best-funded of the Democratic contenders for nomination in 1992, and he used this advantage to buy Super Tuesday ads that attacked Paul Tsongas's modest proposals to control spending on federal entitlement programs. Clinton's ads were an attempt to scare retirees into believing that Tsongas planned to cut their Social Security benefits. Tsongas did not have sufficient funds to counter the exaggerated claims with ads of his own.

The night of the 1988 New Hampshire primary, a defeated Bob Dole was asked on national television whether he had a message for Vice President Bush. "Tell him to stop lying about my record," Dole blurted. Michael Dukakis said much the same thing about Bush during the general election. Bush inflated pieces of his opponents' records and turned them into broad allegations. Dole was tax-happy; Dukakis lacked patriotism and was soft on crime. But if Bush misrepresented their policies, Dole and Dukakis let him get away with it by not defending themselves adequately. Kirk O'Donnell, a Dukakis adviser, later said, "We had the opportunity to change the dialogue. We can take responsibility [for not doing it] on our shoulders."[13] Partisan skirmishing is nothing new. Thomas Jefferson's opponents in 1800 tried to scare electors into believing that he would sell the country into France's hands if elected. Abraham Lincoln was called a "Liar, Thief and Baboon" by *Harper's Weekly*, and the Albany *Argus* described him as "the ugliest man in the Union"—a statement he used in his defense against charges that he was "two-faced": "I leave it to my audience," Lincoln said. "If I had another face, do you think I'd use this one?"[14]

Other campaign lies involve hiding painful truths that voters do not want to hear. Talk of an across-the-board tax increase was suicidal for a candidate until Ross Perot came along. With his own money on the line, he convinced some Americans that they would have to accept a hefty tax increase if they were serious about getting the federal deficit under control. Walter Mondale hurt his campaign when he said in accepting the 1984

Democratic nomination, "Let's tell the truth. Mr. Reagan will raise taxes, and so will I. He won't tell you. I just did."[15]

There are some lies that candidates tell because the truth would destroy their career. These are falsehoods about the skeletons in their closets. When Gennifer Flowers made her charges, Bill Clinton could just as well have packed up and retired to Little Rock if he had told all. He said, "Her story is just not true," and during his appearance on "60 Minutes" he asked for understanding: "I think most Americans who are watching this tonight, they'll know what we're saying, they'll get it, and they'll feel that we have been more than candid. And I think what the press has to decide is, are we going to engage in a game of 'gotcha'?"[16]

In such instances, a relevant question is the balance between the harmful effect of the lie on public morality and the damaging impact of the truth on the candidate and the interests he represents. Not everyone will agree as to how a candidate should act in these instances, but most people would concede that the nature of what is being concealed should weigh heavily in determining the public's response (a serious violation of the public trust would be a graver issue than a private indiscretion, such as marijuana use in one's youth).

All of the above forms of lying do not seriously harm the democratic process, except in severe cases. At no point in life is the truth always prized; nor is the truth always knowable. To expect candidates to bare their souls voluntarily or to say things that people do not want to hear or to rise above emotional subjectivity is to ask them to behave in a way in which no one behaves.

There is one type of campaign lie, however, that has no place in a democratic election. In terms of motive and context, this form of lying destroys the bond of trust between candidates and voters. It consists in making a promise to take a given course of action, to pursue a particular policy or program, that the candidate has no intention of keeping, and which is made not only to deceive the voters but to trick them into acting in a manner—voting for the candidate—that is contrary to their interests.[17] Voters act on the promise and then get something else which they did not want. Such lies, if commonplace, turn free and fair elections into a sham.[18]

The press makes such lies appear to be the norm. Candidates are said to change their positions as they campaign in different regions or talk with different groups, make promises they plan to break, make commitments that cannot be honored even if they try. Cynical manipulation is the story that is told of candidates' efforts to woo the voters. "The journalists' instinct," the sociologist Michael Schudson writes, "is that there is always a story *behind* the story, and that it is 'behind' because someone is hiding it."[19]

Do candidates routinely lie when they make promises about the policies they will pursue? The importance of this question to the integrity of the democratic process has prompted scholars to investigate it. This research has involved extensive analysis, in which winning candidates' campaign promises were systematically catalogued and compared to what they did as presidents. At least four such studies have been conducted, each spanning a minimum of seven presidencies. Each of these studies reached the same conclusion: *Presidents keep the promises they made as candidates.*

The political scientist Gerald Pomper's exhaustive study of party platforms in nine presidential elections found that victorious candidates, once in office, attempt to fulfill nearly all of their policy commitments and succeed in achieving most of them.[20] When they fail to deliver on a promise, it is usually because they cannot get Congress to agree; because the pledge conflicts with a higher-priority commitment; or because conditions have changed (as in the case of Reagan in 1980, who promised to settle the Iranian hostage crisis, which was resolved by the time he took office).

Another political scientist, Michael Krukones, reached the

same conclusion after comparing the campaign speeches and in-office performances of eleven recent presidents.[21] In yet a third study, Ian Budge and Richard I. Hofferbert found "strong links between postwar (1948–1985) election platforms and governmental outputs."[22] A fourth study, conducted by American University's Jeff Fishel, concluded that presidents in the period 1960–1984 signed executive orders or submitted legislative proposals corresponding to a large majority of their campaign pledges; in the case of legislative proposals, Congress enacted most of them (Johnson's 89 percent was the high; Nixon's 61 percent was the low).[23]

These studies are less conclusive than they might appear. Candidates focus on consensual issues, sidestep some controversial issues, and frame many of their positions in general or ambiguous terms.[24] The studies also do not distinguish the candidates' promises in terms of their scope or impact. These considerations do not, however, invalidate the general conclusion that presidential candidates make important promises and act on them when elected. Candidates are not empty vessels who have no ideas about policy and no plans about what to do with political power. The record of campaign pledges largely reveals a trail of promises kept.

Why would it be otherwise? It is not logical to run for the presidency and ask afterward what the job entails. Candidates for the presidency want to govern, and to do so they need the support of the interests they have committed themselves to during the campaign.

Even a cursory review of recent presidencies refutes the press's claim that campaign commitments are empty promises. Ronald Reagan the president did what Ronald Reagan the candidate promised in 1980: he cut taxes, increased defense spending, opposed abortion, reduced government regulation of business, and slowed the escalation of domestic policy spending. There was one major promise that Reagan failed to keep: the balancing of the budget. He made an effort to do so in his first term but misjudged the severity of the recession that had begun under Carter, and he erred in his belief that the revenue generated by the economic stimulus of a steep tax cut would offset the revenue loss directly attributable to the cut.

Jimmy Carter was accused by the press in 1976 of "waffling on the issues" and, ironically, was ridiculed by the press when, as president, he compiled his nearly two hundred campaign promises in a book and proceeded methodically to keep them.

Though George Bush is remembered best for a promise he broke, he did pursue the lean, business-centered economic policies, including global free trade measures, that he advocated in his 1988 campaign. On social issues he stayed true to his pro-life position on abortion and his commitment to a tougher criminal code. And during a presidency that labored under severe budgetary restraints, he persuaded Congress to appropriate significant new funding for two programs he emphasized in his 1988 campaign: HeadStart and the war on drugs. These were two of the three components of Bush's education policy (Head-Start assisted preschool children from disadvantaged backgrounds and the larger war on drugs contributed to drug-free schools); the third was freedom of choice for parents in the selection of the school their children would attend, which was also promoted by Bush while in office.

Perhaps George Bush even intended to keep his 1988 pledge of "no new taxes." He held out for two years against pressure from Congress, conceding when it became necessary to avert a budget crisis, and then only after forcing congressional Democrats to accept a deal that included a lid on discretionary domestic spending. At the time, the move was lauded by many in the press. "The President," said the Washington *Post* in an editorial, "did the right thing."[25]

In 1992 the votes were barely counted when Bill Clinton instructed his transition team to begin the process of implementing his campaign promises. Some commitments did fall by the wayside, including his pledge to open the nation's shores to the Haitian boat people and his promise to raise fees on the ranching and mining interests that lease federal lands. But

Clinton kept, or took initial steps to carry out, a significant number of his promises: humanitarian relief to Bosnia, a tax increase on upper-income taxpayers, an end to the ban on abortion counseling in family-planning clinics that receive federal funds, deep and broad-based spending cuts, health-care reform, a family-leave program, banking reform, an economic stimulus package, tougher ethical standards for presidential appointees, tax incentives for small firms, economic assistance for Russia, a college-loan program, a job training program, among many others.

Press accounts of Clinton's early months in office made it appear otherwise. The news focused on the promises he broke and, more so, on the instances where he was forced to negotiate with Congress. Each compromise was reported as a headlong retreat from principle. This perspective is unfair and inappropriate. American presidents are not like European prime ministers, who operate with a ready-made legislative majority. The president and Congress are separately elected, and share legislative power. For a president to adhere rigidly to his position is to invite deadlock and risk failure. Moreover, compromise in a system of checks and balances is not perfidy; it is a founding principle of American democracy. James Madison in *The Federalist*, no. 48, described this process of accommodation as the proper alternative to the "tyrannical concentration of all the powers of government in the same hands." There is nothing in either the practice or theory of American government that suggests presidents can or should unilaterally dictate policy.

The press sends the wrong message. Its claim that candidates make promises in order to win votes is true, but that is only part of the truth. They make them, *and* work to keep them. What journalists fail to take into account is the constraints affecting these commitments.

Candidates are not free to make any promise they might wish to make, and they must declare commitments they might wish to avoid. They are constrained by the interests that support their party and whose support they need. The Democrat Clinton offered promises to lower-income taxpayers, educators, the unemployed, minorities, gays, labor, and other groups that are aligned with the Democratic coalition. For his part, Bush made commitments to business, high-income taxpayers, religious fundamentalists, and others more closely aligned with the GOP. The assertion that presidential candidates are only reeds in the wind ignores their natural leaning toward constituent groups, and therefore toward certain courses of action.

Another basic truth about the candidates' pledges is that they have a stronger incentive to keep them than to break them. Interests that receive promises during the campaign have ties to Congress and to bureaucratic agencies that can cause trouble for a president who fails to honor his commitments.[26] There is no following that is loyal despite broken promises. Bush paid dearly even within his own party for breaking his 1988 promise of "no new taxes."

Finally, candidates have personal philosophies and causes that guide their choices. Political leaders have policy goals in which they believe and which constrain what they are willing to say.[27] The economic program that Bill Clinton began working to implement the day after his election was the same one that he had described in his first major campaign speech on the subject, which he had delivered late in 1991 at his alma mater, Georgetown University. His speech contained the economic proposals that were later expressed in his acceptance speech at the Democratic convention in July 1992, and he explained those same ideas in the televised presidential debates during the general election. The policies were built on Clinton's experience as Arkansas governor, his association with policy experts such as Robert Reich, and his own sense of how to deal with the nation's problems. When Clinton was challenged by a reporter during the general election about one of his economic commitments, he replied: "It is not a promise I cooked up for the election. It is the work of a lifetime."[28]

*   *   *

Journalists are the problem here. They, and not the candidate, are reeds in the wind. The candidates' speeches are filled with pledges of what they will do if elected. Since the outcome of these promises is in the future, journalists are free to say nearly anything they want. How can anyone disprove the journalist's claim that a candidate has no intention of keeping his promises?

The Engberg news story cited at the beginning of this chapter is a case study in the journalistic half-truths that pass for incisive analysis. If Clinton the candidate was circumspect in his support for the North American Free Trade Agreement, so is Clinton the president. In a meeting with Mexican president Salinas, Clinton said, "I reaffirm my support for the North American Free Trade Agreement. And I restate my belief that some trade issues between our nations still need to be addressed."[29]

When Clinton described the trade agreement as "a very long and complex document," he was simply telling the truth. NAFTA is 1,078 pages in length,[30] and the product of a fourteen-month negotiation between the Bush administration and the Mexican and Canadian governments. It is filled with contingencies, exceptions, and technical details. There is probably not a single policy expert in Washington who understands all aspects of NAFTA. To suggest, as Engberg did, that the "policy wonk" Clinton should know every part of it and flatly accept or reject it in its entirety is disingenuous. Worse than that, it is fatuous. It assumes that having a fixed opinion on every aspect of every issue that comes along displays true leadership, and that any hesitation or objection on a candidate's part is a practiced deception. For example, Clinton took exception (as did many Democrats in Congress) to the fact that the agreement did not cover the issues of environmental protection and job retraining for U.S. workers when their firm relocates to Mexico.

Engberg's report was not the dispassionate analysis of a neutral observer. Like countless other news stories of recent campaigns, it betrayed a deeply cynical view of politics and politicians: "Yes, but Clinton doesn't mention . . ."; "True, but only if . . ."; "Clinton has sounded all year like he wants it both ways"; "The candidate is in the middle, and stalling"; "The onetime Rhodes scholar is a conveniently slow learner."

Nor did Engberg hold himself to the same standards that he imposed on Clinton. When Clinton was quoted as saying the poverty rate was 18 percent, and Engberg countered with the Census Bureau's figure of 11 percent, Engberg proceeded to claim that Clinton was trying to make the poverty level "sound twice as bad through statistical chicanery." Whereas 18 percent is more than 11 percent, it is most definitely not "twice" more. And it was not statistical chicanery that led Clinton to the 18-percent figure. As Engberg should know, Democratic leaders have contended for years that the Census Bureau's definition of poverty is too conservative. In 1992, it defined the poverty line as $14,343 for a family of four, or about $1,200 a month. Whether this income is adequate for the housing, clothing, food, health, education, transportation, communication, and leisure needs of a family of four is debatable. Clinton gauged poverty as beginning at a somewhat higher income level, resulting in the 18-percent figure.

Engberg portrays himself as the truth-telling journalist combating the illusion-selling politician—a message contained even in the title of CBS's report, "CAMPAIGN 92, REALITY CHECK." Clinton was blowing smoke ("statistical chicanery"), while Engberg was clearing the air ("true, but . . .").

By reducing the economic issue to a question of "lies, damn lies, and statistics," Engberg robbed it of its real significance. His report seems to promise a careful examination of what Bush has done on the economy and what Clinton would do differently, but the analysis is never provided. Instead, the economic issue was a pretext for an attack on Clinton's credibility. Any programmatic or philosophical differences between the Republican and Democratic contenders were ignored. Instead of providing an assessment of the effectiveness of Bush's programs or an evaluation of the workability of Clinton's proposals, the report restricts its focus to the credibility of a few of the statistical illustrations cited by Clinton in a long stump speech calling into question Bush's leadership on the economy. The report implies, without providing evidence, that Clinton cannot be taken at his word, or, at the very least, is trying to hide his true intentions. The report leaps from minor facts to the sweeping assertion that Clinton "is a conveniently slow learner" when it serves his political ambitions.

It might be argued that the type of reporting the Engberg story exemplifies is skeptical rather than cynical: the journalist is simply alerting the voting public to the pitfalls of accepting a candidate's statements at face value. A problem with this interpretation is that it does not account for the relentlessness of the media's criticisms. Bad news in 1992 was not reserved for the promises made by Clinton, Bush, and Perot. During the general election, more than 80 percent of network news stories on the Democratic party were negative; 87 percent of all references to the Republican party were unfavorable. Congress was portrayed as a human cesspool: 90 percent of news regarding it was bad. The federal government fared even worse: 93 percent negative.[31] If this pattern reflects skepticism, it is skepticism that is facile and hypercritical.

The political scientist Austin Ranney has traced the press's antipolitics bias to the Progressive movement, the turn-of-the-century reform effort that sought to increase political accountability. The Progressive spirit was expressed through muckraking journalism, which found fault with concentrations of power in any form, political or economic. The muckrakers portrayed politics as a struggle between decent citizens and self-serving parties and groups. The aim of reform was to expose corruption and create new institutions, such as the primary election and the initiative, that would enable the people to govern more directly.[32]

The influence of muckraking waned, however, and it was superseded by the rules of objective journalism, which held that reporters should refrain from expressing their opinions and confine themselves to reporting the facts. If journalists still harbored the belief that politicians were scoundrels, they nevertheless stopped saying so in news reports.

The rules of reporting changed with Vietnam and Watergate, when the deceptions perpetrated by the Johnson and Nixon administrations convinced reporters that they had let the nation down by taking political leaders at their word. Two presidents had lied; therefore no politician was to be trusted.[33]

The irony is that politicians played a vital part in Johnson's and Nixon's downfalls. William Fulbright and other senators were ahead of the press in deciding that Vietnam was a quagmire, and although the Washington *Post* broke the Watergate story, it was Congress, through its investigations, that forced Nixon's resignation.

Nevertheless, the press had a one-sided view of who saved the nation. "The press won on Watergate," declared Ben Bradlee, executive editor of the Washington *Post*.[34] *The New York Times's* James Reston said much the same thing about Vietnam: "Maybe historians will agree that the reporters and the cameras were decisive in the end. They brought the issue of the war to the people, before the Congress and the courts, and forced the withdrawal of American power from Vietnam."[35]

The poisonous effect of Vietnam and Watergate on the relationship between journalists and politicians has not dissipated. The antipolitics bias of the press that came out of the closet two decades ago has stayed out. In *See How They Run*, the journalist Paul Taylor acknowledged the change: "Our habits of mind are shaped by what Lionel Trilling once described as the 'adversary culture.' . . . We are progressive reformers, deeply skeptical of all the major institutions of society except our own."[36] If most journalists today would hesitate to call themselves reformers, they take pride in unmasking politicians' images and refuting their claims.

As a result, presidential candidates have increasingly been

Figure 1.1 **"Bad News" Coverage of Presidential Candidates Compared to "Good News" Coverage, 1960–1992**

In the 1960s, candidates received largely favorable news coverage; today, their coverage is mostly negative.

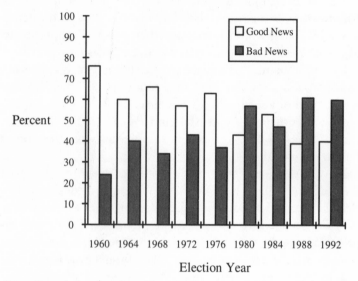

Note: Figure is based on favorable and unfavorable references to the major-party nominees in 4,263 *Time* and *Newsweek* paragraphs during the 1960–1992 period. "Horse-race" references are excluded; all other evaluative references are included.

burdened with negative news. Figure 1.1 shows the good news–bad news distribution for the 1960–92 major-party nominees. Bad news escalated during this period. Candidates of the 1960s got more favorable coverage than those of the 1970s, who in turn received more positive coverage than those of the 1980s. The change is dramatic. Of all evaluative references to Kennedy and Nixon in 1960, 75 percent were positive. In 1992, only 40 percent of reporters' evaluative references to Clinton and Bush were favorable.

The critical span of time in explaining the trend is 1976–1992. *Although Watergate and Vietnam receded with each election, the news coverage of presidential candidates became progressively less favorable.* In three of the last four elections, bad news has out-weighed good news. If Vietnam and Watergate marked a time when the press turned *against* the politicians, the recent period represents a time when the press has turned *on* them.

The cover stories of *Newsweek* and *Time* mirror this trend. *Newsweek*'s cover stories on the 1960 campaign did not include a single negative title; a hefty proportion of its 1992 cover stories did. *Time*'s cover stories on the 1960 candidates carried neutral titles: "Candidate Kennedy" and "Candidate Nixon." Its cover stories in 1992 on Ross Perot were titled "Nobody's Perfect: The Doubts about Ross Perot," "Waiting for Perot: He's Lead-ing in the Polls, But Can He Lead the Nation?," and "He's Back." Bush's cover story was "The Fight of His Life." *Time*'s Clinton covers were "Is Bill Clinton for Real?," "Why Voters Don't Trust Clinton," and "Bill Clinton's Long March."

A basic standard for whether a democratic election serves the people's interest is its legitimacy, or the degree to which it is accepted by the people.

In this basic sense, U.S. presidential elections are legitimate. When the votes are counted on Election Day, the losers accept the outcome. There are no riots in the streets, and tanks do not rumble toward Washington. But legitimacy in a stable democ-racy also requires a public that is satisfied with the election process and the candidates. In this respect, the legitimacy of the presidential selection system is shaky. Opinion polls in recent elections have revealed a people disgruntled with the electoral process and discouraged with their choices.

In June 1992, the presidential race had narrowed to Clinton, Bush, and Perot, and each candidate had the support of 25 to 35 percent of the electorate. The polls also showed that most voters were unhappy with the candidates. All three had high negative ratings, and more than 40 percent of those surveyed in a *New York Times*/CBS News poll said they wished they had other candidates from which to select. In the same poll, 69 percent agreed with the proposition that there is no connection between what presidential candidates promise and what they will do if elected.[37]

In 1988, voters went to the polls to choose what they saw as the lesser of two evils. George Bush and Michael Dukakis were both viewed more negatively than positively by the electorate as a whole. The 1988 situation resembled that of 1980, when the choice was among Ronald Reagan, Jimmy Carter, and John Anderson. Half of the electorate interviewed in a poll said they were dissatisfied with the major-party nominees.[38] Though Reagan won, opinion surveys indicated he was the least popular presidential winner since polling began in the 1930s.[39] He won because the electorate was even less enthusiastic about Carter. Four years later, Reagan's image was positive, but many voters had an unfavorable opinion of his opponent, Walter Mondale.

This pattern of unappetizing choices is without precedent. The Gallup organization first asked voters their opinions of the presidential candidates in 1936. Through the 1960s, the only candidate with an overall negative rating with the voters was Barry Goldwater, in 1964. Since then, most candidates have had a negative rating.

Is it merely by chance that the peak in the public's dissatisfaction with presidential candidates coincides exactly with the peak in the press's negative portrayal of the candidates? Figure 1.2 reveals a close parallel between the two trends.

It would, of course, be a mistake to cite the press's bad-news tendency as the only reason for the voters' increasingly negative impressions of presidential candidates. A number of unfavorable developments in recent years have eroded the public's faith in its political leadership. Yet there can be no doubt that the change in the tone of election coverage has contributed to the decline in the public's confidence in those who seek the presidency. The change is apparent in the sharp contrast between the media's assessments of the 1960 and 1992 conventions. *Time* wrote in 1960:

Kennedy may not be the Democrat best qualified for the
Presidency. But he is mentally keen, vigorous, well-versed
in national and international affairs and more experienced
in them than most Presidential nominees have been. He is
a seasoned and astute politician. In all these respects he is
much like Nixon. They are two of the coolest and toughest
men in our public life.[40]

**Figure 1.2   Relationship Between Election Coverage and Voter
Opinion of Presidential Nominees, 1960–1992**

The voters' opinions of the candidates have become more
negative in recent elections, a trend that follows the
pattern of the candidates' news coverage.

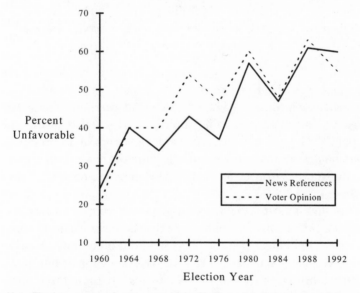

Note: The data on news references are explained in Figure 1.1. Data on voter opinion are
based on available surveys that were conducted at or near the end of each election. Each
data point is the average of the percentage of voters who viewed the Republican nominee
unfavorably and the percentage who viewed the Democratic nominee unfavorably.

The New York Times's Michael Kelly said in 1992:

> There are, as far as can be seen through the fog, four
> serious candidates for the Presidency. On the Democratic
> side, there is Bill Clinton, the big-government, tax-crazy,
> special-interests-loving, old-fashioned liberal; and Bill
> Clinton, the covenant-building, moderate-minded, stand-
> up-to-the-interest-groups New Democrat. The Repub-
> licans have put forward George Bush, the vacillating,
> pawn-of-the-rich, inside Washington, country-clubbing
> middle-of-the-roader who wants everything to stay just the
> way it is; and George Bush, the arch-conservative, deeply
> religious, tax-cutting, Washington-bashing architect of
> bold new change.
>   The embarrassment of candidates was nearly inevitable.
> Men who want to be President, and the men and women
> whose job it is to get them there, are, despite their predilec-
> tion for the language of idealism, strictly in the realism
> business. . . . And what it takes, it has become increas-
> ingly clear, is a campaign of relentless, comprehensive dis-
> tortion.[41]

The late V. O. Key described the impact of communication
in metaphoric terms. "The output of an echo chamber," he
wrote, "bears an inevitable and invariable relation to the
input."[42] The voters begin each campaign without a firm opinion about the candidates,[43] but after months of news that tells
them over and over again that their choices are no good, they
believe it.

Another indicator that election news is at least partly responsible for Americans' low opinion of the candidates is the change
in voters' opinions when the press steps out of the way. Nearly
every presidential debate since 1960 has resulted in an improvement in people's views of the candidates. In 1992, the voters'
opinions of Bush, Clinton, and Perot improved sharply when
the debates gave people an opportunity to view the candidates
through something other than the lens of daily journalism. In

September, before the debates, 23 percent of the voters said they liked Ross Perot, while 45 percent disliked him. A month later, after the debates, 47 percent said they liked him, and 25 percent said they disliked him.[44]

News coverage has become a barrier between the candidates and the voters rather than a bridge connecting them. The press, as Frank Mankiewicz once said, "poisons the well." Election after election, the press tells the voters that the candidates are not worthy of the office they seek. "I know a lot of people who are thinking about this election the same way they think about the Iran-Iraq war," wrote Meg Greenfield in 1980. "They desperately want it to be over, but they don't want anyone to win."[45] George Will said much the same thing in 1992: "The congestion of debates may keep these guys off the streets for a few days. When they emerge from the debates, November—suddenly the loveliest word in the language—will be just around the corner."[46]

Of course, a campaign is sometimes plagued by the candidates' deceit and pettiness, and the media should inform the voters about it. But the press has gone way beyond that point.

The thesis of this book is that the United States cannot have a sensible campaign as long as it is built around the news media. *Out of Order* asks how it is that our presidential-selection system has come to be centered on the news media, explains why such a process cannot serve the nation's needs, and suggests what might be done to put the campaign on a sound footing. I conclude that attempts to convince the press to behave differently can have only a marginal influence on the quality of the campaign. The press is what it is because of news values and imperatives.

This book will no doubt be taken by many in the press as an attack on their institution. It is not intended as such. My argument is that the problem of the modern campaign lies beyond the press, in the electoral system, which asks the media to fill a role it cannot play. Some experienced journalists share this view. "With the demise of political parties," argues Marvin Kalb, the former television correspondent who now heads Harvard's Center for the Press, Politics, and Public Policy, "the press has moved into a commanding position as arbitrator of American presidential politics—a position for which it is not prepared, emotionally, professionally, or constitutionally."[47]

The press's credibility has been weakened in its effort to carry the thankless burden of balancing its traditional role of watchdog with its newfound role of election mediator. Fearful of manipulation by the candidates, and yet charged with the responsibility of providing a channel of communication by which the candidates can reach the voters time and again, the press lashes out at every attempt by the candidates to use its power. This reaction is not watchdog journalism. It is irresponsible journalism and poses a severe threat to the press's watchdog function. What Alexander Hamilton said of the judiciary's power to persuade the people to accept its rulings—"it has only judgment"—applies also to the press. In the long run, the tendency of the press to cry manipulation at every move the candidates make can only weaken its ability to get the voters to attend to its claims. "At this point, I don't care what they [the media] bring out about him," said a Perot voter in an interview. "I'm voting for him."[48]

The press's adversarial stance also threatens its ability to make a constructive contribution to the election dialogue. The press does not have the full confidence of the people it serves. In a Times Mirror poll in the final week of the 1992 election, the public gave the press a C for its performance, which was the same grade given to campaign consultants. Talk shows got a better grade, as did the debates, which received an A.[49]

After the election, Bill Clinton said that future candidates would be "crazy" not to make use of the "new media" to the extent that he and the other candidates had in 1992. The talk and interview shows gave the candidates a chance to get their message across to the voters. The alternative was to go through the campaign press corps, which meant enduring a daily pillorying. Ross Perot went to the extreme length of shunning the press and mocking it. "I've never met a more thin-skinned crowd in my life," he said to reporters in late October. "If you can dish it out, you ought to be able to take it."[50] His fights with the press helped him: each time he criticized the press, the switchboard of his Dallas headquarters lit up with calls from people volunteering to join his campaign.

Although the candidates' 1992 efforts to go around the press were described as a new development by some observers, the same thing had happened in 1984 and 1988, when the Reagan and Bush campaigns had based their communication efforts on televised political advertising. During the 1988 general election, the Washington *Post*'s David Hoffman bought a bullhorn so that he could yell questions at Bush as he gave one speech after another without talking to the press.[51] The closely scripted Bush had a comfortable lead in the polls and a well-oiled ad campaign, and he saw no reason to submit himself to journalists' questions.

Just as a properly functioning campaign cannot be based on the press, the campaign cannot work properly if the press does not have the opportunity to fulfill its watchdog role. The second situation is alarming, and the first is foolhardy. This book tells why.

CHAPTER ONE

The Miscast Institution

> The press . . . has come to be regarded as an organ of direct
> democracy, charged on a much wider scale, and from day
> to day, with the function often attributed to the initiative,
> referendum, and recall. The Court of Public Opinion, open
> day and night, is to lay down the law for everything all the
> time. It is not workable. And when you consider the nature
> of news, it is not even thinkable.[1]
>
> WALTER LIPPMANN

The United States is the only democracy that organizes its
national election campaign around the news media. Even if
the media did not want the responsibility for organizing the
campaign, it is theirs by virtue of an election system built upon
entrepreneurial candidacies, floating voters, freewheeling interest groups, and weak political parties.

It is an unworkable arrangement: the press is not equipped
to give order and direction to a presidential campaign. And
when we expect it to do so, we set ourselves up for yet another
turbulent election.

The campaign is chaotic largely because the press is not a
political institution and has no capacity for organizing the election in a coherent manner. The news can always be made better. Election coverage in 1992 was a marked improvement over
1988, and in a few respects the best coverage ever. The journalist Carl Bernstein, reflecting a widely shared opinion among

members of the press, declared that 1992 coverage closely approximated "the ideal of what good reporting has always been: the best obtainable version of the truth."[2]

Yet news and truth are not the same thing.[3] The news is a highly refracted version of reality. The press magnifies certain aspects of politics and downplays others, which are often more central to issues of governing. During the last six weeks of the 1992 campaign, the economy got a lot of attention from the press, but it still received less coverage than campaign-trail controversies, including disputes over Clinton's draft record, Perot's on-again, off-again candidacy and spats with the press, and Bush's wild charges ("the Ozone Man," "bozos").[4]

The attention that Clinton's trip to the Soviet Union while a graduate student at Oxford received in the closing weeks of the campaign was in itself revealing of the gap between news values and the nation's real concerns. When Bush questioned Clinton's trip on CNN's "Larry King Live," it exploded into the headlines in a way that policy issues seldom do. News of Clinton's Moscow visit overshadowed such October issues as developments on the North American Free Trade Agreement, CIA revelations on the U.S. government's role in the arming of Iraq, and a change in Clinton's health-care proposal.[5]

The press's restless search for the riveting story works against its intention to provide the voters with a reliable picture of the campaign. It is a formidable job to present society's problems in ways that voters can understand and act upon. The news media cannot do the job consistently well. Walter Lippmann put it plainly when he said that a press-based politics "is not workable. And when you consider the nature of news, it is not even thinkable."[6]

Lippmann's point was not that news organizations are somehow inferior to political organizations but that each has a different role and responsibility in society. Democracy cannot operate successfully without a free press that is acting effectively within its sphere. The problem arises when the press is expected to perform the job of political institutions as well.

*   *   *

The press's role in presidential elections is in large part the result of a void that was created when America's political parties surrendered their control over the nominating process. Through 1968, nominations were determined by the parties' elected and organizational leaders. Primary elections were held in several states, but they were not decisive. A candidate could demonstrate through the primaries that he had a chance of winning the fall election, as John Kennedy, the nation's first Catholic president, did with his primary victories in Protestant West Virginia and Wisconsin in 1960.

Nevertheless, real power rested with the party leadership rather than the primary electorate. In 1952, Senator Estes Kefauver defeated President Harry S Truman, 55 percent to 45 percent, in New Hampshire's opening primary. Kefauver then won all but one of the other twelve primaries he entered, and he was the clear favorite of rank-and-file Democrats in the final Gallup poll before the party's national convention. Yet party leaders nominated Illinois governor Adlai Stevenson, in the process rejecting Kefauver, whom they considered a maverick.[7]

The nominating system changed fundamentally after the bitter presidential campaign of 1968. President Lyndon Johnson had entangled the nation in a war in Vietnam that seemed increasingly unwinnable. He was strongly challenged within his party by senators Eugene McCarthy and Robert Kennedy, which led Johnson to make a surprise announcement in a nationally televised address that he would neither seek nor accept his party's nomination. Kennedy's assassination in Los Angeles on the night of the California primary left McCarthy to carry the challenge, but he had lost several primaries to Kennedy and was regarded as a spoiler by party leaders. They nominated Hubert Humphrey, Johnson's vice president, on the first ballot. Humphrey had not contested a single primary and was associated with Johnson's Vietnam policy; his nomination further divided the party. When Humphrey narrowly lost the general election to Richard Nixon, insurgent Democrats demanded a change in the nominating process.

The Democratic party, through its McGovern-Fraser Commission, adopted rules designed to make the nominating process more democratic.[8] The commission contended that "popular participation is the way . . . for people committed to orderly political change to fulfill their needs and desires within our traditional political system."[9] Primaries and open party caucuses (meetings open to all rank-and-file party voters who want to attend) were established as the two acceptable methods by which a state could select its delegates to the national convention.

As a consequence, the nominating system in the Democratic party changed from a mixed system of one-third primary states and two-thirds convention states, controlled by party elites, to a reformed system in which nearly three-fourths of the delegates to the national convention were chosen by the voters in primary elections.* Many Democratic state legislatures passed primary-election laws, thereby binding Republicans to the change as well.[10]

Serious contenders for nomination would now have to appeal directly to the voters. A Humphrey-type campaign for nomination could no longer hope to succeed. The media's influence

---

* The change to a primary-dominated system was not anticipated by the McGovern-Fraser Commission. It assumed that the state parties would merely modify the method of selection they had been using. The smaller number of states that had used the primary method were expected to keep it but to require that the primary vote be binding on delegates. The larger number of states that had relied upon the caucus method were expected simply to open their caucuses to any rank-and-file Democrat who wanted to participate. Unexpectedly, many of the caucus states chose to comply with the rules by switching to the primary-election method of choosing delegates. A basic reason was the judgment of many party regulars that the safest way to comply with the mandated change was to adopt the primary; to retain the open-caucus method (where other party decisions, including the selection of local leaders, could also be made) was to risk a total loss of control of the organization to the insurgents.

correspondingly increased. No amount of backing from party leaders could substitute for support among millions of ordinary people, and if candidates expected to persuade those millions, they had to work through the press.

Some analysts have concluded that the McGovern-Fraser reforms did not significantly alter the presidential selection process.[11] They point to the long-term decline of parties, noting that the bosses had nearly disappeared anyway, that several additional states in the 1960s had adopted the primary election as their means of choosing national convention delegates, and that candidates were already increasingly conducting their campaigns through the media, particularly television. This argument has its facts right, but it draws the wrong conclusion. The McGovern-Fraser reforms were significant because they denied party leaders, most of whom were not "bosses" even in the heyday of machine politics, the power to recruit, evaluate, and select party nominees. The reforms meant an end to the party-centered state delegations that were the basis of brokered conventions. In abolishing a deliberative party process, the McGovern-Fraser Commission took control out of the hands of the party regulars and gave it to those presidential hopefuls who were willing to actively campaign for nomination.[12]

Jimmy Carter's efforts in the year preceding his 1976 presidential nomination exemplified the new reality. Instead of making the traditional rounds among party leaders, Carter traveled about the country meeting with journalists. When the *New York Times*'s R. W. Apple wrote a front-page story about Carter's bright prospects one Sunday in October 1975, his outlook indeed brightened. Other journalists followed with their Carter stories and helped to propel the long-shot Georgian to his party's nomination. Carter would not have won under the old rules.

Of course, the news media's influence in presidential selection had not been inconsequential in earlier times, and in a few instances it had even been crucial. Wendell Willkie was an obscure businessman until the publisher Henry Luce decided that he would make a good president. Luce used his magazines *Time, Life,* and *Fortune* to give Willkie the prominence necessary to win the Republican nomination in 1940. By the time of the fall campaign, Luce was providing him with hot speech ideas and meeting with him regularly to plot strategy. Luce complained whenever one of his editors let slip through any comment critical of Willkie. A *Time* reporter wired from the campaign trail: "Take me off this train. All I can do is sit at my typewriter and write, 'Wendell Willkie is a wonderful man. Wendell Willkie is a wonderful man.' "[13]

Nevertheless, the media's role today in helping to establish the election agenda is different from what it was in the past. Once upon a time, the press occasionally played an important part in the nomination of presidential candidates. Now its function is always a key one. The news media do not entirely determine who will win the nomination, but no candidate can succeed without the press. The road to nomination now runs through the newsrooms.

Reform Democrats did not take the character of the news media into account when they changed the presidential election process in the early 1970s. Their goal was admirable enough. The system required a change that would give the voters' preferences more weight in the nominating process. But the reformers disregarded the desirability of also creating a process that was deliberative and would allow for the reflective choice of a nominee.

In their determination to abolish the old system, they gave almost no thought to the dynamics of the new one. The McGovern-Fraser Commission's report, *Mandate for Reform,* includes no systematic evaluation of the press's role in the new arrangement. The report had one message: rank-and-file voters would be the kingmakers in the new system.[14]

The claim was naïve. The new structure was plebiscitelike, but much too complex to enable the public to understand its choices without guidance. The system did not pose a yes-no vote on a single issue of policy or leadership. Rather, it asked voters to make a complex decision that is difficult even for seasoned party professionals operating in the context of a deliberative national convention.

The voters would have to receive guidance from somewhere. The real choice the McGovern-Fraser Commission faced in 1970 was not between a system with the party leaders in the middle and one without a mediating agent. In any polity of any size, a complex interaction between the public and its leaders requires an intermediary. Since the press was the only other possible go-between, the McGovern-Fraser Commission selected it without any conscious recognition of having made that choice.

The full significance of the change also escaped the notice of the press. Not a single editorial, analysis piece, or news story about the press's power in the new system appeared in the prestige media when the McGovern-Fraser reforms were adopted.[15] The first campaign under the new system did not alter the situation. In *The Boys on the Bus*, Timothy Crouse described a campaign press corps soured by Vietnam and increasingly adversarial, but otherwise engaged in business as usual.[16]

Nevertheless, the reforms had fundamentally changed the press's role. Its new responsibilities were unlike its duties outside the campaign context and had no exact parallel in elections past.[17]

The modern campaign requires the press to play a constructive role. When the parties established a nominating process that is essentially a free-for-all between self-generated candidacies, the task of bringing the candidates and voters together in a common effort was superimposed on a media system that was built for other purposes. The press was no longer asked only to keep an eye out for wrongdoing and to provide a conduit for candidates to convey their messages to the voters. It was also expected to guide the voters' decisions. It was obliged to inspect the candidates' platforms, judge their fitness for the nation's highest office, and determine their electability—functions the parties had performed in the past. In addition, the press had to carry out these tasks in a way that would enable the voters to exercise *their* discretion effectively in the choice of nominees.

The columnist Russell Baker hinted at these new responsibilities when he described the press as the "Great Mentioner." The nominating campaign of a candidate who is largely ignored by the media is almost certainly futile, while the campaign of one who receives close attention gets an important boost. In this sense, the press performs the party's traditional role of screening potential nominees for the presidency—deciding which ones are worthy of serious consideration by the electorate and which ones can be dismissed as also-rans. The press also helps to establish the significance of the primaries and caucuses, deciding which ones are critical and how well the candidates must perform in them to be taken seriously.

The press's responsibilities, however, go far beyond news decisions that allocate coverage among the contending contests and candidates. The de facto premise of today's nominating system is that the media will direct the voters toward a clear understanding of what is at stake in choosing one candidate rather than another. Whereas the general election acquires stability from the competition between the parties, the nominating stage is relatively undefined. It features self-starting candidates, all of whom clamor for public attention, each claiming to be the proper representative of his party's legacy and future. It is this confusing situation that the press is expected to clarify.[18]

A press-based system seems as if it ought to work. The public gets a nearly firsthand look at the candidates. The alternatives are out in the open for all to see. What could be better?

The belief that the press can substitute for political institutions is widespread. Many journalists, perhaps most of them, assume they can do it effectively.[19] Scholars who study the media also accept the idea that the press can organize elections. Every four years, they suggest that the campaign could be made coherent if the media would only report it differently.[20]

However, the press merely appears to have the capacity to organize the voters' alternatives in a coherent way. The news creates a pseudocommunity: citizens feel that they are part of a functioning whole until they try to act upon their news-created awareness. The futility of media-based public opinion was dramatized in the 1976 movie *Network*, when its central character, a television anchorman, becomes enraged at the nation's political leadership and urges his viewers to go to their windows and yell, "I'm mad as hell, and I'm not going to take this anymore!" People heed his instructions, but the chief result of this verbal venting of anger is merely to intensify the public's sense of futility. The press can raise the public's consciousness, but the news itself cannot organize public opinion in any meaningful way.

The press is in the news business, not the business of politics, and because of this, its norms and imperatives are not those required for the effective organization of electoral coalitions and debate. Journalistic values and political values are at odds with each other.

The proper organization of electoral opinion requires an institution with certain characteristics. It must be capable of seeing the larger picture—of looking at the world as a whole and not in small pieces. It must have incentives that cause it to identify and organize those interests that are making demands for policy representation. And it must be accountable for its choices, so that the public can reward it when satisfied and force amendments when dissatisfied.[21]

The press has none of these characteristics. The media has its special strengths, but they do not include these strengths.

The press is a very different kind of organization from the political party, whose role it acquired. A party is driven by the steady force of its traditions and constituent interests, which is why the Democratic leadership in 1952 chose Stevenson, a

New Deal liberal, over Kefauver, a border-state populist. The press, in contrast, is "a restless beacon."[22] Its concern is the new, the unusual, and the sensational. Its agenda shifts abruptly when a new development breaks.[23]

The party has the incentive—the possibility of acquiring political power—to give order and voice to society's values. Its raison d'être is to articulate interests and to forge them into a winning coalition. The press has no such incentive and no such purpose. Its objective is the discovery and development of good stories.[24] Television-news executive Richard Salant once said that his reporters covered stories from "nobody's point of view."[25] What he was saying, in effect, was that journalists are driven by news opportunities, not by political values.

The press is also not politically accountable. The political party is made accountable by a formal mechanism—elections. The vote gives officeholders a reason to act in the majority's interest, and it offers citizens an opportunity to boot from office anyone they feel has failed them. Thousands of elected officials have lost their jobs this way. The public has no comparable hold on the press. Journalists are neither chosen by the people nor removable by them. Irate citizens may stop watching a news program or buying a newspaper that angers them, but no major daily newspaper or television station has ever gone out of business as a result.

Other democracies have recognized the inappropriateness of press-based elections. Although national voting in all Western democracies is media-centered in the sense that candidates depend primarily on mass communication to reach the voters, no other democracy has a system in which the press fills the role traditionally played by the political party.[26] Journalists in other democracies actively participate in the campaign process, but their efforts take place within an electoral structure built around political institutions. In the United States, however, national elections are referendums in which the candidates stand alone before the electorate and have no choice but to filter their appeals through the lens of the news media.

*   *   *

The United States was once the very model of a properly constructed political system. In 1878, the British statesman William Gladstone declared the U.S. Constitution to be "the most wonderful work ever struck off at a given time by the brain and purpose of man." The writers of the Constitution recognized the importance of properly constructed institutions.[27] Because majorities can act rashly, majority power would work through checks and balances; because public opinion can be shallow and whimsical, the public interest would be sought through the slow workings of deliberative processes; because factions are driven by narrow self-interest, the sphere of government would be enlarged from state to nation, ensuring that no single interest would have the size and strength to gain majority control. According to James Madison in *The Federalist*, no. 10, the goal was to seek "a republican remedy" for the pitfalls inherent in popular government.

Presidential selection was part of this remedy. The Electoral College was a concession to the demands of the smaller states for a major voice in the selection of presidents, but it was also designed to give the country presidents of high character and ability. In *The Federalist*, no. 68, Alexander Hamilton said there was "a moral certainty" that the choice of a president would rest on the candidates' "requisite qualifications," and not on their "talents for low intrigue, and the little arts of popularity."

The same claim would be laughable today. "The little arts of popularity" are the heart of the modern media campaign. Candidates today cannot afford to ignore the merest ripple of public opinion. Even lesser issues, when they are exploited by opponents and amplified by the press, can have a major impact on a nominating or election race.

One such issue nearly forced Bill Clinton to abandon his candidacy early in 1992. Governor Mario Cuomo had finally said he was not a candidate, and Clinton was widening his lead in New Hampshire, when Gennifer Flowers laid claim to a twelve-year sexual affair with Clinton in a weekly supermarket tabloid, *The Star*. The story spread quickly to the mainstream press. Soon thereafter the *Wall Street Journal* reported that Clinton had manipulated an ROTC commitment in order to avoid service in Vietnam. The candidate's own poll in New Hampshire showed a drop of 17 points. Former senator Paul Tsongas had surged into the lead, and the Clinton camp feared that they might finish third. If that happened, said Clinton strategist James Carville, their campaign was "toast"—"You could have gone ahead and buttered us." A second-place finish with 23 percent of the New Hampshire vote kept Clinton in the race.[28]

In no other era has the course of presidential campaigns been so unpredictable or hinged so much on small issues as in recent years. There are certainly examples of astonishing twists and turns from the past. In 1884, for instance, the GOP denied nomination to its own incumbent, Chester A. Arthur, and turned instead to James G. Blaine ("the Man from Maine"); Blaine might have won if he had not sat in silence on the same platform while a fellow Republican launched a bigoted attack on the Democrats as the party of "rum, Romanism, and rebellion."[29] But such incidents, once the exception, are now commonplace. The constant presence of reporters, the endless appearances on the campaign trail, and the complexity of modern policy issues have all increased the odds that an unexpected statement or revelation will send the campaign careening in a new direction. Every presidential campaign in the past two decades has experienced its share of surprises, including the following:

1988. Vice President George Bush is the odds-on favorite to win Iowa's caucuses. He finishes third, behind Senator Robert Dole and televangelist Pat Robertson. "Bush is dead," intones television correspondent Ken Bode. The columnist Robert Novak grants him a little more life: "I think Bush, if he's not dead, the pulse is very light."[30] Before the Iowa vote, Bush had led Dole by 15 points in New Hampshire, but he fell 8 points behind with his Iowa loss. During a televised debate in New Hampshire, former Delaware governor Pete duPont pulls from his pocket a written pledge not to raise taxes. He thrusts it toward Senator Dole, saying that the other Republican contenders have signed it. "Will you?" he demands. A surprised Dole takes the petition, stares at it, hands it back unsigned, saying, "Give it to George." Dole's lead in the polls slips away, and Bush wins the New Hampshire primary 38 percent to 29 percent.

1984. In a front-page *New York Times* article, Hedrick Smith declares: "With Senator John Glenn continuing to fade and no new challenger emerging strongly, Walter F. Mondale now holds the most commanding lead ever recorded this early in a presidential nomination campaign by a nonincumbent."[31] A day later, Mondale loses the New Hampshire primary to Gary Hart, 41 to 29 percent. A desperate Mondale borrows an advertising line from Wendy's hamburgers to ask of Hart: "Where's the beef?" Reporters pick up the line even though Hart has provided them with a score of detailed, innovative position papers. The press concludes that Mondale is back in the thick of the race after primary wins in Georgia and Alabama, despite losses in six other states on the same day.

1980. Ronald Reagan has a four-to-one lead in national polls for the Republican nomination and decides not to participate in a televised debate in Iowa, which becomes a leading news story and a point of attack for his Republican rivals. Reagan loses to George Bush, 32 percent to 29 percent, in the Iowa caucuses, and a 45–6 percent lead in New Hampshire polls shrinks to nothing.[32] *Time* quotes a Republican insider as saying, "If Reagan wins [big] I'm the Easter Bunny." The weekend before the primary, Reagan rents an auditorium for a debate with Bush, then surprises him by asking the other Republican contenders onto the stage to join them. Bush had expected a one-on-one debate and protests the arrangement. The moderator warns Reagan that because he has broken the ground rules, the microphone will be turned off. With that Reagan thunders at the moderator, "I'm paying for this microphone, Mr. Green!" dispelling the notion that he was too old to fight hard for his party's nomination. The incident becomes the lead story out of New Hampshire; one observer is quoted as saying, "There were cells in Reagan's body that hadn't seen blood for years. He was terrific." A few days later, Reagan wins a convincing victory over Bush, 50 percent to 23 percent.[33]

1976. Senator Henry "Scoop" Jackson, the early leader for the Democratic nomination, decides to make his first stand in the Massachusetts primary, thus bypassing New Hampshire's contest. George Wallace also skips New Hampshire, which leaves the relatively unknown Jimmy Carter as the lone Democrat of the center or right in a field that includes four liberals—Morris Udall, Sargent Shriver, Fred Harris, and Birch Bayh. The liberals dominate the New Hampshire vote but divide it among themselves, enabling Carter to edge the leading liberal, Udall, by a scant 28 percent to 23 percent. CBS News declares Carter "the clear-cut winner," and the press awards him a publicity bonanza in the week that follows. The extreme cases are *Time* and *Newsweek,* which feature Carter on their front covers and give his candidacy a combined 2,600 lines of coverage, compared with Udall's 96 lines. The media's attention helps to turn a Carter boomlet into a bandwagon.[34]

1972. Public-opinion polls in January place Senator Edmund Muskie ahead of the rest of the Democratic field in 29 of the 50 states.[35] On January 9, David Broder, one of Washington's most influential political writers, reports from Manchester, New Hampshire: "As the acknowledged front-runner and a resident of the neighboring state, Muskie will have to win the support of at least half of the New Hampshire Democrats in order to claim a victory."[36] Three weeks before the New Hampshire

primary, a poll shows Muskie with 65 percent of the vote.[37]
News stories, later discovered to have been planted by the
Nixon "dirty tricks" team, are printed in the conservative Man-
chester *Union-Leader* that accuse Muskie of laughing at a joke
about French-Americans, who form a large part of New
Hampshire's population. Another story brings up rumors that
Muskie's wife is foul-mouthed and drinks too much. During
Muskie's emotional defense of his wife at a speech in front of
the *Union-Leader*'s building, Muskie says that the newspaper's
editor and publisher, William Loeb, "doesn't walk, he crawls."
While speaking, Muskie dabs at his cheeks, appearing to cry.[38]
Reporters interpret Muskie's outburst—"the crying incident"
—as a sign of emotional instability.[39] Although Muskie places
first in New Hampshire, with 46 percent of the vote, the press
claims the "real winner" is George McGovern, with 37 percent.[40] The press begins to focus on unfavorable aspects of
Muskie's campaign. Muskie's subsequent decline is accelerated
when he places fourth in the Florida primary two weeks later.
Within a few weeks, he quits the race.

As these examples illustrate, the presidential election system
has become unpredictable. The nominating phase is especially
volatile; with relatively small changes in luck, timing, or circumstance, several nominating races might have turned out differently.

There is no purpose behind an electoral system in which
the vote is impulsive and the outcome can hinge on random
circumstance or minor issues. Stability and consistency are the
characteristics of a properly functioning institution. Disorder is
a sure sign of a defective system. Although pundits have explained the unpredictability of recent elections in terms of
events and personalities peculiar to each campaign, the answer
lies deeper—in the electoral system itself. It places responsibilities on its principals—the voters, the candidates, and the
journalists—that they cannot meet or that magnify their
shortcomings.

*   *   *

The voters' problem is one of overload. The presidential election system places extraordinary demands on voters, particularly during the nominating phase. These races often attract a large field of contenders, most of whom are newcomers to national politics. The voters are expected to grasp quickly what the candidates represent, but the task is daunting. Early in the 1992 campaign, the talk-show host David Letterman related a joke about Senator Bob Kerrey and actress Debra Winger. The audience did not get the joke, since few of them knew who Kerrey was.[41]

Nor can it be assumed that the campaign itself will inform the electorate. At the time of nomination, half or more of the party's rank-and-file voters had no clear idea of where Carter (1976), Mondale (1984), Bush and Dukakis (1988), and Clinton (1992) stood on various issues.[42]

The Republicans' nomination of Ronald Reagan in 1980 is particularly revealing of the public's lack of information. Reagan had achieved political prominence as a two-term governor of California and had run for president twice before, in 1968 and 1976. He was certainly no Johnny-come-lately to the political scene, nor was he a man of weak convictions: for more than a decade, he had been a forceful advocate of conservative principles. Yet political scientists Scott Keeter and Cliff Zukin discovered in conducting their study *Uninformed Choice* that the public in 1980 did not know all that much about Reagan's ideas before the nominating campaign, and learned very little during it. When asked to place Reagan on an ideological scale, 43 percent said they did not know where to place him, 10 percent said he was a liberal, and 6 percent identified him as a moderate.[43]

Nominating campaigns are imposing affairs. They are waged between entrepreneurial candidates whose support is derived from groups and elites joined together solely for that one election. Primary elections are not in the least bit like general elections, which offer a choice between a "Republican" and a

"Democrat." If these labels mean less today than in the past, they still represent a voting guideline for many Americans. But a primary election presents to voters little more than a list of names.[44] There is no established label associated with these names, no stable core of supporters, and typically the appeals that dominate one election are unlike those emphasized in others. The Clinton campaign of 1992 had almost no connection to the Dukakis campaign of 1988, which in turn was largely unconnected to the Mondale effort of 1984. Thus, the voters begin anew to discover the nature of their choices in the nominating phase of each election. The situation is similar to the one that V. O. Key described in his classic 1949 study of one-party politics in the South: "The voter is confronted with new faces, new choices, and must function in a sort of state of nature."[45] Voters are not stupid, but they have been saddled with an impossible task.

The news media consistently overestimate the voters' knowledge of the candidates and the speed with which they acquire it. In late 1991, before a single vote had been cast, journalists prematurely declared Bill Clinton the pre-emptive Democratic frontrunner. His face was on the covers of *Time, The New Republic,* and *New York* magazine—and this at a time when half the public were telling pollsters that they had never heard of a man named Bill Clinton. Even New Hampshire voters, who get a closer look at the candidates, struggled to make sense of their options. In a Boston *Globe* poll conducted a few weeks before the 1992 New Hampshire primary, 79 percent of the state's Democrats said they had not yet picked a candidate. When the same respondents were given a list of candidates and were essentially forced to make a selection, Clinton got 29 percent of the total, Paul Tsongas had 17 percent, Bob Kerrey received 16 percent, and the other Democratic contenders fell off from there. Flimsy poll results of this second kind are a sharp contrast with the inevitable news stories from New Hampshire that suggest many of the state's voters have talked personally with the candidates and are having trouble deciding because of an overload of information.

Voters would not necessarily be able to make the optimal choice even if they had perfect information. A poll of New Hampshire voters in 1976 reportedly showed that when each Democratic candidate was paired off successively with each of the others, Jimmy Carter came out near the bottom; head to head, he lost out to several of his rivals.[46] Yet he won the primary. New Hampshire's voters divided their support somewhat evenly among the other Democratic contenders, enabling the less favored choice, Carter, to finish first with 28 percent of the vote. The possibility that someone other than the consensual alternative will emerge victorious exists in every multicandidate primary.

There was a time when America's policymakers understood that the voters should not be assigned this type of election decision, even if they were able to make it. Citizens are not Aristotles who fill their time studying politics. People have full lives to lead: children to raise, jobs to perform, skills to acquire, leisure activities to pursue. People have little time for attending to politics in their daily lives, and their appetite for political information is weak. Few Americans have not read, heard, or seen news reports about the secretary of state, the Speaker of the House, and the chief justice of the United States. However, opinion polls show that more than half of all Americans cannot recall these officials by name. How, then, can we expect primary-election voters to inform themselves about a half-dozen little-known contenders and line them up on the basis of policy and other factors in order to make an informed choice?

Of course, voters *will* choose. Each state has a primary or a caucus, and enough voters participate to make it look as though a reasoned choice has been made. In reality, the voters act on the basis of little information and without the means to select the optimal candidate in a crowded race.

The modern system of picking presidents also places burdens on the candidates that they should not be required to carry. Some of the demands are grotesque. A U.S. presidential campaign requires nearly a two-year stint in the bowels of television studios, motel rooms, and fast-food restaurants. "Somehow it's hard to imagine François Mitterrand doing living rooms in New Hampshire," quipped Representative Barney Frank.[47]

The system can make it difficult for a person who holds high office to run for nomination. In 1980, Howard Baker's duties as Senate minority leader kept him from campaigning effectively, and he was easily defeated. In 1992, Mario Cuomo withdrew as a possible Democratic contender on the day of the filing deadline for the New Hampshire primary, saying he could not fulfill his responsibility to the people of New York and simultaneously conduct a presidential campaign. "It would have been nice to run for president," said Cuomo wistfully.[48] The strongest candidate for nomination is often someone, like Carter in 1976 and Reagan in 1980, who is out of office. As a member of Congress noted: "The out-of-office guy is often the one who's way ahead. It's a little wacky."[49]

Advocates of the present system argue that the grueling campaign is an appropriate test of a candidate's ability to withstand the rigors of the presidency. This proposition is a dubious one. It is easy to imagine someone who would make a superb president but who hates a year-long campaign effort or would wilt under its demands. "The self-nomination system does test a few of the abilities we want in a president," observes Alan Ehrenhalt in *The United States of Ambition*. "[But] it ignores countless others, ones that can be measured only over the course of a long public career, and by those who have a chance to watch that career close up."[50]

The current system makes it impossible for the public to choose its president from the full range of legitimate contenders. The demands of a present-day nominating campaign require candidates to decide far in advance of the presidential election day whether they will make the run. If they wait too long to get into the race, they will find their funding and organization to be hopelessly inadequate. Moreover, a candidate who wins the nomination but then loses the general election is likely to acquire a loser's image which may hinder any subsequent run for the presidency. As a consequence, any potential candidate is forced into a strategic decision long before the campaign formally begins. Should I run this time? Or should I wait until next time? The situation makes it likely that the party in the weaker position a year or two before the election will field a relatively weak group of contenders for nomination.

The 1992 campaign is a case in point. In the spring of 1991, after the successful Persian Gulf war, George Bush had the highest presidential approval rating in polling history and seemed nearly unbeatable in a re-election bid. Several Democratic possibilities, including House majority leader Richard Gephardt and senators Bill Bradley and Al Gore, concluded that they should sit 1992 out. They may have regretted their decision by early in the year, when the nation's economy, contrary to expert forecasts, failed to recover, and Bush's approval rating dropped below 50 percent.

For those who run, the electoral system is a barrier to true leadership. Candidates are self-starters who organize their own campaigns. Says Alan Ehrenhalt, the voice they hear is "the voice of self-nomination."[51] As entrepreneurs, they look for support from wherever they can plausibly get it. In the past, the parties buffered the relationship between candidates and groups. Today, it is very difficult for candidates to ignore the demands of interest groups or to confine them to their proper place.

Indeed, the modern candidate has every reason for tirelessly courting interest groups—nominating campaigns *are* factional politics. In 1984, the Democratic frontrunner, Walter Mondale, was attacked by his opponents for the preprimary endorsements he received from labor, women's, and civil-rights groups. He was tagged "the captive of special interests"—a label that stuck with him throughout the campaign. But his opponents were equally diligent in courting special interests. Each of them had actively sought the same group endorsements that they criticized Mondale for accepting.

Contrary to the press's chronic complaint, the central problem of the modern campaign is not that presidential candidates make promises they do not intend to keep; instead, it is that candidates make scores of promises they ought not to make but must try to keep.[52] Politicians with a reputation for breaking promises do not get very far. They attract votes by making commitments and fulfilling them. But it is the nature of the modern campaign to encourage them to overpromise. In this sense, the campaign brings them *too* close to the public they serve. More than a century ago, Abraham Lincoln frequently told voters that he was not prepared to say everything he would do as president, that he wanted to wait until he got to Washington before committing himself on some issues of the day. This is a posture denied to the modern candidate.

The first months of the Clinton presidency demonstrated the consequences all too clearly. The debts he accumulated on the campaign trail came due when he took office, diffusing his attention across a wide range of policy areas. Energies that could have been better spent on his economic stimulus package were diverted toward lesser matters. Some of these initiatives were controversial, which weakened his capacity to hold together the Democrats in Congress. Many of the programs required new or additional funding, exposing him to Republican charges of being yet another "tax and spend" Democrat. Clinton's public approval rating dropped precipitously as a result; at 36 percent, it was a record low for the first one hundred days of a presidency. When in a meeting a Democratic congressman asked the president to "stop the policy-a-day nonsense," the other legislators present burst into applause.[53] Pundits blamed the situation on Clinton's personality and his appointments. But the real cause of his difficulties lay less in his presidency than in his campaign.

Politics, like the marketplace, cannot function without ambition. The challenge, as the political scientist James Ceaser notes, is "to discover some way to create a degree of harmony between behavior that satisfies personal ambition and behavior that promotes the public good."[54] All of the nation's great presidents—Washington, Jefferson, Jackson, Lincoln, Franklin D. Roosevelt—were men of towering ambition, but their drive was directed toward constructive leadership.

The electoral reforms of the early 1970s have served to channel ambition in the wrong direction. Today's nominating system is a wide-open process that forces candidates into petty forms of politics. Without partisan differences to separate them, candidates for nomination must find other ways to distinguish themselves from competitors. They often rely on personality appeals of the ingratiating kind. Jimmy Carter set the standard in 1976 when he said: "I'll never tell a lie. I'll never knowingly make a misstatement of fact. I'll never betray your trust. If I do any of these things, I don't want you to support me."[55]

In 1992, Clinton bridled at reporters' questions about his personal life but posed for *People* magazine and bared family secrets at the Democratic national convention. His running mate, Al Gore, invoked his sister's death and his son's brush with death after being hit by a car. Gore described "waiting for a second breath of life" from his son, linking it to the nation which "is lying in the gutter, waiting for us to give it a second breath of life." George Bush and Dan Quayle mimicked the Democratic nominees' performance a month later at the Republican convention with tales of their childhood and family life. All this was shameless self-revelation, in the tradition of Richard Nixon's 1952 Checkers speech. The difference in 1992 was that all of the candidates did it, and few people thought it remarkable.[56]

Arguably, no candidate better reflects the style of leadership fostered by the modern campaign than George Bush. In 1980, Bush accused Ronald Reagan during the nominating race of advocating "voodoo economics," but as Reagan's running mate in the general election he supported the same economic philosophy. There was no constituency demanding that Bush stick to his principles; he was self-nominated and responsible primarily to himself.[57] In 1988, Bush tore into Robert Dole in the primaries and then pummeled Michael Dukakis with a mean-spirited campaign based on taxes, crime, and the environment —issues that were not big in 1988 until Bush's pollsters identified them as his best options. Shortly after his election, Bush remarked: "That's history—that doesn't mean anything anymore." As his 1992 re-election campaign was about to begin, Bush said: "I'm certainly going into this as a dog-eat-dog fight, and I will do what I have to do to be re-elected."[58]

If Bush the candidate was the victor in 1988 through his tactics, Bush the president was the loser. The writers of the Constitution designed the presidency, as Hamilton expressed it in *The Federalist*, no. 71, "to act his own opinion with vigor and decision." Bush's presidency was robbed of its flexibility by the same tactics that helped gain him the office. His acceptance speech at the 1988 Republican convention contained a populist pledge to hold the line on taxes. "My opponent won't rule out raising taxes. But I will and the Congress will push me to raise taxes, and I'll say no, and they'll push, and I'll say no, and they'll push again. And I'll say to them, Read my lips, no new taxes."

Although it was politically effective, Bush's promise made no sense as a governing principle. The nation had huge budget deficits and was certain to face unforeseen spending needs during the next four years. However, Bush was locked into a position that prevented a constructive relationship with the Democratic Congress to achieve deficit reduction and program initiatives. Bush held the line for two years, yielding only when a compromise with Congress was necessary to avert budgetary paralysis. His retreat from his 1988 promise was a political mistake, but the graver error was the promise itself. It initially paralyzed his presidency and then discredited it, contributing to his failed bid for re-election.

An electoral system should strengthen the character of the office that it is designed to fill. The modern system of electing presidents undermines the presidential office.[59] The writers of the Constitution believed that unrestrained politicking encouraged demagoguery and special-interest politics,[60] and would degenerate eventually into majority tyranny. If we know now that the Framers were wrong in their belief in the inevitability of a tyrannical majority, we also know that they were right in their belief that an overemphasis on campaigning results in excessive appeals to self-interest and momentary passions.

More than in the candidates or the voters, the problem of the modern presidential campaign lies in the role assigned to the press. Its traditional role is that of a watchdog. In the campaign, this has meant that journalists have assumed responsibility for protecting the public against deceitful, corrupt, or incompetent candidates. The press still plays this watchdog role, and necessarily so. This vital function, however, is different from the role that was thrust on the press when the nominating system was opened wide in the early 1970s.

The new role conflicts with the old one. The critical stance of the watchdog is not to be confused with the constructive task of the coalition-builder. The new role requires the press to act in constructive ways to bring candidates and voters together.

The press has never fully come to grips with the contradictions between its newly acquired and traditional roles. New responsibilities have been imposed on top of older orientations, with the result that news about presidential candidates is more likely to sour the electorate on its choices than create an understanding of the nature of those choices.

In his classic study of judicial power, Donald Horowitz identified the issue of capacity as the critical question of many modern institutions. Developed out of the conditions of the past, these institutions operate in the present. Can they do what is required of them? The question is most compelling when, as in the case of the media's role in presidential elections, the responsibilities include new tasks. If the media are capable of organizing presidential choice in a meaningful way, it would be despite the fact that the media were not designed for this purpose. "Institutions are often a step behind the tasks they must perform," Horowitz wrote. "This is especially likely to be true if new tasks have been added to the old, rather than displacing them, so that the problem is not simply one of transformation but of performing both tasks."[61] The public schools, for example, have been asked to compensate for the breakup of the traditional American family. The prospects for success are as hopeless as the task is thankless.

The same is true of the press in its efforts to fill the role once played by the political party. In the next four chapters, I will try to demonstrate why this is so. I will deal with separate aspects of election news, but they are linked by three themes:

1. Journalistic values and political values are at odds with one another, which results in a news agenda that misrepresents what is at stake in the choice among the candidates.

2. Journalistic values, though supposedly neutral, introduce an element of random partisanship into the campaign, which coincidentally works to the advantage of one side or another.

3. Election news, rather than serving to bring candidates and voters together, drives a wedge between them.

The conclusion that flows from these tendencies is that the press is not a substitute for political institutions. A press-based electoral system is not a suitable basis for that most pivotal of all decisions, the choice of a president.

CHAPTER TWO

Of Schemas—Game
and Governing

Every newspaper when it reaches the reader is the result of
a whole series of selections as to what items shall be printed,
in what position they shall be printed, how much space
each shall occupy, what emphasis each shall have. There
are no objective standards here. There are conventions.

WALTER LIPPMANN[1]

On the last major stop of his New York primary campaign, Bill
Clinton addressed a crowd of an estimated four thousand people
on the campus of Syracuse University. Despite a voice hoarse
from nonstop campaigning, Clinton spoke for 22 minutes, out-
lining his differences with the Bush administration and providing a detailed description of his economic-recovery plan. His
speech addressed affordable health care, a universal student-
loan program with various payback options, tax incentives to
spur industrial development, and an ambitious jobs-training
program. Afterward, Clinton stepped down from his platform,
took off his coat, and discussed issues for more than an hour
with the students and townspeople who stayed around to meet
him.

Dozens of reporters traveled with Clinton to Syracuse, but
the news stories that filled the television broadcasts and
morning papers said almost nothing about his policy ideas.

ABC's "World News Tonight" referred to his appearance on "Donahue" and to tabloid headlines featuring his wife, Hillary; but his economic, health-care, and education initiatives were not mentioned.[2]

The Clinton story reported in the press was based on the possibility that his campaign could collapse if he finished second in New York. The previous week, Jerry Brown had beaten him in a stunning upset in Connecticut, and Paul Tsongas was hinting that he might re-enter the Democratic race. A wire-service story claimed the New York primary "has come to be seen as a referendum on Clinton's long-term viability and his ability to prevail over several character issues."[3]

Three days earlier, Jerry Brown had brought his campaign to Syracuse. He was wearing the union jacket handed to him earlier in the day when he had received the endorsement of the New York City subway workers' union. Speaking at Syracuse University, Brown lashed out at Clinton for his ties to Wall Street interests and spoke out for the homeless ("parts of New York City look like a Third World country"), minorities ("we've got to stop the racism that's tearing this country apart"), and the jobless ("Roger Smith [chairman of General Motors] takes thousands of jobs out of the country . . . and gets for his retirement over a million a year—that's not fair"). He advocated a universal health-care policy ("access to good health care should be a birthright") and affordable housing ("there is no American dream for many young people"). He concluded with a blistering attack on congressional trade policy ("let's send Congress to Mexico and pay its members $10,000 a year").

News reports on Brown's appearance virtually ignored his policy themes. He was portrayed as a spoiler with a chance of derailing Clinton's campaign but without a hope of winning the nomination himself. Said the Associated Press: "Clinton hopes on Tuesday to deliver a convincing enough blow to Brown in primaries here and in Wisconsin and Kansas to transform the former California governor into a marginal candidate."[4]

I attended both the Brown and Clinton rallies and asked several dozen people in the crowds a simple, nondirective question: "What do you think?" Not one of them talked about the candidate's strategy. They spoke about his oratorical skills, policy ideas, group stands, wit, savvy, and the fervor of his beliefs. Only one individual said he was unimpressed (by Brown), and nearly all of them said that the candidate was better than they had expected.

The difference in the way reporters and the public see the candidates was evident later in the campaign, when voters had the opportunity through television call-in programs to interrogate the candidates directly. Their questions were problem-oriented, as opposed to the strategy-oriented questions that reporters tend to ask candidates at press conferences. The following are paraphrased versions of the first seven queries that callers asked Bill Clinton on CNN's "Larry King Live":[5]

1. What is your view on trade between the United States and Mexico?
2. Why didn't you attend a meeting of black newspaper publishers, and why do you not speak about black nations?
3. Would you give money to Russia?
4. Would you release loans to Israel?
5. How would you make the economy more competitive?
6. Have you changed your campaign approach by going on talk shows?
7. What would you look for in a Supreme Court nominee?

By comparison, here are paraphrased versions of the first seven questions asked of George Bush by members of the press at a news conference:[6]

1. Ross Perot claims you're hiding from him. Will you commit yourself to debating him and Bill Clinton?
2. Is it proper for Perot, with vast wealth and no spending limits, to use that to attain the presidency?

3. You say you haven't been good at getting your message across, but don't the polls indicate a rejection of the message in and of itself?
4. Hasn't the pattern of the primaries been such that the American people are looking for an alternative to you?
5. You've put Pat Buchanan behind you, but isn't Perot the inheritor of the anti-Bush vote?
6. Do you share the view of Ross Perot as a man who if he doesn't get his way stomps off and goes home?
7. It looks like you'll get a hostile reception at the Rio environmental conference. If that's so, why go?

The differences in outlook between reporters and voters reflect what psychologists describe as a difference in schemas. A schema is a cognitive structure that a person uses when processing new information and retrieving old information.[7] It is a mental framework the individual constructs from past experiences that helps make sense of a new situation.

Schemas are a way of coping with complexity.[8] The world would be a buzzing confusion of unfamiliar information if we had no way of deciphering it. Schemas help us to understand new information, provide us with a framework within which to organize and store it, enable us to derive added meaning from the new situation by filling in missing information, and provide guidance in selecting a suitable response to what we have just seen.[9] When a child has a fit, we recognize it as a temper tantrum, and not as a sign of some deep emotional disturbance. We are able to identify it because the combination of new information (the child's behavior) and our past experiences (we have seen this pattern before in children) tells us what it is.

Schemas are powerful. People who "see" the same activity but apply a different schema to it "see" different things. In the second presidential debate of 1976, Gerald Ford's answer to a foreign-policy question vaguely suggested that the Soviet Union had less control of its satellites than commonly assumed, and he then added there was "no Soviet dominance of Eastern Europe." Polls taken immediately after the debate showed that viewers did not attach much significance to Ford's remark. By 44 to 33 percent, they thought Ford had won the debate. So did Ford, who was greeted by a cheering crowd as he left the scene.[10]

The press viewed the outcome differently. They saw Ford's remark as a costly blunder that cost him the debate and could potentially derail his campaign. All three networks focused on his Eastern Europe statement in their postdebate analyses, and it was headline news the next morning. At a Ford press conference the day after the debate, the first eleven questions tried to force Ford into admitting his mistake. Within twenty-four hours, another poll showed that Ford's 44 to 33 percent win had turned into a 17 to 63 percent loss—a swing of more than 50 percentage points.[11] A voter who was part of the political scientist Doris Graber's 1976 study of media effects said: "I thought that Ford had won. But the papers say it was Carter. So it must be Carter."[12]

The dominant schema for the reporter is structured around the notion that politics is a strategic game.* When journalists encounter new information during an election, they tend to interpret it within a schematic framework according to which candidates compete for advantage. The candidates play the game well or poorly. Ford's Eastern Europe statement was seen as a gaffe that would cost him votes. That Ford was trying to say something other than the meaning conveyed by the actual words he used was irrelevant. "We figured out what he was trying to say," said ABC's Sam Donaldson. "But at best Ford was ambiguous, and at worst his statement suggested he didn't

---

* The singular term "schema" is used here for ease of discussion. In actuality, the press has a number of game schemas. A campaign promise may invoke a schema that presumes the candidate is trying to gain favor with a particular interest; a change in media strategy may be seen as an attempt by the candidate to project a more favorable image; the results of a primary election may be viewed as altering the competitive balance between the contending sides; and so on.

understand what was happening in Eastern Europe."¹³ In less
than the few seconds that it took him to say "no Soviet dominance of Eastern Europe," Ford had made a costly tactical
blunder.

The core principle of the press's game schema is that candidates are strategic actors whose every move is significant. Paul
Weaver described the schema in these words:

> [According to the press's view,] politics is essentially a
> game played by individual politicians for personal advance-
> ment, gain or power. The game is a competitive one and
> the players' principal activities are those of calculating and
> pursuing strategies designed to defeat competitors and to
> achieve their goals (usually election to public office). Of
> course, the game takes place against a backdrop of govern-
> mental institutions, public problems, policy debates, and
> the like, but these are noteworthy only insofar as they
> affect, or are used by, players in pursuit of the game's
> rewards. The game is played before an audience—the elec-
> torate—which controls most of the prizes, and players
> therefore constantly attempt to make a favorable impres-
> sion. In consequence, there is an endemic tendency for
> players to exaggerate their good qualities and to minimize
> their bad ones, to be deceitful, to engage in hypocrisies, to
> manipulate appearances; though inevitable, these tenden-
> cies are bad tendencies . . . and should be exposed. They
> reduce the electorate's ability to make its own discriminat-
> ing choices, and they may hide players' infractions of
> the game's rules, such as those against corruption and
> lying.¹⁴

The reporter's instinct is to look first to the game. In October
1991, CNN provided live coverage of Bill Clinton's announcement speech from the steps of the Old State House in Little
Rock, Arkansas.¹⁵ The cameras stayed on him as he spoke of
his intention to seek the presidency. As he began talking about
the programs he would pursue as president, however, CNN
broke away to its Washington studio so that the commentators

David Broder and William Schneider could discuss Clinton's chances of winning the Democratic nomination. They gave Clinton high marks relative to candidates like Brown, Douglas Wilder, and Tom Harkin but warned that Mario Cuomo's entry into the race could turn all of them into also-rans.[16]

The voters possess a different schematic outlook. They view politics primarily as a means of choosing leaders and solving their problems. As the voters see it, policy problems, leadership traits, policy debates, and the like are the key dimensions of presidential politics.[17] When watching the Ford-Carter debate, viewers had independently judged the candidates on 90 minutes of foreign-policy questions and answers. A Market Opinion Research Center poll taken immediately after the debate indicated that more viewers (50 to 34 percent) agreed with Ford's "statements during the debate" than with Carter's.

Of course, voters want their side to win, and they have an interest in the question of who will win. But they do not see victory as an end in itself. They view it in terms of the implications it has for them. They are moved, said V. O. Key, "by concern about central and relevant questions of public policy, of governmental performance, and of executive personality."[18]

The common thread in the voters' schematic structure is the broad question of governance. We will use the simplified term "governing schema" to indicate the voters' perspective on campaign politics. The political scientist Samuel Popkin uses the term "reasoning voter" to describe what takes place in people's minds. "Voters actually do reason about parties, candidates, and issues," Popkin writes. "They have premises, and they use those premises to make inferences from their observations of the world around them. They think about who and what political parties stand for; they think about the meaning of political endorsements; they think about what government can and should do. And the performance of government, parties, and candidates affects their assessments and preferences."[19]

The game and governing schemas are linked. The quest for victory and power is connected to issues of leadership and policy in the minds of both journalists and voters. It is not that journalists lack a governing schema or that voters do not have a game schema. But the game schema dominates the journalist's response to new information far more than the voter's response. The governing schema is, by contrast, a larger part of the voter's response than the journalist's.

A consequence is that the press's version of the campaign does not mesh with the voters' concerns. The press does in fact communicate a lot of substance during the campaign, but the focus of news buries much of it and distorts much of the rest. Governance concerns work their way into election coverage but never really shine through.

This tendency is worse today than it was in the past. As will be demonstrated later in this chapter, the press's game schema is more pervasive now than it was even a few decades ago. This change coincides with the shift to an electoral process that depends upon the press as its chief intermediary. In the same period that the press has taken on the mediating role once performed by the political party, a number of trends within journalism have combined to make election news a less suitable basis for voter choice.

The game schema dominates the journalist's outlook in part because it conforms to the conventions of the news process. The first fact of journalistic life is that the reporter must have a story to tell.[20] "It's like the pull of gravity," the Boston *Globe*'s Christine Chinlund says. "If you don't write, you don't exist for that day."[21] The news is not a mirror held up to society. It is a selective rendition of events told in story form. For this reason, the conventions of news reporting include an emphasis on the more dramatic and controversial aspects of politics. Above all else, reporters are taught to search for what is new and different in events of the past twenty-four hours.[22] *The New York Times*'s James Reston once described it as "the exhilarating search after the Now."[23]

The game is always moving: candidates are continually adjusting to the dynamics of the race and their position in it. Since it can almost always be assumed that the candidates are driven by a desire to win, their actions can hence be interpreted as an effort to acquire votes. The game is thus a perpetually reliable source of fresh material. A Washington *Post* story in 1992 which began with a strategic reference ("In a bold bid to shake up the presidential campaign, President Bush . . .") typified the format of a great many campaign articles.[24]

The plotlike nature of the game makes it doubly attractive. The campaign "is a naturally structured, long-lasting dramatic sequence with changing scenes."[25] The game provides the running story in which today's developments relate to yesterday's, and probably to tomorrow's events. When Jesse Jackson appeared on NBC's "Meet the Press" during the 1984 primary campaign, he was asked nine straight questions about the damage that his refusal to repudiate the militant Muslim leader Louis Farrakhan was doing to his campaign. After the ninth question, Jackson protested: "I want to talk, if I might, about industrial policies to put people back to work, or about African policy, which most of you tend to ignore, or South African oppression. I think that continuing to raise this [Farrakhan] issue, frankly, is overspending my time."[26]

Policy problems lack the novelty that the journalist seeks. A new development may thrust a new issue into the campaign, but problems tend to be long-standing. If they came and went overnight, they would not be problems. Thus, although the candidates base their appeals to voters on policy issues, what they say has marginal news value. The first time that a candidate takes a position on a key issue, the press is almost certain to report it. Further statements on the same issue become progressively less newsworthy, unless a new wrinkle is added. In *The Boys on the Bus*, Timothy Crouse described a scene in the 1972 campaign that illustrates the declining news value in a candidate's policy statements:

> Fullerton Junior College looked like a large complex of parking garages. The sweltering gym was packed with kids who treated McGovern as if he were Bobby Kennedy. The

cameramen surrounded McGovern as he fought his way
to the platform and the kids tried to push through the
cameramen. The heat and commotion energized reporters
as they squatted around the platform. When McGovern
began to speak, they made frantic notes, although he said
nothing new. Gradually they wound down.

"If there is one lesson it is . . ." said McGovern.

Carl Leubsdorf put up his finger. "I know what it is,"
he said to Elizabeth Drew of PBS. "Never Again."

"It is that never again . . ." said George.

By the end of the speech no one was taking notes.[27]

The story about McGovern that made news this day was a
newly released California poll which indicated McGovern had
surged ahead of Hubert Humphrey by 20 points, with only a
few days left in the state's primary campaign.[28]

The strategy schema is "an event schema."[29] In *Over the Wire
and on TV*, Michael Robinson and Margaret Sheehan note that
"journalism has, for a century and a half, defined news as *events*,
as happenings. 'Horse races' happen; 'horse races' are themselves filled with specific actions. Policy issues, on the other
hand, do not happen; they merely exist. Substance has no
events; issues generally remain static. So policy issues, or substance, have been traditionally defined as outside the orbit of
real news."[30]

Policy issues are rooted in social conditions, which are harder
to enliven than events.[31] When George Bush held a press conference in 1988 on a boat in Boston Harbor to attack Michael
Dukakis's environmental record, the press reported his accusation, and the event dramatized it. A straightforward policy
story would have portrayed Bush's and Dukakis's environmental records in a very different way. Even after the press was
criticized by environmental groups for its coverage of Bush's
claims, its follow-up was weak. The Chicago *Tribune*'s Jon Mar-
golis explained: "When I tried to deal with it later, [I found]
that the environmental groups were not helpful, either. That

they spoke in jargon, that they nitpicked. When you asked them . . . specifically about Bush, decisions that Bush may have made, they . . . did a lot of nitpicking, a lot of very esoteric kind of stuff that I found difficult to understand, much less to explain to readers."[32]

The game embodies the conflict that journalists prize in news —what Jules Witcover has called the "I said—he said—I said" type of story.[33] In the game schema, the focus, is on a few individuals—the candidates—rather than on the larger interests they represent and the broader political forces that shape the campaign.[34] In the journalists' eyes, the campaign at times boils down to little more than a personal fight between the candidates.[35] Shortly before the 1992 New Hampshire primary, Bob Kerrey gave a speech that was billed as a major statement on foreign policy. When it was over, reporters ignored what he had said and asked Kerrey, who was awarded a congressional Medal of Honor for his heroism in Vietnam, for his views on allegations that Clinton had dodged the draft in order to avoid serving in Vietnam. After Kerrey responded, the reporters left; they had their story.[36]

Like any schema, the game schema not only directs attention toward certain activities and away from others but also affects the significance attached to these activities. When Ross Perot held a daylong session with advisers and policy experts for work sessions on four issues—crime, the economy, women, and foreign affairs—*The New York Times* listed the issues in one sentence and devoted the rest of the story (which was headlined, "Seeking Better Image, Perot Shifts Campaign") to strategic considerations, which included a rhetorical question ("An effort to keep reporters too busy to dig for exposés?").[37] To the press, strategy and maneuvers are not merely a component of the campaign; they are a decisive element. "Reporters like to concentrate on campaign tactics and devices," writes *The New York Times*'s Tom Wicker. "In their usual foot-race or game perspective on politics, they and their editors see these as being more critical to the election results than most issues."[38]

Reporters are, of course, aware of the larger forces that influence election campaigns. In 1992, reporters regularly said that the economy would determine the outcome. Yet the economy was often secondary in the news to strategic concerns. During the 1992 general election, campaign controversies such as Clinton's trip to Moscow as a student at Oxford got more television news coverage than the economy.[39]

Issues are played as much for their strategic value as for their relevance to people's needs. The press heavily reported McGovern's income redistribution plan in 1972 and Reagan's opposition to a Panama Canal treaty in 1976 because these appeared strategically significant.[40] In 1992, the health-care issue had staying power as long as its chief advocates, Democrats Bob Kerrey and Tom Harkin, were in the race. When they dropped out, so did the issue. By May, health care was mentioned in only 3 percent of network news stories on the campaign.[41]

The issue of the public's alienation from government also had a roller-coaster ride in 1992. It had surfaced in the 1990 elections in the form of term limitations and a 5 percent drop in support for incumbents. Although surveys showed that as the 1992 campaign began Americans were even angrier about government, alienation was not a leading news item. A political analyst said from New Hampshire that the two candidates who had tied their campaigns to the alienation issue, Jerry Brown and Pat Buchanan, were "irrelevant" and ought to leave the field to the "heavyweights."[42]

Buchanan's better-than-expected showing in New Hampshire gave some force to the issue, but it faded with his Super Tuesday defeats. Brown's candidacy, meanwhile, was treated with about as much derision as the press could muster. A *New York Times* story in late March quoted a Brown worker as saying: "I got involved with Jerry Brown because I think this campaign is psychotherapy on a national cultural scale."[43] Not until Brown won the Connecticut primary was his message taken more seriously. His victory was attributed in a *New York*

Times editorial to "a wave of voter protest against the political process."[44]

The first stories about the Ross Perot candidacy took little note of the public's alienation. The press concentrated on Perot's personal wealth and ego, underplaying the fact that an outsider like Perot could have broad appeal only when people were angry at government. There were exceptions to the general pattern.[45] CBS's James Hattori labeled Perot's following the "mad-as-hell insurgency campaign," and *The New York Times* and the Washington *Post* had several stories about the electorate's angry mood. But the larger story for the press was Perot's personality and his unconventional strategy of bringing his message to the people via talk shows. The rising tide of Perot's support eventually forced the press to confront the issue. The executive producer of ABC's "World News Tonight," Paul Friedman, said in June: "I don't know why, but we really missed the amount of frustration and anger out there." In a decision unusual for network television, Friedman prepared a week-long series of news stories on the alienation issue.[46]

The issue declined when Perot dropped out of the race in July. He returned on October 1 but had less than 10 percent support in the polls, and so the press made no real effort to analyze his support. When he gained momentum later that month, the explanation was found in his debate performance ("folksy, straight-shooting, a master of one-liners")[47] and his money ("his millions of dollars have dictated the course of the campaign").[48] The alienation issue stayed in the background, even though it was still very much in the picture. On Election Day, Perot drew his support disproportionately from voters who were angry with the political process.

Ironically, the press's emphasis on the game was a part of Perot's appeal. The irrelevance of the strategy-driven, scandal-laced coverage of the primaries made Perot appear to many voters in the spring to be the only candidate to share their frustrations. Whenever he attacked the press, new people volunteered to help in his campaign.[49]

*   *   *

Of course, the election includes gamelike elements, and has contained them since the 1830s, when Jacksonian democracy brought with it grassroots rallies and party conventions. "The campaign as sport and spectacle" was how Alexis de Tocqueville described it.[50] The game schema, however, dominates election news in a way that it did not in Jackson's day, nor even a few decades ago.

The press in the 1830s was overtly partisan. Newspapers were aligned with one party or the other and openly used their influence to advance that party's agenda. Their concern with the game was embedded in their conflict with the opposing side. Said Tocqueville of the press, "Its eye is constantly open to detect the secret springs of political designs."[51]

The partisan press gave way to a commercial one as technological and social change made possible the high-circulation newspaper, with its lucrative advertising base.[52] Rabid partisanship restricted a newspaper's circulation—a factor that contributed to the development of objective journalism, with its emphasis on facts rather than opinions, and its commitment to partisan neutrality on the news pages.

The press's game schema acquired a new meaning. Attention to the game kept reporters in the political fray without requiring them to take sides. The election was treated not as an issue but as an event; its strategic dimension could thereby be reported "fairly." There was no overt partisanship in factual news reports on the candidates' attempts to acquire votes.

However, since the "facts" were usually determined by the content of campaign speeches, the candidates had the power to set the agenda.[53] A standard formula for a campaign story was a descriptive account of what the candidate said and whom he said it to. Reporters did not ordinarily delve into why he said it, for that would take them into the realm of subjectivity. At the very least, the journalist took pains to separate the facts of an event from his interpretation of it. The result was a form of election news in which the governing schema—the context in which candidates frame their speeches—was at least as prominent as the game schema.

Today, facts and interpretation are freely intermixed in election reporting. Interpretation provides the theme, and the facts illustrate it.[54] The theme is primary; the facts are secondary. Since the themes are usually constructed from the game schema, it pervades election news.

This transformation is apparent from a study that political scientists Kristi Andersen and Stuart Thorson conducted on news coverage of the 1896, 1928, 1960, and 1984 elections. Andersen and Thorson found that the candidates' speeches were a featured news subject in the first three of these elections.[55] In 1896 and 1928 particularly, the candidates' words carried the story. A news report might begin with a paragraph or two that set the scene, perhaps including the size and mood of the crowd, but the story would then consist mainly of long, unbroken quotes from the candidate's speech. There was almost no analysis of the candidates' strategies. News of the game was plentiful, but it was made up of separate stories that speculated on who would win (many of these opinions were provided by state party leaders) and how the vote would divide among key groups and in the crucial electoral states.

By the 1960 election, candidate strategy had become a major part of election news, but it was usually discussed in articles explicitly labeled "News Analysis." In one article so labeled, *The New York Times* on October 14, 1960, said of a Kennedy-Nixon debate:

> Mr. Nixon's presentation was general and often emotional; Mr. Kennedy's curt and factual. Mr. Nixon, whose campaign is based on his reputation for knowledge of the facts and experience, was outpointed on facts.
>
> Mr. Kennedy, who was supposed to be the matinee idol lacking experience, seldom generalized, plunged into his answers with factual illustrations, and made no appeal to emotion other than the usual Democratic we-take-care-of-the-people argument.[56]

By the time of the 1984 election, the news was firmly rooted in the strategic game. It dominated the schematic structure of most election stories and was the main subject of nearly one-third of the stories in 1984, as opposed to fewer than one-fifth in 1960 and fewer than one-twentieth in 1928 and 1896.[57]

Compared with the three previous elections, straightforward reports of the candidates' speeches were a small part of 1984 election news; barely more than 10 percent of the stories were in this category.[58] The synthetic nature of news stories in 1984 constituted another change. Articles combined events involving the opposing sides and placed them together, as if the candidates were engaged in a direct debate. Such stories were largely absent in the 1896 and 1928 coverage, and constituted a measurably smaller proportion in 1960.[59]

Election news had acquired a very different look by 1984. The candidates had less of a chance to speak for themselves, events were compressed and joined, reporters questioned the candidates' actions, and commonly attributed strategic intentions to them. Andersen and Thorson cite the example of a *New York Times* report of a Reagan campaign stop at a Roman Catholic shrine in Pennsylvania:

> The mixture of religious symbolism and partisan political statements today appeared to contradict the recent assertions of top Reagan campaign aides that the President would ease up on his use of religion in his re-election effort. . . . Some of Mr. Reagan's advisers have said that it was a mistake for him to denounce opponents of government-mandated school prayer as "intolerant of religion."[60]

The change in election news from a governing schema to a game schema is so fundamental that it constitutes a quiet revolution in the campaign that Americans see through the lens of the press. The world of election news has been turned upside down. Whereas the game was once viewed as the means, it is now the end, while policy problems, issues, and the like are mere tokens in the struggle for the presidency.

This conclusion is not the usual complaint that the press is obsessed with the horse race. For nearly a century the press has reported on who is winning and losing. What is different about today's news is a far deeper and more troubling phenomenon. The strategic game is embedded in virtually every aspect of election news, dominating and driving it. The game sets the context, even when issues are the subject of analysis. The game, once the backdrop in news of the campaign, is now so pervasive that it is almost inseparable from the rest of election content. ("Yesterday, [Clinton] told almost everyone what they wanted to hear. He advocated tax relief as well as new tax incentives. He said he favored expanding education programs but pledged to streamline government bureaucracy. He promised that he would maintain a strong defense while reducing military spending.")[61]

As late as the 1960s, the news was a forum for the candidates' ideas. Looking back at election coverage of the 1960s, one is struck by the straightforward reporting of the candidates' arguments. Of course, there was plenty of game coverage in the 1960s as well. The horse-race aspects of the election received close attention. Nevertheless, the press also gave the candidates regular opportunities to present their issues as they wished them to be seen. The candidates' statements had significance in their own right—an arrangement that no longer holds.

The change is apparent in a comparison of how the press reported John F. Kennedy's speech in 1960 at the annual Alfred E. Smith Memorial Dinner and its coverage of Bill Clinton's address in 1992 to the B'nai B'rith International Convention.

It was through media events that Kennedy confronted those who said his Catholicism disqualified him for the presidency. The evening before he was to appear on a paid telecast in largely Protestant West Virginia, Kennedy asked an aide, Ted Sorensen, to write down a list of the fears that Protestants had about his religion. During the telecast, Franklin D. Roosevelt, Jr., son of the former president, enumerated these concerns in a question from the audience. Kennedy devoted nearly half of the telecast to the question, stating his commitment to the separation of church and state. Roosevelt was a Kennedy supporter, yet the press did not report that his question was planted or that Kennedy's answer was a calculated ploy. *The New York Times* said simply, "He declared in one television program last night that he would and should be impeached if he took orders on governmental policy from his church. He stressed, however, that such orders would not be forthcoming."[62]

Later in the campaign, Kennedy received an invitation from Francis Cardinal Spellman to speak along with Richard Nixon at the annual Alfred E. Smith Memorial Dinner in New York. Kennedy discussed his views on religion and politics with a mixture of serious argument and light humor. In one line, responding to former President Truman's suggestion that those who intended to vote for Nixon could "go to hell," Kennedy said, "I think it is important that our side try to refrain from raising the religious issue."[63]

In its coverage of Kennedy's speech, the press emphasized what the candidate said rather than how he came to say it. *The New York Times* printed the entire text of Kennedy's speech on page 27 and in a front-page article reported:

CANDIDATES TERM RELIGION
LESS OF AN ISSUE THAN IN '28

Senator Kennedy, who like the late Governor Smith is a Roman Catholic, remarked that many of the issues in this campaign were similar to those in 1928, when Mr. Smith was defeated by Herbert Hoover. Mr. Hoover is a Quaker, as is Vice President Nixon.

But, Senator Kennedy said, the people this year are different from those in 1928, when religious bigotry played a large part in Mr. Smith's defeat.

"I am confident," he said, "that, whatever their verdict, Republican or Democratic, myself or Mr. Nixon, that their judgment will not be based on any extraneous issue but on the real issues of our time, on what is best for our country, on the hard facts that face us, on the convictions of the candidates, and their parties, and on their ability to interpret them."[64]

Like Kennedy, today's candidates use the media to get their message across, but the message is refracted through the press's game schema. In the 1992 general election, Bill Clinton addressed the international convention of B'nai B'rith, a prominent Jewish organization. *The New York Times* reported:

CLINTON SWIPES AT BUSH FOR LACK OF JEWISH AIDES

Gov. Bill Clinton of Arkansas, seeking the support of Jewish voters, today painted the Bush Administration and the Republican Party as institutions that were virtually devoid of Jews and dominated by fringe religious and right-wing elements hostile to Jewish concerns.

Alluding to the fact that there are virtually no Jews in the upper reaches of the Bush Administration, the Democratic Presidential candidate told the B'nai B'rith International Convention, "I think I ought to give you an administration that looks and feels like America—a Cabinet, a White House staff, appointments to the judiciary and to other major positions that reach across racial, and religious, and ethnic, and regional lines, an administration committed to the highest standards of excellence."

These remarks, made by way of a satellite hookup, underscored the different approach Mr. Clinton adopted in his effort to woo Jewish votes from that employed by President Bush, who addressed the same audience in person on Tuesday. Mr. Bush's appeal to the Jewish audience was a traditional national security approach, focused on how as Commander in Chief he had been ready to use force to confront Israel's enemy Iraq, how he had worked with the former Soviet Union to organize Arab-Israeli peace

talks and how he had helped Russian Jews emigrate to
Israel.

Mr. Clinton, by contrast, made a domestic-focused appeal to American Jews. . . .[65]

The press has been criticized for its strategic approach to election reporting. After the 1988 campaign—one widely regarded
as the most poorly covered in modern times—the press promised that 1992 would be a different story. The news in 1988
focused not on the great issues of global security and the nation's economy, but on such minor issues as Michael Dukakis's
gubernatorial veto of a Massachusetts bill that would have required students to recite the Pledge of Allegiance at the beginning of each school day.

In postelection conferences at dozens of universities, including Harvard, Columbia, and De Pauw, prominent journalists
vowed that coverage of the 1992 campaign would be meatier.
Gloria Borger, senior editor at *U.S. News & World Report*, said:
"We looked back at the last campaign and asked what prison
furloughs and flags had to do with the real world."[66]

These avowals notwithstanding, the 1992 campaign proved
not to be fundamentally different. In the period before New
Hampshire, a lot of stories did get written about the candidates'
backgrounds and comparisons of their health-insurance programs, their economic positions, and the like. But this pattern
changed abruptly with the New Hampshire primary.[67] The
primary results took over the news, as did game-centered speculation: Would Cuomo get in? Would Clinton survive the Flowers incident? Was Brown anything but a spoiler? The horse
race and campaign controversies outplayed policy issues as a
news subject by a ratio of three-to-one,[68] and the issues the
stories covered were embedded in the game schema.

During the general election, the news was even more game-
driven than for the same period in 1988. According to the Center for Media and Public Affairs, the horse race was the major

subject of election news, accounting directly for 35 percent of network evening news stories (up from 27 percent in 1988). The tracking polls that underpinned this coverage also buttressed the news of the candidates' strategies and tactics, accounting for an additional 33 percent of the coverage. Campaign controversies were another major theme. Policy issues accounted for fewer than one-third of campaign stories (down from two-fifths in 1988) and were laced with game analysis.[69]

There were exceptions to the general pattern. ABC's "World News Tonight" devoted more than 20 percent of its election coverage to an "American Agenda" series. Its nineteen features were lengthy by television standards and would typically describe a social problem and then analyze Bush's and Clinton's records and proposals on the issue, with a short reference to Ross Perot.[70] CBS and NBC, however, gave less attention to issues as compared to their coverage in the 1988 general election.

When policy issues were covered in 1992, they were sometimes labeled "analysis." In 1960, strategy stories bore that label. The significance of the press's stories on issues in 1992 should not be dismissed, but the dominant message of election news was the game, just as it had been in all the recent campaigns.

Figure 2.1 (next page) shows the pattern. A random sample of 1960–1992 *New York Times* front-page stories was coded for the schema that framed the report. ("Framing" refers to the way in which a situation is described to an audience.[71]) As the figure shows, there was a steady increase after 1960 in the application of the game schema in election reporting, such that twice as many stories were framed with this schema in 1992 as in 1960. In this period, the proportion of stories framed within a policy schema declined from more than 50 percent to less than 20 percent.

It is also the case that the candidates' statements have become a smaller part of election news. Candidates have been given steadily fewer chances to speak for themselves through the

Figure 2.1   The Schematic Framework of Election Stories on the Front Page of *The New York Times*, 1960–1992

In the 1960s, election stories were frequently framed in the context of a policy schema; today, they are nearly always framed within the context of a game schema.

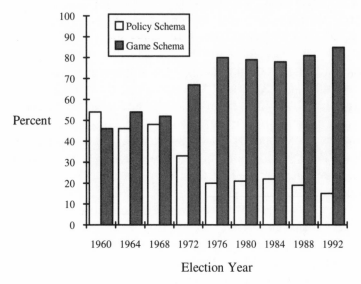

Election Year

Note: News stories were placed in the game category if they were framed within the context of strategy and electoral success. Stories were placed in the policy category if framed within the context of policy and leadership problems and issues. Stories based on other schemas (such as human interest) accounted for about 15 percent of election coverage during the period, and have been excluded from the analysis.

news. In 1968, when presidential candidates appeared in a television news story they were usually pictured speaking; 84 percent of the time, candidates' images on the television screen were accompanied by their words.[72] The average "sound bite" —a block of uninterrupted speech by a candidate on television news—was 42 seconds.[73]

By 1988, the 42-second sound bite had shrunk to less than 10 seconds.[74] The average sound bite in 1992 was also less than 10 seconds in length.[75] The voiceless candidate had become the norm: for every minute that the candidates spoke on the evening news in 1988 and 1992, the journalists who were covering them talked 6 minutes.[76]

The total speaking time allotted to the candidates on the evening newscasts during the 1992 general election was paltry. A viewer watching a nightly newscast every day between Labor Day and Election Day would have been able to hear George Bush and Bill Clinton for a total of 20 minutes each, and Ross Perot for a total of 8 minutes, which is less exposure than would be gained from watching a single presidential debate.[77]

Presidential candidates have also been squeezed out of newspaper coverage (see Figure 2.2, page 76). In 1960, the average continuous quote or paraphrase of a candidate's words in a front-page *New York Times* story was 14 lines. By 1992, the average had fallen to 6 lines. The candidate's words are now usually buried in a narrative devoted primarily to expounding the journalist's view, as in this Washington *Post* story:

> The meaning of last week's riot lay like a shard of glass in Bill Clinton's path here today. Through it, he saw clearly the chance to drive home the idea that things are going badly wrong in America, but it was jagged at the edges and dangerous to grasp.
>
> And so he considered it gingerly and spoke of it cautiously during a day spent consulting with community leaders and viewing the bare, ruined wreckage of Vermont Avenue.
>
> Wary of charges that he was playing politics with disaster, Clinton met in two closed sessions with firefighters and community leaders and spoke privately with Mayor Tom Bradley. When he faced the news media, his remarks were guarded. And though his walks along scarred streets made grimly powerful pictures, the likely Democratic presidential nominee gave no bold speeches about the spasm that left more than 50 people dead and stunned the nation.
>
> "We're never going to have enough money or enough

Figure 2.2   Length of Candidate Statements in Election Stories on Front Page of *The New York Times*, 1960–1992

The average length of candidate quotes in 1992 news articles was less than half of the average length in 1960.

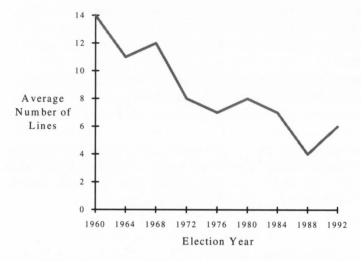

Note: Based on the length in number of lines of continuous quotes or paraphrases of candidate statements in news stories. In the mid-1970s, *The New York Times* changed from an 8-column format on each page to one of 6 columns, resulting in a roughly 25 percent increase in the number of words per line in a column, and a corresponding decrease in the number of lines devoted to any given subject. The pre-1976 data have been adjusted to reflect the change; thus, the average length of a candidate's statement in 1960, with the 8-column format, was actually 19 lines rather than the 14 lines indicated in the figure.

wisdom to solve all these problems," Clinton said to reporters. "Unless we have a grass-roots effort in every community . . . to give all sectors of the community a fair say, it's going to be hard to succeed."

Caution was necessary, campaign officials suggested, because talk was dangerous. It might look like political grandstanding. Or worse, from their perspective, it could sound like tired liberal hand wringing. So Clinton listened more than he spoke, and when he spoke, spoke quietly, in the dry, detailed terms of a policy paper.[78]

Election news in the 1960s gave candidates the opportunity to present themselves on their own terms to the voters. Today, journalists do most of the candidates' talking for them.* The American case is unique. In other democracies, the press is the secondary voice in election news. The principle that governs British election coverage is that "politics belongs to the politicians," and the job of the press is to "hold the ring"—that is, to offer a forum in which the candidates can express their views in their own way.[79] In Britain, there is "no equivalent to [U.S.] reporters' concern with exposing the manipulative publicity motives and machinations of leading campaigners."[80] The level of issue coverage in Britain is twice that in the United States.[81] A comparative study of U.S. and British election coverage found that most news items in Britain originate with the politician, whereas in the United States they originate with the journalist.[82] In Britain, quoted material from political leaders accounts for roughly 30 percent of television coverage of elections; in the United States, it accounts for only 10 percent.[83]

What happened between the 1960s and today? What turned election news into a journalist-centered, strategy-centered form of communication?

Part of the answer lies in the nature of the modern campaign. Strategy became more important as political parties carried less of the burden of electioneering and the candidates assumed more of it. They must fend for themselves, creating personal identities that will distinguish them from their competitors. They try to stay ahead of politically dangerous issues and seek to exploit advantageous ones.

The manner in which candidates present themselves has

---

* The voters' voice has also receded in news coverage. The research of Dan Hallin of the University of California at San Diego indicates that their voices accounted for 20 percent of sound bites in 1968 but less than 4 percent in 1988, and were used primarily to illustrate poll results rather than to add another dimension to the coverage.

changed. In their speeches, they continue to emphasize their policy positions, problem-solving know-how, and ability to build coalitions and get things done in a leadership role. However, they also work on building images and managing the media. "We tried to create the most entertaining, visually attractive scene to fill the [news]," said Michael Deaver, Reagan's image maker.[84] Compared with times past, manipulation and imagery are a larger part of the campaign, and the candidates' party ties are less central.[85]

To expect the press to ignore the strategic aspects of the campaign and report solely on enduring questions of national policy and leadership is to inaccurately assume that the substance of a campaign is all that matters. Tom Hannon, CNN's political director, says rightly: "We've recognized that the horse race has a place in our coverage, a legitimate place."[86]

There are times when strategic calculations are so obviously the basis for a candidate's actions that the press would be irresponsible not to say so. In 1992, George Bush went to the General Dynamics Corporation plant in Fort Worth to announce his decision to sell 150 of its F-16 fighter planes to Taiwan and at the same time dropped his opposition to the development of the V-22 Osprey tilt-rotor aircraft and modernization of the Army's M-1 tank. The press described the trip as politically motivated. The Washington *Post* headlined its story "Military Moves with Political Overtones" and reported: "After repeatedly saying that politics should not affect the nation's approach to reshaping the post-Cold War military, the Bush administration has made a series of decisions and policy reversals that carry obvious benefits for the president's reelection campaign."[87]

Changes in the way candidates conduct their campaigns, however, are not nearly as significant as changes in journalism in explaining the shift to game-immersed news.

Reporters in the 1960s began to chafe at the restrictive rules of objective journalism, partly as a result of their newfound status. There have always been celebrity journalists, such as Joseph and Stewart Alsop and Walter Lippmann, but television greatly increased the number of reporters whose names and faces were widely known to the public. As they soared in the public's esteem, so did their profession. Journalism became a prestigious calling. National correspondents were celebrities— some more than others, but all were exalted by television's influence on the public's perception of their importance.

It was one thing for nameless, faceless journalists to defer to politicians, and another thing for well-known television corre- spondents and bylined reporters to do the same. Journalists became more assertive. They were getting accustomed not only to asking the questions but to answering them as well. When V. O. Key wrote in 1961 that the press was a "common carrier" of neutral political information,[88] he was applying a description that would soon be outdated.

The Pentagon Papers and Watergate further boosted the rep- utation of journalists and gave a twist to their relations with politicians. The press responded to the trickery of the Johnson and Nixon administrations with a style of reporting that was decidedly more aggressive. If the politician was going to lie to the journalist, then the latter would scrutinize the former's every word and action.[89]

If before Watergate and Vietnam the game had been a theme of election news, it was now also a *theory:* candidates did not merely seek to win; they would do anything to win.[90] Their motives were suspect, their images false, their promises empty. CBS News correspondent Leslie Stahl said in 1980, "We didn't want their campaign to dictate our agenda."[91]

Journalists had been silent skeptics; they became vocal cyn- ics. This was particularly true among the "elite" national jour- nalists. "The way of advancement in journalism is to attack," as Theodore H. White said.[92] The game schema was a potent weapon. It offered, within the rules of journalism, a ready means of undermining what candidates were saying. The candidates' promises could be exposed as little more than vote-getting ploys.

The emergence of this more aggressive style of reporting coincided with and was exaggerated by the impact of commercial television on journalism. Television relies on an interpretive style of reporting that emphasizes the "why" more than the "what." When television news shifted from a 15-minute to a 30-minute format in 1963, NBC's Reuven Frank informed his correspondents: "Every news story should, without any sacrifice of probity or responsibility, display the attributes of fiction, of drama. It should have structure and conflict, problem and denouement, rising action and falling action, a beginning, a middle and an end."[93]

This emphasis on narrative stems from commercial television's need for tightly structured stories. In a medium that depends on the spoken word and large audiences, stories that are to be readily understood must be given a narrative form; they cannot be allowed to trail off in the fashion of the traditional newspaper story.[94] Most television news stories are built around interpretive themes. Facts become "the materials with which the chosen theme is illustrated."[95]

Consistent with the tendency of journalists to see the campaign through a game schema, television's dominant themes are the status of the race and the candidates' strategies. For this reason, the game was more prominent on television than in newspapers even in the 1960s. The newspaper was wedded to its traditional inverted-pyramid style. Most newspaper reports were descriptions of events (and many today still are, particularly those of AP and UPI). Although selection and editing were important, newspaper stories did not have a tight story line. They were a string of related facts presented in descending order of importance that an editor could cut almost anywhere in order to fit the story into the available space. Since the newspaper relied less on a central theme and more on events themselves, substantive content had greater prominence in newspapers than on television.

The television model gradually affected the print media, to the point where the difference in the styles of television and newspaper reporting is now relatively small. Of course, newspaper stories are longer and more detailed than television stories, but they also rely heavily on the interpretive style of reporting, as Figure 2.3 (next page) indicates. From 1960 to 1992, the proportion of interpretive election reports on the front page of *The New York Times* increased tenfold, from 8 percent to 80 percent. The change took place in two stages. In the 1970s, interpretive reporting increased to account for half of all election articles. In the 1980s, it jumped to the 80 percent level.

The interpretive style of reporting greatly increases the reporter's influence on election news. Campaign coverage is always a mixture of straight reporting of what the candidates say, investigative reporting of the candidates' backgrounds and of issues, and analysis of the campaign situation. As a consequence of the trend toward interpretive reporting, the analyst's role has come to overshadow the rest.[96]

Opinion polls have abetted the process. Gallup, Harris, and other commercial pollsters increased their polling efforts in the 1960s, and by the 1970s most of the major news organizations —including CBS News, NBC News, *The New York Times*, and the Washington *Post*—were conducting their own polls. By 1980, more than 10 percent of election news stories on television and in the newspaper were based wholly or in significant part on poll results.[97] The number of poll stories has since increased, to the point where they now take up more space than candidates' speeches. In a three-week period during October 1988, polling information appeared in 53 percent of Washington *Post* stories and 37 percent of *New York Times* stories about the election. In the last month of the 1988 campaign, the *Post* had thirteen poll stories on its front page, and the *Times* had ten.[98]

The press relies on polls to maintain a running tally on the game.[99] Political scientist Anthony Broh studied a sampling of

Figure 2.3   The Reporting Framework of Election Stories on the Front Page of *The New York Times*, 1960–1992

In the 1960s, the vast majority of election stories were descriptive in nature; today, the vast majority are interpretive in nature.

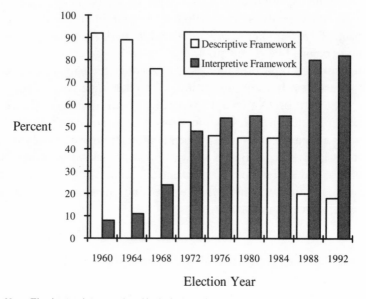

Election Year

Note: Election stories were placed in the interpretive category if they mainly told "why," and in the descriptive category if they mainly told "what."

130 poll stories from *The New York Times*, the wire services, and the national news magazines during the 1976 election and found that the status of the race was by far the dominant theme.[100] In the last month of the 1992 campaign, CNN in conjunction with *USA Today* conducting a tracking poll and released the candidates' standings daily.

Poll stories get top billing. Half of all poll reports on the network evening news during the 1984 election were broadcast as either the lead or the next-to-lead story.[101] They also rate high in newspapers; a study of fifty papers during the 1980 campaign found that nearly a third of poll stories appeared on the front page.[102]

The extreme case of a poll story was a report on ABC's "World News Tonight" during the 1988 campaign. The piece lasted twelve-and-a-half minutes, which is an eternity on television news. The story showed Bush leading Dukakis 51 percent to 45 percent nationally, and then proceeded to analyze each candidate's strength state by state (Bush had a "firm" lead in twenty-one states and a smaller one in fifteen others). Included in the report was an explanation of the poll, an analysis of how the Electoral College operates, and interviews with members of the Bush and Dukakis campaigns on their reactions to the poll.[103]

Dukakis's press secretary. Dayton Duncan, observed that "a new cure for cancer" might not have received the same news coverage and then pointed out the significant truth underlying the story: *"nothing had actually happened."* A poll story is entirely manufactured. It is pseudo-news created by the news media to report on the game: "They create it, pay for it, and then report on it." The poll story is the press's analogue to the pseudo-events that the candidates create to dramatize their policy positions.[104]

Theodore White's model of behind-the-scenes reporting has also contributed to game-based reporting. White's *The Making of the President 1960* was a fascinating bestseller about a part of the campaign never before seen in such detail, and it was nearly inevitable that his perspective would make its way into daily election coverage. If, as the political scientist James David Barber noted, few of White's imitators had his graceful prose and storytelling ability, they at least shared his fascination with the inside story of politics.[105]

White, for one, regretted the influence of his books on daily news. "It's appalling what we've done to these guys," White told Timothy Crouse. He was reacting to a scene in George McGovern's suite in the Doral Hotel in Miami during the 1972 Democratic convention. White said to Crouse:

"McGovern was like a fish in a goldfish bowl. There were three different network crews at different times. The still photographers kept coming in in groups of five. And there were at least six writers sitting in the corner—I don't even know their names. We're all sitting there watching him work on his acceptance speech, poor bastard. He tries to go into the bedroom with Fred Dutton [an adviser] to go over the list of vice presidents, which would later turn out to be the fuck-up of the century of course, and all of us are observing him, taking notes like mad, getting all the little details. Which I think I invented as a method of reporting and which I now sincerely regret. If you write about this, say that I sincerely regret it."[106]

In its tendency to portray the candidates as strategists more than as leaders of electoral coalitions, the press makes it difficult for them to get their message across to the voters.[107] By looking behind the scenes, reporters expose the candidates' plans and foil their attempts to communicate with the voters. "Those school children didn't just happen to be there, it was planned by [Mondale's advance team]" was a line from a news story on a 1984 campaign stop that the Mondale campaign had hoped would dramatize the nominee's commitment to education reform.[108]

The communications scholar Michael Levy uses the phrase "disdaining the news" to describe the tendency of reporters to distance themselves from the candidates' efforts to communicate their ideas through the press.[109] A study of the 1984 campaign found that roughly 10 percent of election stories contained overtly disdaining comments.[110]

Studies of the 1988 and 1992 campaigns documented the same tendency.[111] On the basis of her study of the 1988 campaign, the sociologist Kiku Adatto concluded that "time and again reporters called attention to the politicians' use of television imagery," thereby implying that the candidates were trying to manipulate the voters. "So attentive was television news to the way the campaigns constructed images for television that political reporters began to sound like theater critics,* reporting more on the stagecraft than the substance of politics."[112]

Candidates are strategists, of course. But the fact that they dramatize their appeals and adjust their messages does not per se constitute manipulation. The assumptions of the game schema, rather than a trail of broken campaign promises, are the basis of the press's conclusions to the contrary. Consider this CBS News report from the 1980 campaign:

> WALTER CRONKITE: Since setting out on this Campaign '80 trail, Reagan has been shifting from the right to the center of the political spectrum. More on that from Bill Plante.
>
> BILL PLANTE: As he rode through New Hampshire nine months ago, Ronald Reagan still carried high the conservative banner. For 16 years he had promised a clean sweep of liberal programs and philosophies in government, leaving a trail of conservative rhetoric in his wake. That rhetoric is what Jimmy Carter has been using for ammunition. But Reagan has proved to be a moving target. As he searches for the votes of Democrats and independents, many of those conservative positions have changed. Take the question of abolishing federal programs.
>
> RONALD REAGAN: [*On-screen caption:* January statement] I think we should get the federal government out of the classroom.
>
> PLANTE: Reagan promised repeatedly to abolish the new Department of Education, along with the Department of Energy. No more is heard about that, and he takes pains to promise no cutbacks in existing programs such as Social Security.

---

* In 1992, *The New York Times* actually sent its chief theater critic, Frank Rich, to report on the election.

REAGAN: [recent statement] This strategy for growth does not require altering or taking back necessary entitlements already granted to the American people.

PLANTE: For years, Reagan has promised to do away with such taxes as the inheritance tax.

REAGAN: [February statement] That's a tax that should be canceled.

PLANTE: But there was no mention of it in his comprehensive economic program. He talked about taxes on interest. . . .

REAGAN: [May statement] I, in principle, do not believe in government bailing out businesses and industries—private businesses and industries—that failed.

PLANTE: But he told Chrysler workers he supported this particular bail-out on the grounds that it was excessive government regulation which had done the company in. Similarly, in 1975, Reagan was quoted as saying, "I include in my morning and evening prayers that the federal government will not bail out New York City." Though he did give New York credit for getting its economic house in order, it wasn't until two weeks ago that he said in a statement, "I believe that to pull the rug from under New York City, which is halfway through the financing program approved by the Congress, would be a mistake."

Which is the real Ronald Reagan? Does he plan to deliver on his conservative promises, or is he a closet moderate? His aides say that it's simply that he understands the politics of getting elected. In any case, it presents Jimmy Carter with the problem of convincing voters that he's talking about the same Ronald Reagan who looks and sounds so much more moderate today. Bill Plante, CBS News, with the Reagan campaign in Philadelphia.[113]

As Plante spoke, an X was drawn across Reagan's face at each mention of a broken promise. However, Reagan's message had, in fact, hardly changed during the campaign. He spoke throughout the campaign of his commitment to free enterprise, low taxes, a beefed-up military establishment, and less government regulation, which were the same things that he had been saying ever since he made his name politically with a nationally televised speech in behalf of Barry Goldwater during the 1964 campaign. As president, he would hold fast to these conservative principles. Nothing in Reagan's political record or campaign message justified Plante's portrayal of Reagan as unprincipled.

Plante was not trying to mislead. He was following the rule of journalism that the news is what is new and that any change in a candidate's position is a ploy. If there were five thousand words in Reagan's campaign speech and ten of them were new, these ten words would be the journalist's target. For his own part, Reagan did nothing more than what all presidential candidates do during the course of a year-long national campaign. He made a few marginal adjustments in the application of his basic ideas. Plante caught the tinkering and failed to see the essential Reagan. Indeed, much of Plante's report is based on what Reagan had not said in recent weeks compared with statements made earlier in the campaign. In the news game, candidates are discredited not only for not saying anything new but also for not repeating everything old.

Plante applied an all-or-nothing standard to Reagan's positions. When the complexity of politics confronts the simplicity of news, it is the complexity that gives way. Reagan's reasons for supporting the New York City bailout ("to pull the rug from under New York City, which is halfway through the financing program approved by the Congress, would be a mistake") did not invalidate his claim that he was opposed in principle to government bailouts. Opposing the termination of an existing program in midpassage is not the same as supporting a new initiative promoting the program.

In the game schema, a change in a candidate's position, however slight, is a calculated attempt to manipulate the electorate. In a different schema—that of governing—flexibility and compromise are a vital part of the political process. Campaigns have historically served an educative function for candidates. As they travel the country, their ideas are tested against public opinion and regional problems. They learn which of their ideas are sound and which need adjustment if they are to garner the support necessary to make their programs work if and when the voters put them in office. The campaign would be a failure if the public's reactions did not feed back into the candidates' programs.

Journalists understand this basic principle at some level, but their game schema cannot easily accommodate it. The idea that candidates "learn" from their campaign experiences is not part of that schema. The feckless candidate who is so prominent in the news is largely the creation of a reflexive application of the game schema. If the truth be told about Ronald Reagan, his problem was less a penchant for expediency than a stubborn adherence to his principles.

The press is the critical link in election communication. The media do not entirely determine what the voters think of the campaign. But it is no exaggeration to say that the press is the link to what is happening in the campaign for the large majority of voters.

This connection is weakened by the press's reliance on the game schema. The voters, as noted previously, bring a governing schema to the campaign. Their chief concerns are what government has done before the election, what it will do after the election, and how this will affect them. The game schema, however, asks them to concentrate on who is winning, and why. The result is a breakdown in the type of communication that should occur during the course of the election.

In her best-selling book *You Just Don't Understand*, Deborah Tannen describes the difficulty that men and women have in talking with each other.[114] The analytical schema that men bring to interpersonal communication clashes with the emotion-based schema that women rely on. Men and women converse without fully understanding what the other is saying, and sometimes misunderstand each other completely. A similar conclusion would apply to the relationship between media and voters in a presidential campaign.

Although voters also have a game schema, which includes elements of the journalists' game schema, it is not as fully developed and is less central to their thinking about the campaign. They respond passively to game-centered news. In a study that I conducted of the 1976 campaign, respondents were asked to recall a news story they had seen within the past twenty-four hours. Consistent with the press's emphasis, the game was by far the most frequently recalled subject.[115] In a follow-up question, the respondents were asked to describe their reaction to the news story they had just recalled. News of the game often elicited no reported reaction at all, either about the game or about governing. On the other hand, governing stories were more than 50 percent likely to draw a reaction from voters.[116]

Other studies provide similar results. Doris Graber found that when news stories "discussed serious social problems," people were inclined to advocate action to address them, but when stories discussed the game, they tended to have less involved reactions, including feelings of resignation about the candidates' behavior.[117]

When voters encounter game-centered stories, they behave more like spectators than participants in the election, responding, if at all, to the status of the race, not to what the candidates represent. On the other hand, stories about the issues and the candidates' qualifications bring out the politics in voters, eliciting evaluations of the candidates' leadership and personal traits and of their records and policy positions. These stories also cultivate more involvement, which is evident in the voters' greater reaction to such stories.

Voters are not mindless recipients of media messages. Just because the press says something or portrays the campaign in a particular light, it does not mean that the voters will always see things in precisely that way.[118] The power of words, however, should not be underestimated. Experiments have shown that preferences can be affected simply by changing the way in which situations are framed.

In one experiment, the cognitive psychologists Daniel Kahneman and Amos Tversky told a group of subjects to imagine that an unusual disease was expected to kill six hundred people and then asked them to choose between treatment program A, which was expected to save two hundred, and treatment program B, which offered a one-third probability of saving all six hundred and a two-thirds probability of saving none of them. By 72 percent to 28 percent, the subjects preferred treatment A. A matched group of subjects was provided the same information about the disease and asked to choose between treatment A, under which four hundred were expected to die, and treatment B, which offered a one-third probability that nobody would die and a two-thirds probability that all six hundred would die. In this case, treatment B was preferred 78 percent to 22 percent. The choice given to both groups was identical, but one choice was framed in terms of the number of people who would live if the action were taken, and the second one was framed in terms of the number who would die. By altering the way in which the choice was framed, people's preferences were completely changed.[119]

In their experiments involving news messages, the political scientists Shanto Iyengar and Donald Kinder found that the media have a substantial capacity to frame political choices. "By priming certain aspects of national life while ignoring others, [the news] sets the terms by which political judgments are rendered and political choices made."[120] Framing is stronger when exposure to a theme is continuous, as in the case of the game, than when it occurs in a single concentrated exposure, as is typical of a candidate's pronouncement of a major policy position.[121] This helps to explain Graber's finding that after a period of time, voters frequently have trouble recalling the details of a candidate's statements about an issue. One of Graber's subjects said: "I've just forgotten. I'm sure they're things at one time I knew the specifics on, and I just forgot."[122]

The press's tendency to frame the election within the schematic structure of the game has an effect on how voters see the campaign. By portraying candidates as strategists, the news media impress this view on the voters' thinking.[123] Even if the effect of a given media message is small, the same message repeated continuously leaves an imprint. Graber found that even people who trust politicians tend to discount their campaign promises. Whatever is said is "swallowed with the proverbial grain of salt."[124] The press's game-centered news is a key to understanding the paradox that Americans trust their own member of Congress but distrust members of Congress in general. The second opinion is derived almost entirely from a broad-based view of politicians that has been constructed from news messages, largely in the context of the game schema.

All of these things—the press's focus on the game, the candidates' difficulty in getting their message across, and the voters' spectatorlike behavior—became worse with the change in the structure of the presidential campaign in the early 1970s. The primaries were a small part of the contest until then. Fewer than one-third of the states held a primary, and candidates were not required to run in all of them to prove their vote-getting appeal. John Kennedy could not have won the nomination in 1960 without victories in the primaries, but he campaigned in only seven of the sixteen states that held primaries. Adlai Stevenson and Dwight Eisenhower won their party's nomination in 1952 without mounting primary campaigns.

The nominating stage is the period when the game most fully dominates the news.[125] For four months, the weekly parade of nearly forty primaries, with their winners and losers, overshadows everything else. The game dimension is sometimes so consuming of the news that almost nothing else gets through. In the two-week period preceding Super Tuesday in 1988, game

news outpaced issue news by a wide margin in the daily newspapers and by an astounding twenty-to-one on network television newscasts.[126] Super Tuesday, with its enormous pool of
delegates at stake, was a critical juncture; Democrats vied for
delegates in twenty states, while Republicans fought it out in
seventeen. The nominating races of 1988 were crowded, involving thirteen major candidates; in the past, serious candidates
had not numbered more than eight. Never before had primary
voters needed so much help in sorting out their alternatives, but
they received little assistance from the news media. The only
issues to break through the barrage of game news were the wild
claims by televangelist Pat Robertson that George Bush knew
of secret Soviet missiles in Cuba and had masterminded the
Jimmy Swaggart sex-and-religion scandal in order to discredit
Robertson's presidential bid. Robertson was not the leading
Republican contender, but his charges were so sensational and
so calculated that they were irresistible to the media.[127]

Game coverage always peaks during the primaries. My study
of the 1976 campaign found that the game received 30 percent
more news space during the primaries than during the convention and the general election. Robinson's analysis of the 1980
campaign produced similar results, although the disparity between the primary and later stages was less substantial.[128]
Lichter, Amundson, and Noyes's study of the 1988 campaign
found that coverage of the horse race and campaign controversies outpaced issue coverage four-to-one during the primaries.
They concluded that the only time "policy issues received sustained attention was in the last weeks of the primary season.
Even then they were dealt with only about as often as the horse
race, which had become a mere formality."[129] The Center for
Media and Public Affairs reported that in 1992 game coverage
was substantially greater during the primaries than in the general election.[130]

"The power of the press is a primordial one," Theodore
White observed. "It determines what people will think and talk
about—an authority that in other nations is reserved for ty-

rants, priests, parties, and mandarins."[131] I asked voters at different points in a presidential campaign whether they "had talked with anyone about the election during the last 24 hours." If they said yes, they were asked to describe what they had discussed. During the primaries, the game was the subject of 66 percent of the conversations, compared with only 20 percent about substance. During the convention and the general election, substance dominated the game as a subject of conversation 46 percent to 35 percent.[132]

A presidential contest is a very different experience for voters today than it was in the past. In their study of the 1948 campaign, Berelson, Lazarsfeld, and McPhee found that 67 percent of the voters' conversations were concerned with the candidates' positions and qualifications.[133] Today the game is the dominant topic, particularly during the nominating phase. The obvious reasons for this dramatic shift in what people talk about are the changes since 1948 in the structure of the campaign and the content of election news. Faced with contest after contest and exposed to news centered on the competition, election conversation is also certain to focus on the game.

By emphasizing the game dimension day after day, the press forces it to the forefront, strengthening the voters' mistrust of the candidates and reducing their sense of involvement. The press has this effect because the game schema drives its analysis, and its capacity to see the campaign in other ways is limited.

CHAPTER THREE

Images of
the Game They Play

For the most part, we do not first see, and then define, we
define first and then see.

WALTER LIPPMANN[1]

Everyone knows that Harry S Truman charged from behind to
edge out Thomas E. Dewey in 1948 on the strength of a "give
'em hell" style and a barnstorming whistle-stop campaign that
traversed America. Truman's spectacular show of brashness
and endurance captured Americans' imagination, gaining their
confidence and votes.

Truman's closing rush makes a nice story, but it was not
the story told during the campaign itself. Instead, the press
portrayed Truman chiefly as a weak candidate whose stridency
was a sign of desperation. Although there were at least some
favorable articles arguing that the underdog Truman was gaining steam, these were overwhelmed by far more numerous reports of an embattled nominee who had lost the ability to
inspire. *Newsweek* said that he lacked the "stature" of a president: "a woefully weak little man, a nice enough fellow but
wholly inept."[2]

As for Truman's rear-platform speeches, the press noted but
did not accentuate the fact that his crowds were getting bigger

and noisier. *Newsweek* headlined Truman's whirlwind tour at the end of the campaign "Prayer for a Chain Reaction."[3] Truman traveled farther and gave more speeches, but Dewey also did a lot of whistle-stopping, delivering more than one hundred speeches during the general election alone. A *Newsweek* columnist noted: "Dewey's extensive touring and frequent rear-platform talks are putting many Republican candidates for the Senate and House into his debt. This should help him in his relations with Congress."[4]

A Truman victory? In a front-page story the day before the election, *The New York Times* claimed: "The rosy prospect of victory for the Truman ticket on election day finds no credence outside Mr. Truman's kitchen cabinet."[5] *Time* polled the forty-seven journalists traveling with Dewey; all of them predicted he would win. *Newsweek* conducted a poll of "50 of the nation's top political writers" shortly before the election; all of them anticipated a Dewey victory. The *Newsweek* panel predicted a Dewey win of 366 to 126 in electoral votes and by 54 percent to 46 percent in the two-party popular vote.[6] Even after early returns revealed strong voter support for Truman, many news organizations still clung to the conviction that he would lose. "Dewey Defeats Truman" was the famous headline of the Chicago *Tribune*'s early edition.

The Truman whom we know today—the man of give-'em-hell and whistle-stopping fame—did not become the press's story line until after the election. Finding themselves with a surprise winner on their hands, journalists proceeded without hesitation to give him a new image. The aggressive style which had earlier been labeled "intemperate"[7] suddenly became energetic and hard-hitting.

The images in the news of Truman before and after Election Day were not complete fabrications; they were constructed from elements of the candidate's strategy and personality. But they were highly selective images, built on reporters' expectations of the election's outcome. Truman-the-likely-loser was depicted differently from Truman-the-surprise-winner. For a

time during the fall of 1948, the press was operating on a view
of the electorate that did not correspond with what the voters
were thinking, and it concocted images that fit its imagined
world.

Election news in 1948 was fiction of a kind. The last Gallup
poll, conducted a few weeks before the November election,
showed Dewey with an apparently insurmountable lead. State-
by-state assessments by political pundits confirmed the expecta-
tion. Washington insiders were already speculating on the
makeup of President Dewey's cabinet. Reporters accepted and
contributed to the belief in the inevitability of a Truman defeat.
They created images for Truman that matched the assumptions
of the story they were telling. They accentuated Truman's
weaker traits and downplayed his stronger ones. When reporters discovered on Election Day that they had been telling the
wrong story, they constructed a new Truman—"give 'em-hell
Harry"—to fit their new story.

An understanding of the news media's version of reality begins
with a recognition that reporters must have a story to tell. The
news cannot be a jumble of facts tossed together willy-nilly.
The "facts" must cohere, and they must do so in time for the
daily deadline. This assignment cannot be carried out unless the
reporter starts with a story in mind. Raw reality "is a confusing,
confounding blur of information."[8] The reporter who begins
the day in search of a story with no idea of what it will say risks
finding nothing.[9] Journalists are like the rest of us; they define
first, and then they see.[10]

Unlike the rest of us, however, journalists see politics
through a game schema. Paul Weaver describes it as "a narrow
and distinctively journalistic model or theory of politics."[11]
Journalists do not have to see politics in this way. Although
campaigns include political activity and strategy, they en-
compass an entire public and a wide range of governing problems. The story possibilities are endless, which means that

journalists must find some way to narrow the selection. European journalists see the campaign through the lens of party politics.[12] American reporters find the shortcut in their game schema.

Exit polls and electronic vote returns spare modern journalists the embarrassment of the Chicago *Tribune* when the victorious Truman held high its early edition, but the press today is no less inclined to assign candidates an image that is consistent with their position in the race. The central issue of the game schema is the horse race, and it predetermines the answers. The issues, the images, the tactical adjustments—all of these factors at some point must make sense in terms of the race.[13] A reporter cannot routinely say that the candidate who is in second place has the better strategy; to do so is to invite a complex explanation that might not be persuasive and that would call into question the reporter's objectivity.

The need to simplify is magnified by the journalistic tendency to report the news through the actions of individual leaders.[14] "The media," the political scientist Hugh Heclo observes, "amplify what we know to be a predisposition in the general public: namely, an impulse to understand public affairs mainly through a prominent political actor's behavior and not in terms of more complex, situational factors."[15] Although the conditions of society set the parameters of political debate, they are a difficult basis for analysis. Explanations based on the actions of leaders, though less sound, are more easily assembled. If Truman is behind, this must reflect a personal shortcoming or a flaw in his game plan.

The journalist is drawn irresistibly to such inferences. The tendency to say unfavorable things about a faltering candidate is nearly tautological: the candidate is doing poorly; therefore, something is wrong with him. In an article titled "Mondale's Image Is a Victim of Television's Eye," the Washington *Post* wrote in the closing weeks of the 1984 campaign that on television Walter Mondale looked "shrill, harsh—sometimes even menacing. Yet, at the same time—primarily because of his voice—he comes off as somehow 'weak' and a 'wimp.' "[16] In actual fact, Mondale performed well on television. In the first televised debate against Reagan, Mondale beat the "Great Communicator" in the judgment of the audience, and a large majority of viewers said they held a better opinion of him after the debate than they had held before.[17]

Mondale's real problem was his position as the out-party's nominee when the nation's economy was strong. Any challenger would have had trouble in 1984 and would have received the type of "bad press" that is reserved for sure losers, whatever their true nature or the quality of their campaign effort. Mondale was less a victim of "television's eye" than of journalistic inference. After the second presidential debate, in which Mondale, though unable to shake Reagan's confidence, gave a capable performance, *Newsweek* said he looked "grayer and more tired" than in the first debate.[18]

Although the reporters' view is narrow, their claims are broad. There is always something that a losing candidate is doing poorly—or, at least, differently from the leader. Such "facts" furnish the press with its "explanations" for the candidate's weak showing. Mondale was reported to have run a "mistake-free" campaign until he secured the Democratic nomination, at which point he was measured against Reagan and described as "error-prone." *The New York Times* said of Mondale's effort: "Bad ideas [can] get embedded in the strategic thinking of a presidential campaign. A faulty central concept can either kill a candidacy outright or cripple it."[19] Who can dispute the reporter's claim that a losing candidate has the wrong game plan or lacks charisma? (Said *Time*, "Listening to Mondale is like reading a book, and a heavy one at that.")[20] The uncertain truths of electioneering get pushed aside as the press attempts to reconcile the "facts" of the campaign with its call of the race.

There are constraints on the press's explanations. Candidates have traits that limit what can be said of them. Ronald Reagan's skill and ease in public speaking, acquired during his years in

Hollywood, made him the "Great Communicator."* No reporter said the same of his predecessor, Jimmy Carter.

Nevertheless, if journalists were describing candidates "as
they really are," their portrayals would not swing abruptly
when the candidates' fortunes change. But the images do shift.
When George Bush beat Reagan in the Iowa caucuses in 1980,
he got positive press.[21] "There is a gleam in his eye and a spring
in his step," reported UPI's Clay Richards. "The candidate's
energy seems limitless."[22] Bush's strength was said to rest on
ambiguous positions, which allowed voters to see in him what
they wanted to see. Bush then lost the New Hampshire primary to Reagan, and the tone changed. Voters were said to
have deserted Bush because they had only "vague reasons for
supporting him."[23]

---

* The "Great Communicator" label indicates that the press's image-making is
not confined to campaigns. In the first months of his presidency, Reagan had
success with Congress but lost public support because of the country's economic problems. Although inflation and interest rates fell, unemployment
reached a postwar high. Reagan's approval rating declined faster than that of
any president in the history of the Gallup poll. The "Great Communicator"
label made no sense in this context and was not a news theme. Instead, the
"Great Persuader" appeared in news stories and columns as a description of
Reagan's ability to get Congress to accept his leadership. "The wooing came
at the end of a month-long campaign by Reagan that once again showed why
he is known as the Great Persuader," concluded *Time* in late 1981, after Reagan
had convinced Congress to sell AWACs planes to Saudi Arabia. Toward the
end of Reagan's second year in office, his political fortunes changed. The
economy turned upward, and so did his public support; meanwhile, congressional Democrats had begun to contest his policies. A new image was required.
The "Great Communicator" came forth. The term began to appear regularly
in opinion columns, spread to news-analysis pieces, and then showed up in
routine news reports. In this context, it is interesting to speculate on how
Mondale would have been portrayed if the 1984 presidential election had been
held two years earlier. Opinion polls in 1982 indicated that Americans preferred any Democrat to Reagan. If the election had been held in 1982, and
Mondale had led throughout, would reporters still have described him as
"somehow 'weak' and a 'wimp' "? During his vice-presidential and Senate
years, words like "thoughtful" and "dedicated" were used in press descriptions
of Mondale.

Post-hoc reversals of this type are routine in the early stages of a nominating campaign. My study of the 1976 election found that press statements about a candidate's character, strategy, and organization were significantly less favorable in weeks when the candidate had lost a primary or slipped in the polls.[24]

Press judgments acquire credibility because of "pack journalism"—the tendency of reporters to concentrate on the same developments and interpret them in the same way.[25] When reporters speak with one voice their judgments seem accurate, but are no more true because of it. After Reagan lost the 1980 Iowa caucuses to Bush by 3 points, reporters believed he was finished. CBS's Walter Cronkite began an interview with Reagan by showing a film clip of the candidate contradicting himself. Cronkite observed that "some of his opponents like to say his ideas haven't changed in a decade."[26] At a National Press Club luncheon in Washington, reporters were asked to predict who would win the presidency. Jimmy Carter got the most votes, 197, and Bush was second, with 65. Reagan received fewer votes than Edward Kennedy and John Connally, each of whom was selected by 19 reporters. When asked about the GOP nomination, 185 chose Bush, while 29 named Reagan, which was the same number who picked Connally.[27] At the next stop on the campaign trail, New Hampshire, Reagan crushed Bush, 50 percent to 23 percent, and then breezed to his party's nomination.

"Has the press gone soft on Bill Clinton?" The question was posed by the Washington *Post*'s Howard Kurtz during the 1992 general election, after many Republicans and some journalists had asked whether Bush was being held to a higher standard than Clinton.[28] Reporters had given Clinton a rough time earlier in the campaign: their stories about his draft record, marijuana use, and relationship with Gennifer Flowers nearly derailed his candidacy. He was called "Slick Willy" because of his evasive answers ("I did not do anything wrong [on the draft], and I certainly did not do anything illegal"; "I didn't inhale it [marijuana], and never tried it again"; "The [Flowers] story is just not true").

Clinton was third behind Bush and Perot in June, and reporters were ready to write him off. The Washington *Post*, in a front-page story, said, "On the morning after Bill Clinton clinched his party's presidential nomination, words that he had often used to evoke the frustrations of America's middle class seemed more applicable to the candidate's own predicament."[29] He was nearly ignored by the press for a three-week period in June, during which he resorted to television appearances on call-in shows, MTV, and Arsenio Hall.

Clinton's coverage changed dramatically in July, when Ross Perot's abrupt withdrawal, the continued weakness of the economy, and a show of unity at the Democratic convention gave him a 27-point lead over Bush. His "Slick Willy" image gave way to admiration for his tireless campaigning. *Newsweek* called him "Clinton the Survivor."[30] The Washington *Post* said that "through better and worse . . . Clinton just keeps going."[31] On the nightly newscasts in August, three-fifths of the references to Clinton by nonpartisan sources were neutral or favorable, compared with fewer than half earlier in the campaign.[32] The Clinton-Gore bus tour across middle America produced a string of glowing stories. "New Heart Throbs of the Heartland" was the headline of a story in the Washington *Post*'s Style section.

Bush's coverage was substantially different; only a third of the network news references to Bush during August were neutral or favorable.[33] According to the press, Bush was doing nearly everything wrong. His campaign staff was in shambles. The appointment of James A. Baker III as White House chief of staff was labeled a "desperate" move by CBS's Susan Spencer, who added that there was "some doubt even Jim Baker can rescue this one."[34] Bush's strategy was inept. "Under savage criticism from Republican officeholders and strategists for a tardy, flaccid and unimaginative campaign, President Bush headed into the Midwest. . . ."[35] His demeanor was sluggish.

"But unless the President conveys new energy . . . he may as well take the fall off and retool his old campaign slogan to read: 'Ready on Day One to Be a Great *Ex*-President.' "[36] His record was lousy. "Bush has not put forth a positive reason for people to elect him to a second term, other than his foreign policy record, which is not enough."[37]

By the general election, Clinton's coverage had turned negative again, but Bush's coverage was even more so. At no time was Bush accorded a comment like the one NBC's Lisa Myers made about Clinton: "Throughout his life, Clinton has been committed to public service and doing good."[38]

The third candidate in the 1992 race, Ross Perot, rode a roller coaster of news and polls. "He was a phenomenon when he had 30 percent support in late spring, a fake when he dropped out of the race in July, an egomaniac when he returned in September, and paranoid when he searched for his base in October," wrote Jeffrey Katz in the *Washington Journalism Review*.[39]

However, Perot's press ride did not fit the normal pattern, because his opponents hesitated to attack him, fearing they would alienate his followers. During the primary-election phase, Perot had 36 percent bad press on network television, compared with Bush's 78 percent and Clinton's 59 percent. Negative evaluations of Perot came chiefly from supposedly neutral sources, mainly reporters.[40] When he made statements that seemed to conflict with the record, the press brought forth the discrepancies—most of them about small matters, but a few about important things, such as whether he had launched several investigations of President Bush.[41] Perot's refusal to discuss issues in detail was criticized ("Trying to pin down Perot on specifics is like trying to nail Jell-O to the wall," NBC's Lisa Myers complained),[42] and his history of playing politics was contrasted with his antipolitics image ("Perot has a penchant for military solutions, covert operations, and intimidation," said CBS's Eric Engberg).[43]

In June, Perot's bad press sharply increased, which he

blamed on Republican "dirty tricks."[44] This bad press may be the most plausible explanation for his quitting the race in July. But this coverage was based on generally good reporting and was followed by a slippage in the polls. Perot was stunned by the press's handling of his "you people" remark at the NAACP convention. "This sound bite has made me sound like David Duke," Perot complained to the president of CNN. "I consider every person in the country my equal. . . . This is the last straw. I'm living in a world of setups."[45]

Paradoxically, the bad press that then accompanied Perot's withdrawal in July ("The Quitter" was how *Newsweek* dubbed its cover story)[46] contributed to his decision to return. Perot had not expected to become a laughingstock, and he had to undo his decision in order to restore his reputation. He was below 10 percent in the polls upon his return, and Clinton and Bush held back their criticisms. Overall, Perot's good press–bad press ratio in the general election period was better than Clinton's or Bush's, because there were not many "partisan" attacks to report. The press itself, however, was still highly critical of Perot. *Newsweek* greeted his return in October with the cover story "Ego Trip."[47] CBS's Bill Lagattuta claimed that Perot's televised ads "don't show how temperamental, thin-skinned and downright mean Perot can be."[48] According to the Center for Media and Public Affairs, 81 percent of the evaluative comments about Perot by television correspondents during the general election were negative.[49]

During all three stages of the 1992 campaign—the primaries, the convention, and the general election—Bush led the pack in bad news.[50]

A possible explanation of this pattern was the press's determination to contribute to the president's defeat. A Bush advisor said, "I think we know who the media want to win this election —and I don't think it's George Bush."[51] Bush operatives were not the only ones who griped. ABC News correspondent Brit

Hume, seen by many other journalists as a conservative, complained, "Some reporters are smitten with Clinton. . . . I think there has been a double standard."[52]

The allegation of press bias during presidential campaigns has been made before. In *The News Twisters*, Edith Efron charged that the television networks in 1968 "actively opposed the Republican candidate, Richard Nixon."[53] She tracked the amount of television good press and bad press received by Nixon and his opponents, Hubert Humphrey and George Wallace, and concluded that "network coverage tends to be strongly biased in favor of the Democratic-liberal-left axis of opinion, and strongly biased against the Republican-conservative-right axis of opinion."[54]

Studies have shown that most journalists are liberal and Democratic in their personal beliefs.[55] A 1992 survey of journalists found that they identified with the Democratic party three-to-one—an increase from three-to-two in the pre-Reagan period.[56]

No scholarly study, however, has definitively linked journalists' partisan views to a systemic bias in favor of Democratic presidential candidates. Efron, a conservative columnist, did her own content analysis rather than using trained coders, which is the accepted method. Scholarly studies employing the latter method have concluded that partisan bias plays a relatively small part in election news. The political scientist Doris Graber's studies found no clear favoritism toward either Republican or Democratic candidates in the 1968, 1972, and 1976 elections.[57] In *Over the Wire and on TV*, Michael Robinson and Margaret Sheehan concluded that good and bad press in 1980 were distributed impartially to candidates of both parties.[58]

The most detailed study of bias is C. Richard Hofstetter's *Bias in the News*.[59] Hofstetter's analysis, which covered more than four thousand television news references to the 1972 campaign, produced no evidence of significant bias against Republicans. Hofstetter's study did detect one kind of bias, however, which results from journalistic values: good or bad press stems from decisions based on independent news standards, which apply to Republicans and Democrats alike. Paul Weaver made a similar observation, concluding that "if the news confers advantage or disadvantage on any candidate, it does so primarily because of the inherent biases of [journalism] as a distinctive form of discourse."[60]

Journalistic bias helps to explain Bush's bad press in 1992.* The prevailing story line was an incumbent president whose reelection bid was in trouble. This news theme was unfavorable, and so, therefore, were the "facts" that reporters used to support it.

In the early phase of the campaign, the theme was defined in terms of the unexpectedly strong showing of the Republican challenger Pat Buchanan and public concern about the economy. "President Bush has used the word 'free-fall' in talking about the economy," said CBS's Susan Spencer. "Free-fall may apply to his popularity as well."[61] The Washington *Post* reported, "An angry New Hampshire electorate issued a powerful cry of protest against President Bush today, giving him victory in the state's presidential primary but casting a large vote for Patrick J. Buchanan, the conservative commentator who invited voters to use him to 'send a message' of discontent."[62] On network television, Bush got more bad press (76 percent negative) than Buchanan (53 percent) from "nonpartisan" sources (pundits, voters, and journalists).[63]

In the second phase, around the time of the national conventions, the theme of a beleaguered incumbent was played out in news of Bush's dismal standing in the polls and his failed attempts to revitalize his campaign. ABC quoted an economist as saying, "He has articulated no vision of where this country should go in an economic sense."[64]

* Much of the analysis that follows is patterned on Paul Weaver's seminal article on news bias.

The third phase was the fall campaign, which showed a candidate who was far down in the polls ("The President, clearly, is in desperate trouble"),[65] grasping wildly in search of tactics and issues that would work to his advantage ("The Bush camp has relied on frenzied action, a show of crisis management and a shower of subsidies to cloud the voters' attention, diverting it from the economy, and also from the lack of a clear Bush agenda"[66]). Evaluations of Bush's campaign style and strategy were singularly negative. Almost no reporter suggested that Bush was campaigning effectively. According to an analysis of the Center for Media and Public Affairs, "93 percent of 'nonpartisan' [mostly reporters'] comments about Bush's campaign were negative."[67]

There was nothing overtly partisan in most of this reporting. The press treated the campaign more as an event than as an issue; the contest was the main subject.[68] Moreover, Clinton's views did not get more attention than Bush's; in fact, Bush got slightly more news coverage during the general election than Clinton.[69]

Bush's bad press was mainly a function of journalistic values. The news form itself affected both the content and the slant of most of his coverage. Bush's story was that of a re-election campaign in deep trouble—much like the story of a baseball team that was favored to win the pennant but stumbled early and never regained its stride. Bush was saddled with a stagnant economy, and each new indicator of the economy's poor condition (government agencies issue nearly fifty such indicators each month) brought more bad news to his campaign coverage. Each new poll did the same.

The impact of the economy on Bush's re-election bid was so basic to the press's game commentary that the president's efforts to raise other subjects were treated as attempts to hide the real issue. A Knight-Ridder wire-service story a month before the election said: "But barring a last-minute 'October surprise' all the tactical maneuvers on the surface of the [Bush] campaign probably cannot alter the underlying forces driving the election:

a dismal economy and a widespread demand for change, both of which bode ill for Bush."[70]

Perhaps journalists' opinions of Bush influenced their coverage of his candidacy. Journalists felt they had been manipulated in 1988 into reinforcing Bush's mean-spirited attacks on Dukakis. By 1992, the media had also soured on Bush's handling of the presidency. Editorials and opinion columns were generally critical of his leadership and policies.

This view crept into the reporting of the election. When issues were covered in election stories, reporters sometimes took sides. Many of the criticisms of Bush were voiced through others—Clinton partisans, policy analysts, and voters. NBC News pictured a voter saying, "He's not done anything, he don't stand for anything."[71] However, there was also a great deal of anti-Bush sentiment within the context of supposedly straight news reports. Bush's campaign, said an ABC correspondent, "has succeeded so far in solidifying its position—10 or 15 points behind."[72] *Newsweek* said, "On the big question—the economy —he has little more than gimmicks to offer, and his advisors know it."[73] When Bush's veto of the cable-television bill was overridden, NBC's Odetta Rogers remarked, "The override makes Bush look like a lame duck."[74]

These statements go beyond any reasonable definition of aggressive reporting. They represent advocacy journalism. Whether they also constitute partisan bias—a systematic attempt by a liberal press to defeat a Republican president—is a question that will be dealt with later in this chapter.

The argument that journalistic bias was the primary source of Bush's bad press is strengthened by the parallel with 1980, when the embattled incumbent was a Democrat, Jimmy Carter. Carter's approval rating, like Bush's, was below 40 percent during much of the election year.

In the early phase of the 1980 nominating campaign, Carter got favorable news out of his primary victories over Edward

Kennedy, but Kennedy's persistent challenge ("He has at last become a forceful, zesty campaigner"),[75] weaknesses in the economy ("Inflation is not only a frightening economic problem but it is rapidly becoming Carter's most dangerous political liability as well"),[76] and challenges to America's international standing from the Iranian hostage crisis and the Soviet invasion of Afghanistan ("More than at any point in the postwar period, the U.S. seems to be on the defensive in a dangerous world"),[77] combined to make the overall tone of the president's coverage unfavorable.

In the summer, when Carter fell far behind Reagan in the polls, the bad news continued ("The president begins the race against Reagan on the defensive, leading a troubled party that shows few signs of enthusiasm for his style of leadership").[78] When Carter gained momentum in the fall, the possibility of a dramatic comeback was a source of good news, but it was outweighed by continuing problems with the economy and in the world ("The worsening inflation is bound to . . . help Ronald Reagan in his attempt to convince voters that President Carter has mismanaged the economy").[79] Carter's attempts to claw his way back into the race through attacks on Reagan led the press to nickname him "Jimmy the Mean." Reagan supposedly responded to the attacks with a "lofty calm."[80]

Carter's coverage was less favorable than Reagan's,[81] which prompted his advisers to complain that he was being treated unfairly. In an essay titled "Rooting for Reagan," the journalist Jonathan Alter suggested that reporters assigned to Reagan gave him "good press" because they would get the coveted White House beat if "their man" won.[82] The Washington *Post*'s Howard Kurtz wrote that reporters covering the Clinton campaign in 1992 may have had the same motive.[83]

Although some correspondents in 1992 and 1980 may have been trying to advance their careers, the major reason the challenger got more favorable coverage was his opponent's association with a sagging economy. The incumbent president as weak candidate: this theme dominated the stories of Bush's and Carter's re-election bids.

The same story line was prominent in 1976, when Republican Gerald Ford presided over an ailing economy. Ford's story was one of high unemployment and inflation, as well as a loss in public confidence after the Nixon pardon. Like the coverage of Bush and Carter, Ford's bad press included personal ridicule. Bush was the rudderless president; Carter, the inadequate one; and Ford, the awkward one. He was pictured as slow-witted and clumsy, even though he had a law degree from Yale and had played football at Michigan. He was shown falling on the slopes of Aspen and tripping on the ramp of Air Force One— metaphors for an inept president.

The news coverage of each of these candidacies was superficial and nasty. It was also biased in its effects; the re-election prospects of Bush, Carter, and Ford were diminished by news of their campaigns. When presidents lose popularity, they not only, as David Broder observed, lose "the ability to govern";[84] they also lose the ability to campaign effectively. They struggle against the news image of a floundering, ineffective politician.

This news bias has political consequences. Truman was able to overcome it in 1948, but he was the majority-party nominee in an era of stronger partisanship and a mannerly press. Today's embattled president must surmount weakened partisanship and an activist press that faults his every move. Ford could not prevail over them, nor could Carter or Bush. Perhaps no hard-pressed modern president can be expected to do so.

The validity of a journalistic explanation of bias becomes more persuasive when the 1988 election is examined. That year Bush's opponent got the worst of the bad news.

A *Newsweek* reporter wrote that Michael Dukakis lost largely because he failed to "de-ice his image."[85] But the issue of Dukakis's personality did not become a news theme until after the primaries. Dukakis's early coverage offers a sharp contrast to what reporters said later on. When, after the Republican convention, he fell 15 points behind, his news image deteriorated. The same candidate who had been described by *Newsweek* as "relentless in his attack" and a "credible candidate"[86] was suddenly recast by the same magazine as "reluctant to attack" and "trying to present himself as a credible candidate."[87] This "new" Dukakis, "losing the lilt of his acceptance speech, is in an unappetizing eat-your-peas pose."[88]

Dukakis's campaign was portrayed as a series of missteps. Everything was fair game. In mid-October, ABC's Sam Donaldson showed Dukakis playing the trumpet with a local band. He was facing away from reporters. "He played the trumpet with his back to the camera," chortled Donaldson, who could be heard in the story calling to Dukakis, "We're over here, Governor." Donaldson concluded his story with a picture of Dukakis rolling a gutter ball at the local bowling alley.[89] When Dukakis failed to mention his wife, Kitty, in response to a debate question about whether he would favor the death penalty for an assailant if she were raped and murdered, reporters took it as confirmation of his "iceman" image.[90] *Time* remarked, "It may take until springtime to raise Dukakis to room temperature."[91]

Bush fared better, at least in the late summer and early fall. *Newsweek* said, "Somehow, with his formal nomination at the August convention, [Bush] stepped out of Reagan's long shadow and became his own man."[92] Bush had carried the label of "wimp" during the spring campaign. When he announced his candidacy in October 1987, *Newsweek*'s cover story was headlined, "Fighting the Wimp Factor," which the magazine justified by saying it was the chief question that campaign strategists were asking about Bush.[93] After he won the nomination, *Newsweek* said the wimp factor was "banished, as long as Bush is on the attack." Bush had now become everything Dukakis was not: "Duke seems a sourpuss compared to this new Bush person."[94]

It is conceivable that Bush changed between the spring primaries and the summer conventions. But in view of his many years in politics, including eight years as vice president, it is more likely that the journalists' portrayal of Bush was all that had changed. The "wimp" label was easier to pin on a vice president than on a candidate who had just taken a solid lead in the presidential race (*Newsweek* said he looked "relaxed, authoritative, even presidential").[95]

During the general election, Bush's coverage turned sour. His frontrunner's position brought favorable comments about his association with a Republican administration that was presiding over the longest upturn in the economy since World War II. However, the theme that developed from his use of the Willie Horton, Boston Harbor, and flag issues was not favorable. Since these aspects of the fall campaign were tied most closely to the game, Bush got bad press: 65 percent of evaluative comments on the nightly television newscasts were negative. Dukakis's coverage was marginally worse.[96]

Where does this analysis leave the issue of partisan bias in news coverage of the 1992 campaign?

The charge of bias cannot be dismissed entirely. Reporters turned strongly on George Bush in 1992. The analysis of the Center for Media and Public Affairs reveals Bush as a candidate who received almost nothing but negative coverage. It concluded:

> During the primaries, the summer, and the general election, Bush received more negative evaluations than his rivals. Bush's 22 percent positive press during the primaries was worse than that received by any other candidate in the field. His [slight] upswing in good press during the conventions and the general election mainly reflected the visibility of partisan Republican sources. Yet even during his best period (the general election), more than 70 percent of non-partisan news sources criticized Bush, a figure no other candidate matched even during their worst periods.[97]

A key indicator here is the evaluations provided by supposedly nonpartisan sources—mainly journalists, but also some policy experts and voters. Their assessments were filtered through the news-editing process. In Bush's case, many reporters and editors selected particular evaluations without making any attempt to balance the good with the bad. When Bush threatened a veto of a congressional package filled with pork-barrel projects, CBS's Bob Schieffer harked back to Bush's favors for defense contractors: "What was he handing out? Chopped liver?"[98] Voters interviewed on the nightly news nearly always spoke ill of Bush, even though the polls were not nearly so one-sided. The voters allowed to speak on the news were typically harsh on Bush. A voter on CBS said, "I will not trust my future and my child's future to someone who has done such a poor job for the past four years."[99]

A comparison of Bush's evaluations by nonpartisan sources (including journalists) and partisan sources is also revealing: 71 percent negative as opposed to 67 percent negative. In contrast, criticism of Clinton originated mainly from partisan sources—mostly Bush himself. About 75 percent of partisan assessments of Clinton were negative. Nonpartisan evaluations of Clinton were evenly divided—48 percent negative, 52 percent positive.[100] Reporters themselves made proportionally fewer negative statements about Clinton than about Bush, and by a wide margin. When questioned about this, Erik Sorenson, executive producer of the "CBS Evening News," gave an incredible response: "We had trouble finding people, even Republicans, who would say nice things about George Bush."[101]

Bush did not even get the honeymoon coverage that normally accompanies a candidate's nomination. Clinton's press was 68 percent favorable during the week of the Democratic convention—nearly the same as the 69 percent favorable coverage that Dukakis received in 1988. In comparison, Bush had 84 percent positive evaluations in 1988, but only 49 percent in 1992.[102]

Even ostensibly good news was sometimes made to seem bad. ABC's Stephen Aug reported in October, "The unemployment rate came down for the wrong reasons—fewer jobs and far more people too discouraged to look for them."[103] CBS did much the same thing a week before Election Day with the positive information that gross domestic product had risen by an estimated 2.7 percent during the third quarter of 1992. After Dan Rather announced it, correspondent Eric Engberg shouted "Time out" and presented four less significant economic indicators that seemed to dismiss the possibility that the economy would be moving out of recession.[104] After the election, when the actual figure turned out to be a healthy 3.4 percent jump, the press declared that the economy was growing again.

The economy was the backdrop to the Bush candidacy, and, like Bush, it was represented in a consistently negative light. During the general election, more than 90 percent of references to the economy on network news were negative, as opposed to 75 percent in the immediately preceding period—a remarkable statistic.[105] *The networks' portrayal of the economy got worse as the economy improved.* Bush was forced to run not only against a bad economy but against negative coverage of an economy that was in fact getting better.

In 1988, the Yale economist Ray Flair predicted the outcome of the Bush-Dukakis race within less than 1 percent of the actual vote. His model was based on the condition of the nation's economy six months before the November election, and included nothing about Willie Horton or the personal characteristics of the nominees. In 1992, Flair's model predicted another Bush victory, since the economy was in good shape relative to the Carter 1979–80 recession. According to the media, however, the economy was in grave condition, and Bush's policies were a major reason why. "The problem for Bush and for Flair's model was that many people thought conditions were worse than they were," Seymour Martin Lipset writes. "Even if it were true that the recession was not as bad as some previous ones, Americans thought it was the worst they had experienced since World War II."[106]

While the pattern of Bush's news coverage in 1992 does not prove partisan bias, it strongly suggests it, as does the more general trend in election news toward journalist-led criticism. In the 1960s, the "tone" of a news story (whether favorable, unfavorable, or neutral toward its subject) was usually deter-

Figure 3.1   Source of Tone of Election Stories on the Front Page of
**   *The New York Times*, 1960–1992**

In the 1960s, the tone of most election articles was set by the words of partisan sources, mainly the candidates themselves; today, the tone is usually set by the journalist who prepares the story.

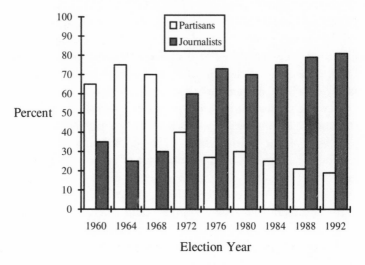

Note: Stories were coded in terms of tone (favorable, unfavorable, or neutral) and the principal source of this tone (the journalist who wrote the story or partisan sources—candidates and their supporters—who were mentioned in the story). Analysis excludes 10 percent of stories where the tone was set by other actors, such as experts.

mined by the quoted words of the candidates themselves and other partisans. Attacks on a candidate typically came from the mouths of opponents, praises from his supporters. As Figure 3.1 shows, partisan sources accounted for the tone in 70 percent of election articles on the front page of *The New York Times* in the 1960s. By the 1970s, the words of the journalists were setting the tone of most articles, and that tone was increasingly negative. In 1988 and 1992, journalistic sources determined a story's tone in about 80 percent of the cases—a complete reversal from the 1960s.

Today's journalism offers more opportunities for advocacy. The restrictive rules of objective reporting are weak, when they apply at all. It is no longer safe to assume, as Richard Hofstetter did of coverage in 1972, that partisan bias is insignificant. Perhaps it still is. However, journalists would have to exercise an extraordinary restraint, which they do not otherwise demonstrate, to keep their personal views out of their interpretive stories. There is a good probability that partisanship has become an integral part of election news.

If so, it should not be confused with the partisanship that once characterized the American press and that still marks the European media. Partisanship in those cases is an acknowledged factor in reporting. Most American journalists today are possibly unaware of how their partisan biases can affect their news coverage. National Public Radio's Cokie Roberts said after the election: "The losing party always whines. The best thing to do is just cover the campaign and not worry about what eighteen institutes on the media and politics think. We're not here to be loved. . . . And when you say the Bush campaign was a disaster, it's simply a fact. It's not our fault."[107]

But reporters are no more able than anyone else to set aside their ingrained predispositions. To some extent, they will see what they want to see when observing the campaign. Believing is seeing. Extensive scientific research has confirmed the powerful influence of the human tendency toward "selective perception."[108] If the conventions of the news process deny to the American journalist the more blatant modes of partisanship, the vogue for interpretive reporting encourages the less conscious forms of bias.

The coverage that Bush received was unusually negative, but all candidates get a lot of bad press. As was noted in the Prologue, the press has an antipolitics bias, which contributes to news that is harshly critical of those who seek the presidency.

The deep skepticism that reporters bring to the campaign

takes shape within the context of a story-driven news process. The social scientists Dan Nimmo and James Combs describe news reporting as "a literary act, a continuous search for 'story lines.' "[109] As the situation changes, so does the story line, and with it the news image in which the press envelops a candidate. What is said of the candidate must fit the plot.

Since the press is focused so tightly on the candidates and their standing in the game, it has for the most part only four stories to tell: a candidate is leading, or trailing, or gaining ground, or losing ground. The press has a distinctive narrative for each situation. Although there are positive aspects to all of them, the underlying assumption of the press's game schema is that candidates are in the game to win and will do almost anything to accomplish their goal. Thus the dynamic of the story line is furnished by the candidates' efforts to gather votes. Strategy and manipulation are the major themes of the plots built around the candidates' positions in the race.

In order to demonstrate the effect of a candidate's position on the tone of his news coverage, I conducted a content analysis of *Time*'s and *Newsweek*'s election coverage in the 1960–1992 period. All paragraphs that made reference to a major-party nominee were evaluated by trained coders; they were instructed to judge whether, on balance, the content was favorable or unfavorable to the candidate. For my analysis, I deleted all paragraphs judged to be neutral in tone and also those that referred to the horse race, since these evaluations naturally coincide with the candidates' positions in the race. Included in my analysis are all other paragraphs (3,279 in total) which made evaluative references, good or bad, to the candidates, including their ideas, issues, campaign deportment, personality, public records, and competence.

The next step was to categorize the candidates' positions in the race. Gallup polls conducted in the 1960–1992 period were used as the basis of classification. Candidates who gained substantial voter support within a relatively short span of time were placed in the "bandwagon" category for that period. Those who lost significant support were in the "losing ground" category. The "frontrunner" category consisted of nominees who had a large lead and held their position. Finally, the "likely loser" category covered candidates who trailed by a wide margin throughout a particular period of time.

These categories were then related to changes in news coverage. For example, what *Time* and *Newsweek* said about a candidate when he was in the frontrunner's position was compared with what was previously reported about him. In this way we were able to correlate the news coverage of given candidates with their positions in the race.

The most favorable coverage was received by those in the "bandwagon" category. The news of a candidate who has gained momentum and is rapidly gathering support takes the form of a compelling drama, particularly when the candidate has come up from far behind. The portrayal, to be sure, is not entirely positive. It includes mention of personal and political reasons why the candidate was trailing earlier, and the explanations offered for his present success typically include references to calculated manipulation.[110] But the overall portrayal of a candidate who is succeeding in his battle to get ahead is at least relatively favorable.[111]

"The bandwagon" was the story of Bill Clinton ("on a roll")[112] in midsummer 1992. It also describes other recent candidates at various points in their campaigns, including Hubert Humphrey in the closing weeks of the 1968 race. Humphrey's earlier coverage had included a great number of unfavorable statements surrounding his association with the Johnson administration's Vietnam policy and the divisions within his party after the Chicago convention. He was portrayed as a candidate whose "Happy Warrior" image was out of step with the political climate of the time, and the media focused primarily on the circumstances of his nomination and the disorganized condition of his campaign. However, as Humphrey's campaign straightened itself out, it attracted the support of dissident Democrats and gained momentum. His news image sharply improved. Toward

Figure 3.2   News Portrayal of the "Bandwagon" Candidate

When a candidate's support in the polls increases sharply, the news of his candidacy becomes more favorable.

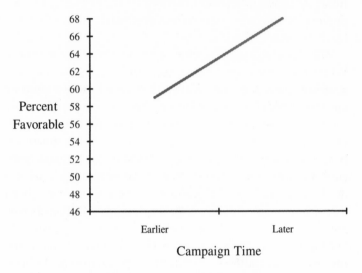

Campaign Time

Note: The figure is based on a composite of the May–October news coverage of major-party nominees in *Time* and *Newsweek* during the 1960–1992 period. The favorability of a nominee's coverage in the month before a bandwagon began (the "Earlier" category) was compared with coverage in the subsequent month (the "Later" category). "Horse-race" evaluations are not included in the data; all other evaluative references are included. The data for this figure and the next three are based on 3,279 paragraphs of election coverage.

the end of the campaign, as he closed with a rush and nearly beat Nixon, his "rags-to-near-riches" story was irresistibly positive news.[113]

The general pattern of "bandwagon" news is shown in Figure 3.2. The figure is a composite of the evaluative news references to candidates from 1960 to 1992 when they were moving up rapidly in the polls. The "bandwagon" narrative is good news for the candidate. In comparison with the coverage received previously, he is suddenly more decisive, committed, inspiring, and in general a better candidate and person. He is the same individual he was when the bandwagon started, but his news image is more positive. It is a natural tendency for the press to build him up in a story line that centers on his charge to the front. In statistical terms, his news image undergoes an improvement of about 15 percent over what it was before the bandwagon began.

The "bandwagon" story, however, tends to have a short life. When the bandwagon either sputters to a halt or carries the candidate into a safe lead, the press reverts to its more usual view of a candidate, and bad news begins to take precedence.

The polar opposite of the "bandwagon" narrative is the "losing ground" story line. The reasons why the candidate's support is eroding are highlighted, and there is no good news in electoral weakness. The decline in the candidate's self-confidence and his desperate attempts to reverse the slide become major news topics. The candidate's attacks on the opposition are thus depicted as increasingly wild and irresponsible. The "losing ground" story describes the coverage of many recent candidates, including Carter in the 1976 campaign. As his support plummeted, so did the tone of his news coverage. *Newsweek* reported, "Carter has clearly failed to 'connect' with voters. For a politician whose hand-to-hand, eye-to-eye style has been a major feature of the campaign, this is a disturbing trend and one that the candidate seems uncertain how to remedy."[114]

The "losing ground" scenario is shown in Figure 3.3 (next page). The story line results in a nearly 25 percent decline in favorable news coverage from the level immediately preceding the candidate's slide. No erosion of good news is more substantial than this steep drop. The only saving element is that it does not last forever. Once the candidate's free-fall ends, the bad news slows down. While it is happening, however, the candidate faces a flood of negative coverage embracing everything from his poor choice of issues to his lack of good sense.

The third category, and also one that offers very little pros-

Figure 3.3   News Portrayal of the "Losing-Ground" Candidate

When a candidate's support in the polls drops sharply, the news of his candidacy becomes less favorable.

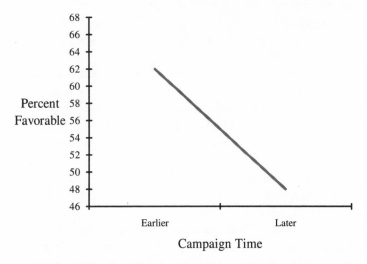

Note: The favorability of candidates' coverage in the month before they began to lose ground (the "Earlier" category) was compared with coverage in the subsequent month (the "Later" category). See Figure 3.2 for additional information.

pect for good news, is "the likely loser." This theme defined the failed re-election bid of President Bush. In its article on the first presidential debate of 1992, *Newsweek* dismissed Bush's chances of re-election even as it dismissed his appearance: "George Bush seemed reluctant to look the camera in the eye— even though 70 million Americans were waiting to be convinced that he should be president for another four years. Whatever was said in St. Louis Sunday night in the first, and probably most pivotal, presidential debate, it was the body language that had a story to tell: Bush, often staring down at his lectern, smiling his oddly apologetic smile, had not convinced himself, and therefore could not convince the country."[115]

It is a theme that can also apply to nonincumbents, such as Barry Goldwater and George McGovern. Goldwater, the

Republican nominee in 1964, was the most conservative major-party nominee of recent times, and McGovern, the 1972 Democratic nominee, was the most liberal. Both faced a strong incumbent. Their respective campaigns took a similar course. Each candidate trailed by a wide margin in the polls throughout the campaign and was defeated in a landslide of historic proportions. Goldwater and McGovern also shared a lousy news image. Both were portrayed as personally flawed, politically naïve, and programmatically unsound.

The pattern of "likely loser" news is shown in Figure 3.4 (next page). The decline in favorable news coverage is not as sharp as it is for a candidate who is losing ground, since the likely loser's coverage starts at a level that is already low. Nevertheless, the decline is still nearly 10 percent.

The fourth narrative is "the frontrunner." It is the story of a candidate with a presumably safe lead, and it contains some positive elements. The candidate is described as a confident leader with solid support. There is, however, a more pervasive and less favorable aspect to coverage of this type of candidacy: the press is critical of the maneuvering undertaken to keep the candidate on top. The candidate is described as overly secretive, and thereby as denying the public its right to know what he will do if he is elected. The candidate's superior resources are said to have funded an almost machinelike campaign. If he is an incumbent, any use of the presidential office by the candidate in a manner that may promote his re-election chances will be described as a calculated ploy.

"The frontrunner" describes the Reagan campaign of 1984 as well as the Nixon effort of 1968. Edith Efron claims the Nixon campaign reflected the press's liberal bias; but according to Paul Weaver, Nixon's press coverage was actually colored by journalistic bias. Weaver found that Nixon's bad press could be explained almost entirely by news values. He wrote:

Many stories on Nixon fixed on the characteristic problems of the front runner: how to maintain his lead and how to do it most effectively. This variation on the front runner

Figure 3.4   News Portrayal of the "Likely Loser" Candidate

When a candidate trails by a wide margin in the polls, the news of his candidacy becomes less favorable.

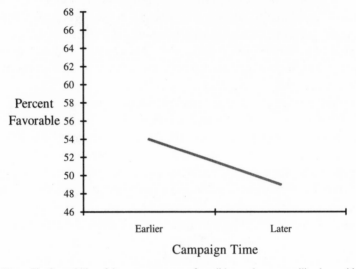

Campaign Time

Note: The favorability of the news coverage of candidates who were trailing by a wide margin was compared from one month (the "Earlier" category) to the next (the "Later" category). See Figure 3.2 for additional information.

theme, of course, focuses directly on the campaign as an exercise in the calculated, organized, well-funded manipulation of appearances and public opinion; and stories built around this theme emphasized the deliberateness, the lack of spontaneity, and the deceptiveness of all campaign events—the fact that behind every enthusiastic rally there are advance men at work creating and directing an audience, that in every public statement on some issue there lurks a tactical intelligence calculating what position will gain the most votes or lose the fewest, and so on.[116]

The pattern of the "frontrunner" narrative is shown in Figure 3.5. The average decline in a frontrunner's good news during

Figure 3.5   News Portrayal of the "Frontrunner" Candidate

When a candidate leads by a wide margin in the polls, the news of his candidacy becomes less favorable.

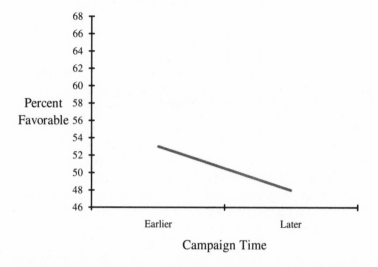

Note: The favorability of the news coverage of candidates who were leading by a wide margin was compared from one month (the "Earlier" category) to the next (the "Later" category). See Figure 3.2 for additional information.

the period 1960–92 was roughly 10 percent. Newswise, being out in front is not an advantage.

Of course, these composite pictures of how the press reports candidates according to their position in the race do not exactly describe any one candidate in this period. Each major-party nominee made a transition at some point in the campaign from one type to another. The composites do provide, however, a glimpse into the dynamics of presidential election coverage. The press dumps on losers and those who are losing support, criticizes frontrunners, and praises those who catch fire—at least for as long as the bandwagon lasts. But since most of the press's narratives are dominated by unfavorable evaluations of the candidates, so too is their news coverage.

The pattern of news coverage is somewhat different during the nominating phase. The "bandwagon" and "losing ground" narratives have a more extreme character than in the general election. A candidate who catches fire can expect highly favorable news coverage for a brief period. A candidate who starts to slide is quickly written off as a loser in nearly every respect.[117]

There are several variations to the "likely loser" narrative during the nominating phase. The weaker contenders usually do not receive much coverage, either good or bad. A candidate with the apparent potential to pull ahead may be accorded the status of "underdog," resulting in sympathetic and mostly favorable coverage.[118] Finally, a few losing candidates get a torrent of bad news. In 1980, CBS's Bernard Goldberg said that Jerry Brown's campaign was following "the path of Skylab"— the orbiting satellite that had crashed to earth.[119] The news for Brown was no better in 1992.[120] In a front-page *New York Times* article, Maureen Dowd described a Brown campaign stop in which a baby with a dollar bill tucked in her sweater as a campaign contribution was handed to Brown. As the crowd yelled "Kiss the baby," Brown drew back and then reached out and poked her arm with his finger. "The Zen of the Brown campaign," wrote Dowd, "is that the fiery populist, riding the tiger of rage in American politics, still has a hard time with the concept of actual human contact."[121]

A major difference between the nominating and general election phases is in the coverage afforded the frontrunner. In the general election, the frontrunner and his opponent receive roughly similar levels of negative coverage, although the content of the bad news is different.* The frontrunner's coverage,

---

* In some general elections, the frontrunner received the more favorable coverage and in other elections the likely loser did. For example, Goldwater (1964), McGovern (1972), Carter (1980), and Dukakis (1988) were losing candidates who fared less well in the news than their opponents. Nixon (1968) and Reagan (1984) were frontrunners who received more unfavorable coverage than their opponent.

however, is decidedly less favorable during the nominating phase. In this situation, the frontrunner may be under attack from four or five opponents at once, which fuels his negative news. In addition, the press appears to apply a double standard of scrutiny to a candidate who breaks from the pack. Such a candidate is usually not well known to the voters and may become president. The television commentator Jeff Greenfield has argued that the journalists' watchdog role takes over the coverage of such a candidate: "They are looking with more critical and skeptical eyes at a figure who may well hold the power of life and death over the world."[122] Robinson and Sheehan's study of the 1980 election concluded that the "thesis about double-standards is accurate."[123]

The stories that the journalists tell of the candidates are not harmless little tales that mix fact and fiction. They are narratives with real consequences, because they affect the images that voters acquire of the candidates. The press is the message.

A more conventional view of image formation is "The medium is the message." The print media are "hot," said Marshall McLuhan, and television is "cool." Platforms and issues are suited to the newspaper, but not to television, which rewards the inclusive image. "Without TV," McLuhan wrote of the 1960 race, "Nixon had it made." McLuhan concluded that Nixon lost because of the televised presidential debates—the first of their kind. Kennedy was said by McLuhan to project the image of a fictional hero—something like "the shy young sheriff"—while Nixon's dark eyes and circumlocutions made him resemble "the railroad lawyer who signs leases that are not in the interests of the folks in the little town."[124]

McLuhan's thesis was also applied, ironically, to Nixon's political comeback in 1968. In *The Selling of the President*, Joe McGinniss described how Nixon's managers had used audience research and television techniques to artfully create "a new Nixon."[125]

McLuhanesque analyses still surface during every presidential election. In 1988, after noting that Senator Sam Nunn had decided not to seek the presidency, the Washington *Post*'s David Broder said: "I believe that as far ahead as we can see, American presidential campaigns will be dominated by television, and no one can win the Oval office who is not 'photogenic,' who does not exude charm, and who lacks a facile, anecdotal usage of the English language. I think Nunn is smart enough to know this, and that this influenced him not to run."[126] In 1992, some pundits said that the Democrat Paul Tsongas might have won the nomination had he not talked like Elmer Fudd and looked like the guy next door.

Whatever the merits of this type of argument—and the evidence is largely circumstantial[127]—the critical influence of mass communication on the candidates' images is the narratives provided by the press. What these say about the candidates is more important than how they look on television. A candidate is helped or hurt far more by the tone of news messages than by being "telegenic" or not.*

The 1976 Carter candidacy illustrates how journalistic portrayals can significantly influence the voters' judgments of a candidate. Carter was a political unknown outside his home state of Georgia; hence the nation's voters began the 1976 campaign with virtually no impression of him at all. When he emerged as the surprise winner of the Iowa caucuses and the New Hampshire primary, and then rose rapidly in national polls, the news media cited Carter's apparent trustworthiness

---

* Even the examples generally cited to support the presumed effects of television have obvious flaws. Although the crowds at Kennedy's rallies increased after his debates with Nixon in 1960, research indicated that few voters chose their candidate on the basis of the debates. Some observers claim that Kennedy won only because the Daley machine stuffed enough ballot boxes to steal Illinois's crucial electoral votes from Nixon. As for the "new Nixon" of 1968, he nearly blew a 15-point lead during the general election. It is doubtful that the "medium is the message" argument would now have much support if Nixon had won in 1960 and Humphrey in 1968.

as a key to his success. He was at the crest of a "bandwagon" narrative. His candor and image as a "Washington outsider" reportedly appealed to a public disillusioned by Watergate and Vietnam.

Later, when Carter began to lose primaries, the "losing ground" plot took over. The electorate was reportedly becoming disenchanted with Carter, because despite saying repeatedly that he would "never lie to the American people," he spoke in vague generalities when addressing the issues and therefore was accused of waffling. *Newsweek* claimed in June that "the most common complaint of anti-Carter voters has been that he is fuzzy on the issues" and then quoted a voter who said, "We just got rid of one fellow [Nixon] who said he told the truth. I don't know how Carter can prove his integrity."[128]

Although Carter's status as a Washington outsider contributed to his initial success, it was only part of the story. His early wins were the product of many factors, not the least of which was a disorganized liberal wing of the Democratic party. In Iowa, Carter got 26 percent of the vote, while 37 percent was cast as "undecided," which was understood mainly to be a vote for Hubert Humphrey, who was considering entering the race. The press ignored the undecided ballots and declared Carter the winner. "He was the clear winner in this psychologically crucial test," declared CBS's Roger Mudd.[129]

In New Hampshire's critical primary, Carter, as the lone centrist, narrowly edged Morris Udall, who was competing with Bayh, Harris, and Shriver for the liberal vote. Although Carter won by fewer than five thousand votes and with barely more than one-fourth of the total New Hampshire vote, *Newsweek* reported: "On the Democratic side, former Georgia Governor Jimmy Carter was the unqualified winner."[130]

Because Carter was a new face and an early winner, he got the lion's share of the news coverage. In the period between New Hampshire and the decisive ninth primary, in Pennsylvania, he received as much coverage as all his Democratic rivals combined.[131] Since Carter's competitors were also not well known to the public before the campaign, Carter's publicity advantage provided an extraordinary edge in the first nine contests, eight of which he won.[132] Without this boost, according to an analysis by Larry Bartels of Princeton, Carter could have won the primary in only two states—New Hampshire, which gave him the boost, and Georgia, his home state.[133]

Later in the primary period, the liberal opposition to Carter coalesced around the late entrants Frank Church and Jerry Brown, both of whom beat Carter in nearly every head-to-head contest they had with him. However, Carter had already accumulated so many delegates that for all practical purposes the race was over.

Although the press misinterpreted the Carter candidacy to a large degree, the story it told made a difference. Figure 3.6 shows the relationship between news references and the voters' beliefs about Cater's trustworthiness. In the earliest months of 1976, when reporters were claiming that Carter's great popularity stemmed from a public perception of his trustworthiness, most Americans indicated they did not know Carter well enough to judge him. The press had ascribed to the entire electorate an image of Carter which was, in fact, only held by a few voters.[134]

The press's message eventually helped to shape what many voters came to believe about Carter. They came to think of him as trustworthy, and, as Figure 3.6 indicates, the higher their news exposure, the more likely they were to believe it. Later, as his news turned negative, the decline in Carter's image was steeper among those with heavier news exposure.

Perhaps there were McLuhanesque effects somewhere in this process. But if such a phenomenon occurred, its effect was small in relation to the influence of journalistic narratives. They told stories of Carter that were partial truths at best but that eventually affected how voters actually came to view him.

Reporters have considerable leeway in making claims about why candidates succeed or fail. Whether a candidate is doing well or poorly is an obvious fact, but the reasons why he is

Figure 3.6   **Jimmy Carter's Trustworthiness in the Eyes of the Voters, 1976—as Reported by the Media, and as Stated Directly by Voters**

The press's assessments of voters' perceptions of Carter did not correspond to their actual perceptions.

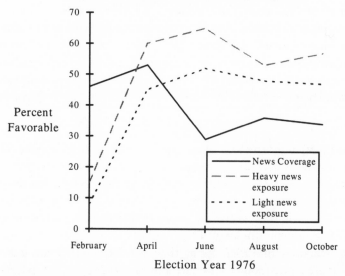

Note: The news data are based on a content analysis of network newscasts and four newspapers. Included are all news references that touched overtly or by clear inference on Carter's trustworthiness. The data on the public's actual perceptions are based on panel-survey questions as to whether Carter was "trustworthy" or "untrustworthy." Respondents were given the opportunity to say they did not know Carter well enough to judge his trustworthiness. A full description of the data is provided on pages 9–17 of the author's book *The Mass Media Election* (New York: Praeger, 1980).

doing well or poorly are not, leaving reporters relatively free to provide explanations of their choosing. When a candidate gains strength, reporters can fix on a favorable aspect and make it a reason for his success. When a candidate starts to slide, a negative quality can be brought forward as a causal factor.

The tendency of reporters to find their narratives in aspects of strategy and personality is inevitable. Their game schema presumes that the candidates' ability to play the game is a crucial factor in their success. If candidates succeed at the game, then, according to this line of reasoning, they must have picked the right strategy or been the right candidate for the time.

Journalists reason from effect to cause. They observe what is happening in the race and then look to the candidates for explanations. Other possible reasons for the electorate's changing support, such as the activation of party loyalties or the intrusion of societal problems, get less attention. Small wonder that election news is a story of triumph and defeat, and of the tactical and personal factors that separate the victors from the vanquished.

The fact that journalistic bias is a greater influence than political bias on the stories the press tells does not eliminate the former as an issue. As Weaver notes, it merely changes the nature of the issue.[135]

Journalistic bias would be a minor concern if the press's stories were inconsequential. They could be dismissed as interesting diversions in a melodrama that is much too long anyway. But these stories sometimes have substantial effects. When Carter is said to be sailing along because he is trustworthy or Bush is claimed to be dead in the water because he is incapable of seeing ahead, the message works its way into the public's consciousness. "This means," says Weaver, "that insofar as we rely on news in forming our mental picture of what is going on in the world, what we are receiving is not a neutral body of information, but rather information gathered and presented to illustrate certain ways of seeing the world, based on certain values and favorable to certain courses of action."[136]

In some ways partisan bias is preferable to journalistic bias, because it can be contested head-on. A partisan vision can be fought or deflected with an alternative one. In the days of the partisan press, the audience knew where a newspaper's opinions were coming from, and the reader could embrace or reject them as it suited his own preferences. "Andrew Jackson is a coarse, venial man of unprincipled ambition" was a charge that Whigs believed and Democrats denied. But what about the modern press's claim that George Bush was a man without vision and of limited talent? "It's tough to lead when you don't know where you want to go," said NBC's Lisa Myers. "Call it a vision; George Bush doesn't seem to have one."[137]

If in some way we recognize that Myers's view is not the whole truth, we have no alternative version of reality to compare or replace it with, so dependent are we on the press for our mental pictures of what is going on in the campaign, and so authoritative is the press in its pronouncements. The media, and television in particular, present "news without ambiguity, equivocation, or uncertainty."[138] The journalist speaks confidently about everything from leadership to particular events to society in general. "All are evidently within his perfect understanding, and he pronounces them without any ifs, ands, or buts."[139]

We are not required to make these authoritative judgments the basis of our vote, and many people do not. The loyal Republicans who supported Bush did so despite what the press was saying about him, not because they had tapped into a parallel news world that offered a different version of reality.

This one-dimensional journalism has served America for a century, and while it is usually "fair" in its reporting (Republican and Democratic candidates are treated about equally well or badly when they are in similar situations), it is not neutral in its effects. Reporters' vision of politics as a strategic game and the narratives they use to tell this story introduce random partisanship into the campaign. Bush in 1992, Carter in 1980, and Ford in 1976 were all hurt by it. Bush in 1988, Carter in 1976, and Clinton in 1992 benefited from the same.

Although the news has always had an influence on voters, only in recent years has this power become sufficiently pronounced to cause major concern. In the days when the parties chose the nominees and the great majority of voters selected their candidate on the basis of party loyalty, the news was less consequential.

Voters today are not as anchored by partisan beliefs and

hence are more easily influenced by developments in the campaign. Most votes are not won or lost as a result of the campaign (committed Republicans and Democrats always find reasons in the end to stay with their party's nominee), but a large percentage of the vote has been up for grabs in recent elections. In 1976, more than 40 percent of the voters at one time or another during the general-election campaign considered voting for the candidate who was not their final choice.[140] Carter came out of the Democratic convention with a two-to-one lead over Ford but had lost nearly all of it by mid-October. The pattern repeated itself in 1980, when a full third of the electorate did not make a final choice until the last weeks of the campaign. In 1988, Dukakis at one time led Bush by 15 points, but he fell 10 points behind a month later. Clinton was trailing Bush in 1992 until he jumped to a 25-point lead in the space of a few weeks.

In each of these cases, the press joined the bandwagon and chipped away at the candidate who was losing ground. Not all of these changes in the vote, or even most of them, are attributable solely to the press's influence. Nevertheless, journalists' narratives surely contributed to the swings in the vote.

The nominating campaigns are especially volatile. There is no partisanship to anchor primary voters, who usually know little about their choices before the campaign begins. When they encounter candidates through the press's narratives of winners and losers, they have only limited means to fend off the images contained in them.[141] The Markle Commission's examination of the 1988 election concluded: "Viewers and readers are implicitly invited to assume that the strategic political game is a worthy and possibly a sufficient test of suitability for office, and that the shrewdest candidate with the most effective campaign both wins and deserves the presidency for that reason alone."[142]

The vote in primary elections can be powerfully affected by the electorate's sense of who is winning and losing; news can fuel nominating bandwagons. (This subject will be examined in greater detail in Chapter 5.) Jimmy Carter's fast start in the

1976 primaries provides a sense of the power of the press's narratives. My study of the 1976 campaign found that half or more of Carter's support came from voters who knew he was leading the pack and had a vague notion he could be trusted, but not much else.[143] Among the opinions expressed by voters were the following:

> He is the person the majority of the public is backing. He seems to be a nice man.

> He seems to be forthright, a good man. The voters like him and he's way ahead.

> I respect him. He doesn't have a machine behind him and yet is going to be nominated.

> I guess we haven't heard as many bad things about him as the others. He's popular, too.

> I know that he's doing good. He seems down to earth. He seems honest and sincere. He has a nice smile.

> He appeals to many people.

> I guess I like him because I hear more about him.

> He seems to be honest. I don't necessarily really favor him, but I think he's going to be the one.

> I don't see anyone else with a chance. He's a fresh and engaging personality. Not committed to Washington, either.

> He must be doing the right thing. He's in popular demand.

The voters, as V. O. Key noted, "are not fools."[144] But their decisions can be foolish when they are forced to choose without adequate guidance. They depend on the press for information about the candidates. Much of the information they receive is useful, but much of it consists of fanciful imagery.

CHAPTER FOUR

Reporters' Issues
versus Candidates' Issues

> If you study the [news] . . . you will find, very often, that
> the issues are rarely in the headlines, barely in the leading
> paragraphs, and sometimes not even mentioned anywhere.
> . . . The routine of the news works that way. . . . The
> news is an account of the overt phases that are interesting,
> and the pressure on the [reporter] to adhere to this routine
> comes from many sides.
>
> WALTER LIPPMANN[1]

"I don't understand why, when in this country we license people to drive automobiles, what is so wrong about proposing that
we license guns to make sure that felons and mental incompe-
tents don't get ahold of them."[2] With these words, John Anderson assured himself of headlines in a Republican debate in New
Hampshire, just as he had made news in an Iowa debate a few
weeks earlier by saying, "I would put an emergency excise tax
on gasoline."[3]

Why the focus on Congressman John Anderson and his issues? Why were they newsworthy in early 1980? Anderson was
not the leading Republican candidate. He ranked last among
the seven active contenders in an Iowa poll taken before the
debate and secured less than 1 percent in a national Gallup

poll.[4] Anderson trailed even Texan John Connally, a former Democrat.

Nor was Anderson in the headlines because his issues were the most important. Gasoline taxes and gun control were relatively insignificant policy matters alongside a slew of domestic and foreign problems, which included double-digit inflation, the worst unemployment and productivity rates since the Depression, the hostage crisis in Iran, and the threat to peace posed by the Soviet invasion of Afghanistan.

The reason for the media focus on Anderson's issues lay in their news value. The other candidates in the Iowa and New Hampshire debates made routine statements that were typically Republican: government is too big, taxes are too high, the free market is the key to a jobs policy. Anderson's proposals for a gasoline tax and gun control were controversial stands for a Republican to take. When Anderson staked out his positions, attracting criticism from his rivals, the press had a story to tell.

It is commonly said that the news is about events, and this is true in a limited sense. Yet events must also have a defining attribute if they are to make headlines. This attribute is newness—not just in the sense of being recent, but also as a departure from the ordinary. A family quarrel is not news—unless it ends in a homicide. Airlines run thousands of safe flights every day; it is the rare disastrous crash that makes news. News of the weather grows in significance when a hurricane is impending.

It is the same with election issues. Candidates spend their days talking about issues, and society always has urgent problems that need the government's attention. Most of these matters are unheeded by the press. They are important, but they are not newsworthy until they take a form the reporter recognizes as news. In most cases, the defining attribute is controversy; it signifies a break in the routine of politics. It did not matter that John Anderson was not the top contender, or that his issues were minor in the context of the larger responsibilities of the presidency. His positions provoked the conflict that reporters seek in a news story.

The reporters' game schema also predisposes them to high-light controversies. Politics is a competitive struggle for power, and the overt forms of this struggle stand out in reporters' minds. Issues and problems are a backdrop to the central drama until they push their way into the forefront. Foreign policy was George Bush's strongest issue in 1992, but it got little notice because no one was challenging his handling of it. Not until the closing days of the campaign, as new revelations emerged suggesting that Bush knew more about Iran-Contra than he would admit, did the media focus on foreign policy, and then in a way unfavorable to the president. Iran-Contra was a live controversy; the Gulf War was mere history.

The press has a predilection for what the British political scientist Colin Seymour-Ure calls "clear-cut issues." Such issues are rooted in controversy and sharply define the candidates. In most cases, they rest on principle rather than complex facts, and they involve ends rather than means. Ideally, they can be reduced to simple terms, usually by reference to a shorthand label, such as "tax increase" or "gun control."[5]

Some "clear-cut issues" become causes célèbres. Vice President Dan Quayle in 1992 prepared a half-hour speech that addressed issues such as race, poverty, abortion, work, and life style. His speech on moral values was not slated for much press attention until Quayle penciled in a single sentence about the television character Murphy Brown. "It doesn't help matters when prime-time TV has Murphy Brown . . . mocking the importance of fathers, by bearing a child alone and calling it just another 'lifestyle choice.' "[6]

The press had a field day. The Murphy Brown issue dominated the headlines and the nightly news. The dispute grew when the show's executive producer fired back at Quayle ("If the Vice President thinks it's disgraceful for an unmarried woman to bear a child . . . then he'd better make sure abortion remains safe and legal").[7] For nearly a week, Murphy Brown was the biggest story in the land. Fact and fiction collided, creating a row that the press found riveting. Said the Washington *Post* in a front-page story, "Quayle's Tuesday comments became the talk of the nation."[8] Other newspapers took great relish in the way the tabloids were handling the story: "Murphy Has a Baby . . . Quayle Has a Cow" (Philadelphia *Daily News*); "Quayle to Murphy Brown: You Tramp" (New York *Daily News*).[9]

For reporters, controversy is the real issue of campaign politics. The press deals with charges and countercharges, rarely digging into the details of the candidates' positions or the social conditions underlying policy problems. It is not simply that the press neglects issues in favor of the strategic game; issues, even when covered, are subordinated to the drama of the conflict generated between the opposing sides. In this sense, the press "depoliticizes" issues, treating them more as election ritual than as objects of serious debate.[10] Quayle's claims about the social consequences of the breakdown of the American family were not seriously examined. Murphy Brown was nearly the whole story.

The greater the potential for controversy, the bigger the story. The tendency is not absolute—there are moments when other, less controversial issues get into the news—but it is the way the process works most of the time. On "This Week with David Brinkley" in March 1992, ABC's Sam Donaldson bore in on Bob Kerrey. "Did you ever use drugs?" asked Donaldson. "No," said Kerrey. "Ever use marijuana?" asked Donaldson. "No," said Kerrey. "Ever use cocaine?" asked Donaldson. "No," said Kerrey. Had Kerrey said yes to any of these questions or replied that it was none of Donaldson's business, the press, as Ken Auletta observed, would have been "buzzing."[11]

Reporters are drawn irresistibly to controversy. They are so attracted to it that they regularly overlook intrinsically more pressing matters. Late in the 1976 campaign, *Newsweek's* White House correspondent, Thomas M. DeFrank, was granted an exclusive interview with President Gerald Ford, the Republican nominee. The nation's economy was then beset with stagflation —an unprecedented combination of high inflation and high unemployment for which the economists had no theory and no solution. In the international arena, the United States was facing the image-shattering consequences of its Vietnam defeat and the threat of an OPEC oil embargo. When DeFrank met privately with Ford in the Oval Office, he ignored these issues, concentrating instead on two campaign controversies:

Q. Would you consider Carter's *Playboy* interview one of his mistakes?

Q. You talk about one mistake after the other. Aside from the *Playboy* interview, what else has Carter done wrong?

Q. Mr. President, what about these allegations concerning the funding of your congressional campaigns? [Five straight questions on this subject follow; Ford categorically denies the allegations.]

Q. Do you think you have a political problem from any of this and do you think these allegations are in any way politically motivated? [12]

The policy ramifications of the candidates' positions are usually underplayed by the press. In the 1984 Democratic race, Walter Mondale campaigned on "economic fairness," Gary Hart on "a new generation of leadership," Jesse Jackson on "social justice," and John Glenn on "bold leadership." [13] Their themes were different, but not contradictory, and reporters quickly tired of what the candidates were saying:

Fritz, John, Jesse, Gary and the other Democratic munchkins for president spent 90 minutes on television in Manchester, N.H., Thursday night with Barbara Walters.

It was about 80 minutes too much. . . . This seemingly 10,000th debate proved that the White House hopefuls have nothing new left to say. They're even starting to bore one another.

They're like the dogs in Pavlov's experiment. Ring a bell and they make stump speeches. . . . Walters tried but failed to inject life into Thursday night's ritual.[14]

Reporters got the type of issue they were searching for a few weeks later, in Atlanta. The Democratic race had winnowed down to Mondale and Hart when they met in a Super Tuesday debate. Hart said, in response to a question: "I've made quite an issue out of the need for a new generation of leadership." Mondale retorted: "When I hear your new ideas, I'm reminded of the [Wendy's hamburger] ad: 'Where's the beef?' "

Mondale's quip dominated television news for the next twenty-four hours. NBC's Lisa Myers began her next day's report by saying, "A noticeably more upbeat Mondale stormed across the South, sounding his new battle cry." Mondale was then shown saying, "Where's the beef? Where's the beef?" On the same newscast, a voter was asked, "Mondale says that Gary Hart has no new ideas. . . . [What do you] think about that?" The voter replied, "That was probably the issue that bothered me most." At no time in the newscast was Hart shown defending or explaining his ideas.[15] Hart had, in fact, developed a series of position papers that offered innovative solutions to national problems. These proposals were not seriously evaluated by the press, either before or after Mondale's blanket assertion that they lacked substance.

Competitive pressures feed the tendency toward controversy. In a footnote in her 1992 book, *The Power House*, Susan Trento related a secondhand story about the possibility that George Bush had been involved in an extramarital affair in 1984. The rumor had been around for years, and several news organizations, including the Washington *Post*, had investigated it without finding confirming evidence. Nevertheless, the tabloid New York *Post* printed a story headlined "The Bush Affair," based on Trento's footnote. This prompted CNN's Mary Tillotson to confront the president with the allegation at a Bush news conference with Israeli prime minister Yitzhak Rabin. "I'm not going to take any sleazy questions like that from CNN," replied an angry Bush. "I'm not going to respond other than to say it's a lie." Bush's response was given extensive play on CNN, and the three broadcast networks ran the story on their evening newscasts. "We wish we didn't have to deal with this," said CBS executive producer Erik Sorenson, "but if our viewers are hearing it all day . . . we sort of have a responsibility to address it."[16]

Commercialism is a crucial factor in determining which election issues get attention from the press. Although many journalists deny responding to commercial influences, these pressures are built into the very definition of news. The sensational is favored over the routine. Why did the news media in 1980 present seven times as many stories on President Carter's wayward brother Billy as on the Strategic Arms Limitations Talks between the U.S. and USSR? Was Billygate more important to the nation than SALT II?[17]

Michael Robinson's study of the 1984 campaign indicates how fully such controversies can dominate the news. Robinson, using a broad definition of these issues ("short-term concerns about how candidates and their campaigns *should* behave"), found they accounted for a larger part of the coverage than did policy issues ("enduring disputes about how government *should* behave").[18] They ranged from Bush's offhand remark to a New Jersey longshoreman that he had "[kicked] a little ass" in his vice-presidential debate with Geraldine Ferraro to Reagan's suggestion that the 1983 Beirut bombing which killed 241 U.S. marines was somehow former president Carter's fault. The 1984 election had the dubious distinction of being the campaign in which the most intensely reported issue—Ferraro's refusal to make public her family's tax returns—was neither a policy matter nor one that involved a presidential nominee.

In 1988, campaign controversies also dominated the treatment of issues. In their study of network coverage, S. Robert

Lichter, Daniel Amundson, and Richard E. Noyes found that "campaign issues like disputes over Dan Quayle's National Guard service, negative ads, and mudslinging" received more news time than issues of policy.[19]

While policy issues received more attention in 1992 than they had in 1988, campaign controversies dominated the election's final month. Short-term flare-ups over such matters as Bush's low-road tactics and Clinton's Oxford activities and draft record got more news coverage in October than the state of the economy, the budget deficit, and other policy issues.[20]

The media's preference for conflict makes the battlefield the dominant metaphor of election news. Fighting words fill the stories.[21] The language of war, says the communication scholar Kathleen Hall Jamieson, is "all but inevitable" in news that rests on controversy. Jamieson's study of the 1988 election identified dozens of variations on the battlefield metaphor, including "search-and-destroy missions" (CBS, September 22), "holding back no ammunition" (NBC, October 6), "under fire" (ABC, March 29), "cut-and-slash candidate" (CBS, September 14), "targets" (ABC, February 19), "the first shot across his bow" (ABC, February 18), "cease-fires" (ABC, January 16), "a war of attrition" (CBS, October 23), "do or die" (ABC, March 12), and "crashed in flames" (ABC, March 11).[22]

Even when candidates refuse to accept the press's conception of the campaign, their statements are made to fit this image. In a *New York Times* article in June 1992, Clinton was quoted as saying it was "pointless" and "totally irrelevant" to answer the questions on Ross Perot that were posed to him on a daily basis. "All it does," Clinton said, "is follow the needs of the press, and has nothing to do with either my objectives or the people of the country." Nevertheless, the newspaper's story was titled "Clinton, Out of the Limelight, Ponders Attack on Perot" and was filled with conjecture about how Clinton might go after Perot, if he decided to do so.[23]

The battlefield metaphor is largely a construct of the press. Although candidates sometimes fight over particular issues, they do not routinely engage in direct debate. The metaphor of the beauty contest is as apt a way of describing a campaign as is the battlefield.[24] In their classic 1954 study *Voting*, Bernard Berelson, Paul Lazarsfeld, and William McPhee found that candidates talked " 'past each other,' almost as though they were participating in two different elections."[25]

Rather than the clear-cut issues favored by the press, candidates emphasize the broad issues of economic prosperity, global security, social justice, national unity, and government efficiency. In a study of twelve presidential elections, political scientists Benjamin Page found that all major-party nominees had built their campaigns around such issues. "Both incumbents and challengers," Page concludes, "enunciate broad goals and conjure up visions of the glorious society which their future administrations will bring into being."[26]

Peace and prosperity dominate the candidates' campaigns because these issues rank highest with the voters. In polls, people express most often a concern with issues such as jobs and national security. These concerns also determine the vote. Over the years, the best predictor of whether the in-party will retain the presidency has been the economy. If the economy is healthy, the incumbent party nearly always wins; if it is weak, the in-party typically loses.[27]

In 1992, Bill Clinton had the best issue a challenger could want—a weak economy. He did not have to persuade millions of voters that he was with them on each and every issue; he had to convince voters that he stood for real change and had the determination to achieve it. He presented a vision of the nation as a community, a broad theme that in a period of economic dislocation and social change appealed to people's desire to pull together and get themselves and the country moving forward. "This is America. There is no 'them,' " said Clinton. "There's only us."[28]

When candidates turn to narrower issues, it is usually to

address the special concerns of their party's constituencies. Although candidates like to appear to be all things to all people, in fact they build a coalition through simultaneous processes of unification and division. If candidates never took sides—if they did not stand for something—they would not have a political base. For this reason, they naturally align themselves with the groups that identify with their party.

These commitments do not ordinarily bring the candidates into direct conflict with one another. Constituent appeals typically involve assurances of continued support or special benefits for a particular group—assurances that do not clash with those of the opposing candidate, because he is appealing to different groups. Only in some instances—for example, a commitment to labor that is a direct threat to business—do the candidates' coalitional promises collide. In a comprehensive study of national convention platforms from 1944 to 1976, the political scientist Gerald Pomper has shown that most campaign pledges are distinctive commitments made by one party or the other. Only one in ten pledges places the nominees on opposite sides of the same issue.[29]

This explains why, contrary to the impression conveyed in news reports, candidates use positive televised ads more often than negative ones. Positive ads focus on the candidates' positions and background, often making glorified claims about their past accomplishments and future goals. The *National Journal's* Jerry Hagstrom describes four major types of positive ads: "the sainthood spot," "the testimonial," "the bumper-sticker policy spot," and "the feel-good spot." Ronald Reagan's 1984 "Morning in America" commercials were of the "feel good" variety; they praised the spirit and vitality of the American nation, and the contributions of Reagan's leadership. Such commercials, however, normally get far less attention from the press than the candidates' attack ads, which, while fewer in number, conform more closely with the press's view of election politics.[30]

Of course, presidential candidates do make use of clear-cut issues. Although the electorate as a whole is moved by larger concerns, elections are sometimes won by a narrow margin, and campaign controversies can be critical. Every candidate has issues on which to attack his opponent. Republican candidates always accuse Democrats of being soft on crime and hard on taxpayers. Moreover, candidates rarely ignore a controversy that may work to their advantage. Democrats jumped on the Murphy Brown issue when they saw it backfiring on Quayle. "The world is a much more complicated place than Dan Quayle wants to believe," said Clinton's press secretary, Dee Dee Myers. "He should watch a few episodes before he decides to pop off."[31] The political scientist Nelson Polsby uses the term "policy crazes" to describe the candidates' exploitation of controversial issues to serve their purposes.[32]

As a rule, however, candidates rely far more heavily on general issues and coalitional appeals than on clear-cut issues. This does not signify that the candidates' policy differences are trivial or irrelevant. But it does indicate that candidates prefer to define their candidacies in their own way rather than as opponents or as the press would have it. Each side, in the words of one study, "tends to campaign on its self-chosen battlefield against straw men of its own devising."[33]

Thus, the battlefield metaphor with which reporters describe the campaign imposes "a false relationship" on the candidates.[34] They are competitors, but only infrequently are they combatants. This may help to explain why the press has expressed dissatisfaction with all recent campaigns: the candidates do not behave as journalists imagine they ought to. In 1992, Bill Clinton proposed an upper-income tax increase, which George Bush said would lead to higher taxes on families with incomes in excess of $60,000. Clinton denied it, without being specific, and reiterated his belief that higher-income families should bear a larger share of the tax burden. Reporters pressed him for an exact accounting of the tax hike that would be necessary to achieve his revenue goals. Clinton provided rough estimates. In the final presidential debate, a frustrated panelist, CNN's Susan Rook, demanded a precise answer: "Will you make a pledge tonight below which, an income level that you will not go below? I'm looking for numbers, sir, not just a concept." When a candidate fails to address an issue in a form agreeable to the press, journalists may claim that he has no plan for dealing with it. This allegation was leveled repeatedly at Bush for his handling of the economy. "Too improvisational to be called a plan," said *Newsweek*'s Jane Bryant Quinn.[35] The allegation made sense only from a journalistic perspective. In their constant search for signs of conflict and change, reporters have trouble seeing continuity. The Bush administration from the start pursued a free-market policy that curtailed economic regulation, reduced barriers to free trade, and emphasized higher capital investment. The policy, said Bush, was designed to make Americans "globally competitive."

The press was not buying. When Bush traveled to Detroit to deliver what was heralded as his major campaign speech on economic policy, ABC's "World News Tonight" dismissed it, saying that "it contained no major new initiative."[36] The Washington *Post* called it "repackaged," while the Los Angeles *Times* said it "offered no new plans or short-term solutions."[37]

In contrast, Bush's attack on Clinton's draft record, based as much on rumor as on fact, was treated as a real issue. The dispute was nourished by inconsistencies in Clinton's recollections of his thought processes a quarter-century earlier. But Bush's attacks kept the issue in the news, even though he was clearly grasping at straws.

The 1988 campaign also had a draft controversy, and it, too, captivated the press. During a twelve-day period in August, there were ninety-three network news stories about Dan Quayle—a number that exceeded the coverage received by any presidential candidate apart from George Bush during the entire primary election period.[38] Why would a vice-presidential nominee get more coverage in two weeks than most presidential candidates received in four months? The answer lies in the

Figure 4.1   The Issue Content of Election Coverage, 1960–1992

In the 1960s, issue coverage focused primarily on policy problems; more recently, it has focused also on campaign controversies.

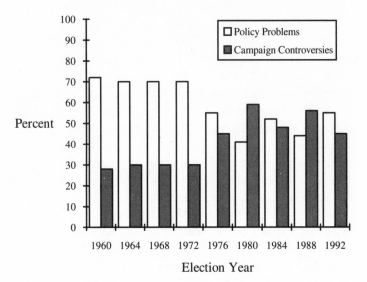

Note: Policy problems refer to enduring issues about how government should act. Campaign controversies refer to short-term concerns about how candidates should act. Figure is based on 3,740 paragraphs in *Time* and *Newsweek* in the 1960–1992 period.

press's zeal for controversy—in this case, the row created by the accusation that Quayle had pulled strings to avoid Vietnam service.

Until the 1970s, the rules of objective journalism limited the press's attempts to shape the issue agenda. However, journalists have since been less willing to let the candidates define the issues. The change is indicated in Figure 4.1, which shows the balance in coverage between policy problems and campaign controversies in the period 1960–92. Policy problems were once far and away the top issues of presidential politics; now they share top billing with campaign controversies. The change reflects the press's increased influence on the agenda.

At the conclusion of every recent presidential campaign, the press has expressed its "weary distaste" for the candidates' handling of the issues.[39] In 1976, *The New York Times*'s James Reston said, "If President Ford or Governor Carter had really raised a new issue, or defined an old one in new terms, the press would have been startled into reporting it. In the whole of the campaign, neither Mr. Ford nor Mr. Carter made a single memorable speech, so the press summarized their dreary clichés and the candidates were lucky that the press didn't print the full text of what they said."[40]

Presidential candidates are always somewhat surprised by such attacks. Their speeches, position papers, and policy statements are carefully prepared and widely presented. Reporters may see the candidates as evasive, but the candidates find it difficult to understand why reporters ignore so much of what they say. After the 1976 campaign, Carter said: "It's strange that you can go through your campaign for president, and you have a basic theme that you express in a 15- or 20-minute standard speech that you give over and over; and the traveling press—sometimes exceeding 100 people—will never report that speech to the public. The peripheral aspects become the headlines, but the basic essence of what you stand for and what you hope to accomplish is never reported."[41]

That each side sees things so differently reflects fundamentally different conceptions of issues. Candidates tend to think in terms of broad policy questions and narrow coalition appeals. Reporters are inclined to view controversies as the real issues of election politics. The difference is irreconcilable. One type of issue does not make for good politics, nor the other for good news.

The press's view was evident early in the 1992 Democratic

campaign, when Bob Kerrey made news in a big way, while Bill Clinton received relatively little attention. The top news of the day was the dispute over a lesbian joke that Kerrey had related at a political roast in New Hampshire. Kerrey had whispered the joke in private, but his words had been caught by a television boom mike aimed his way. Kerrey's blunder, first reported in the San Francisco *Examiner*, quickly became a national story.

At the same time, the press mostly ignored Bill Clinton's first major statement on the economy. Designated as such and delivered in Washington at Georgetown University, his speech called for "a new covenant for economic change." He urged his party to abandon the "tax and spend" politics of the past and proposed a comprehensive plan for revitalizing the economy: expansion of the Earned Income Tax Credit for the poor, more affordable FHA mortgages, a highway bill that would create thousands of construction jobs, lower credit-card interest rates, tax incentives to discourage companies from moving overseas, a fully funded HeadStart program, job training and education programs for workers, apprenticeship programs for high school graduates, an innovative college-loan program, and health-care reform.[42]

The speech was arguably the best single indicator of a Clinton administration's priorities. He gave it repeatedly during the primaries, used parts of it in his acceptance speech at the convention, and made it a blueprint for his presidential transition. Yet his Georgetown speech was not reported at all by some major news outlets.[43] The Washington *Post* described it in a single story on page 4. In contrast, Kerrey's joke was the subject of four *Post* stories and an editorial ("Take My Joke, Please").

Reporters' issues and candidates' issues are different. My study of the 1976 campaign indicated that clear-cut issues accounted for twice as many news references when a journalist was the initiator of the news items (for example, "Ford was asked by a reporter today about . . .") than when a candidate was the initiator ("Ford gave a speech today about . . ."). I also found that clear-cut issues accounted for two-thirds of the issue references in the news but only one-third in the candidates' speeches.[44]

When asked why they pay so little attention to the candidates' speeches, reporters usually claim lack of interest on the part of the voters. While there is some truth to this, it is more accurate to say that journalists are the ones who are not very interested. The first time that a candidate gives a speech on a major policy issue, it is likely to be reported, and may even make the front page. Thereafter, its news value is small. "When candidates say the same things over and over," says television correspondent Judy Woodruff, "it is not news."[45]

Not surprisingly, the press becomes increasingly hostile toward the candidates as the campaign wears on. After a brief honeymoon at the start of the campaign, the press's mood sours. The reporters' major complaint is that the candidates are avoiding the issues. In 1976, Gerald Ford was said to be hiding from the issues by acting "presidential"—that is, by campaigning from the White House, where media access to him was limited. His Democratic opponent, Jimmy Carter, was also said to be fuzzy on the issues—"a moderately liberal conservative" was how the *Wall Street Journal* described him.[46]

Thus, when it was announced that Ford and Carter would meet in televised debates—the first since 1960—the press hailed them as an opportunity for a real dialogue on the issues. However, the debates did not meet the press's expectations. An AP story said of the first debate, "There were no dramatic new proposals." Another news account described it as "side-by-side press conferences." Reporters felt that the candidates had failed to air their differences. The second debate raised a stir when Ford stumbled over a question on Eastern Europe, but "tough talk hides basic agreement," was how UPI summarized its view. The third debate was characterized in the Los Angeles *Times* as "subdued." Another newspaper wrote, "the litanies were familiar." Carter and Ford were said to have framed replies in their own terms, aiming much of what they had to say at their separate constituencies and addressing general concerns in answers sprinkled with statistics ("like pocket calculators," said one news report).[47]

Most presidential debates draw this type of a reaction from the press.[48] The 1980 Reagan-Carter encounter was heralded by NBC's John Chancellor and Tom Brokaw as a chance to get the candidates' "real views, something other than rhetoric." When it was over, NBC's expert panel expressed disappointment: "a scoreless tie," said Tom Pettit; "nothing new was said," said Jack Germond; they talked past each other, said David Broder.[49] In 1988, *Time*'s cover story on the debates was dubbed, "1988 You're No 1960." *The New York Times*'s John Tierney squelched a 1992 Democratic debate by saying: "It might also have left a viewer wishing that the moderators, Robert MacNeil and Jim Lehrer, were running for president. They were the sensible ones, worrying about unpleasant realities like money.[50]

The public does not share the reporters' opinion. Televised debates draw a favorable response from their audiences. Scholarly studies of presidential debates—more than one hundred have been conducted—indicate generally high levels of audience attention, learning, and satisfaction.[51] Postelection surveys by Times Mirror in 1988 and 1992 indicate that of all forms of election communication, the public ranks the debates highest (the news ranks lowest).

What the public sees and hears in a debate is relatively new to them. It may be tired rhetoric to the press, but it is news to the audience. Moreover, the public does not share the press's view of issues. The voters' concerns are closer to those of the candidates. Voters are interested in central questions of leadership and performance.[52] The Markle Commission's study of the 1988 campaign concluded that voters believe they get their best information about the candidates from debates: "Judging from the enthusiastic response of our focus groups, they were the high point of an otherwise uninspiring campaign."[53]

*   *   *

Although reporters cannot force candidates to address the issues that are important to them, they can criticize candidates for not doing so. Richard Salant, who was with NBC and CBS for years, said many times, "Just once, I wish I had the guts to say that, 'Today, Candidate X campaigned at six stops and didn't say a goddamn thing.' "[54] No such restraint exists today. A *New York Times* story during the 1992 general election portrayed a Clinton campaign stop as all show and no substance:

> Campaign officials billed Mr. Clinton's speech today to a group of several thousand people gathered in a great, green meadow here about 20 miles south of Des Moines as the unveiling of a comprehensive economic plan for rural America. But the speech did not include any major new initiatives in rural policy; it was instead a compilation of broad, vague promises to help farmers, along with the usual denunciations of his political opponent, President George Bush. The three-page policy memorandum the campaign provided to reporters outlined Mr. Clinton's farm policy ideas with more specificity, but almost all of those ideas have been around the Clinton campaign for some time. . . . The paucity of new ideas suggests that the point of a lightning visit to a state where Mr. Clinton enjoys substantial support in the polls had much more to do with a new political offensive than with any new policy initiative.[55]

As the example illustrates, for journalists a "new" idea is not one that represents a departure from existing policy but one that has been developed within the past few days. Newness is defined by news standards rather than the standards of politics.

Reporters will sometimes put words into a candidate's mouth when they believe he is not being entirely candid. A *Newsweek* story described what Clinton and Bush would have to do to keep their health-care promises. The article was headlined "Rx for Health Care: Bush and Clinton want to remake the system —but neither is telling the truth about the costs and pitfalls of reform." Statements by policy experts were used to give authority to the reporter's version of the candidates' intentions.[56]

If journalists go too far in this direction, they cross the line that divides journalism from partisanship. Therefore, they seek validation of their opinions, preferably in the actions of the candidates themselves. Gaffes can provide the justification. Gaffes are blunders, misstatements, indiscretions, and other mistakes that supposedly expose a side of the candidate that he seeks to hide.

The press has always had a penchant for episodes that unmask a candidate. In 1940, while speaking to a large crowd in Cicero, Illinois, Wendell Willkie began his speech, "Now that we're in Chicago . . ." When the crowd shouted out that he was in Cicero, the secular Mr. Willkie shouted out, "All right, to hell with Chicago." The statement made front-page headlines throughout the country, alienating Chicagoans and the deeply religious. Reporters called it "one of the worst blunders" of the election.[57]

When a candidate acts out of character, it is likely to make headlines. Gaffes fit what the campaign consultant Roger Ailes describes as "the orchestra-pit theory" of news. "If you have two guys on a stage and one guy says, 'I have a solution to the Middle East problem,' and the other guy falls in the orchestra pit, who do you think is going to be on the evening news?"[58]

A gaffe need only entertain. In a 1988 campaign appearance, George Bush referred to September 7 as the anniversary of the Japanese bombing of Pearl Harbor. All three broadcast networks highlighted Bush's slip of the tongue. Said CBS's Dan Rather, "Bush's talk to audiences in Louisville was overshadowed by a strange happening." NBC's Tom Brokaw remarked that Bush "departed from his prepared script and left his listeners mystified." ABC's Peter Jennings said, "What's more likely to be remembered about today's speech is a slip of the tongue."[59] Bush's misstatement received six paragraphs of coverage each in *The New York Times* and the Washington *Post*, and eight paragraphs in the Los Angeles *Times*, which headlined its story "Bush Disremembers Pearl Harbor."[60]

Talk of Bush's Pearl Harbor slip-up died in a day. Innocent mistakes are bound to occur when candidates give hundreds of speeches during the year-long campaign. On the other hand, when President Bush seemed unfamiliar with computerized checkout equipment during a campaign appearance at the National Grocers Association convention in February 1992, the press had a larger tale to tell. Reporters treated the incident as emblematic, as an indication that Bush had lost touch with the economic realities facing the average American. A Times Mirror survey indicated that only 18 percent of the national press believed the story was blown out of proportion or was unfair to Bush.

Mistakes give reporters an opportunity to reveal to the public the "real" candidate behind the image. The gaffe's significance is symbolic, resting on the contradiction between the impression the candidate tries to create and that suggested by the incident.[61] Vice President Quayle prodded twelve-year-old William Figueroa during a spelling bee to add an "e" to "potato" and had reporters leaping at the opportunity to portray him as a lightweight. They quoted Figueroa as saying that Quayle "is an O.K. guy, but he needs to study."[62] Even the entertainment media got into the act. Jay Leno warned kids that if they did not study, they "could end up a vice president." A few months later, in the final scene of the season premiere of "Murphy Brown," a truck dumped a load of potatoes outside Quayle's residence.

Gaffes tend to make news for several days running. Policy issues rarely get this treatment. My study of the 1976 campaign found that more than 50 percent of gaffes get extended news coverage (at least one story for two consecutive days), compared with 15 percent of policy issues. Television networks were the extreme case: their nightly newscasts gave extended coverage to more than 65 percent of gaffes, but only 10 percent of policy issues.[63]

Gaffes trigger what political scientist Larry Sabato calls a "feeding frenzy." "It has," says Sabato, "become a spectacle without equal in modern American politics: the news media, print and broadcast, go after a wounded politician like sharks in a feeding frenzy. The wounds may have been self-inflicted, and the politician may richly deserve his or her fate, but the journalists now take center stage in the process, creating the news as much as reporting it. . . ."[64]

Never in history have blunders played the large role in election politics that they do today. The greater prominence of gaffes both parallels and results from the expansion of the press's large role in the campaign. Even a partial list from recent elections confirms their increased stature:

1972
crying incident (Muskie)
Eagleton has my "1,000 percent support" (McGovern)

1976
Rhodesian peace-keepers (Reagan)
"Eastern Europe is free from Soviet domination" (Ford)
"ethnic purity" (Carter)
"lust in my heart" (Carter)

1980
Mudd interview (Kennedy)
ethnic jokes (Reagan)
"Taiwan" China (Reagan)
Vietnam was a "noble cause" (Reagan)

1984
family tax returns (Ferraro)
"kicked a little ass" (Bush)
Beirut bombing was "Carter's fault" (Reagan)

1988
"Hymietown" (Jackson)
premarital conception (Robertson)
tank photo-op (Dukakis)
Donna Rice (Hart)
plagiarism (Biden)

1992
"your people" (Perot)
Gennifer Flowers (Clinton)
p-o-t-a-t-o-e (Quayle)
Murphy Brown (Quayle)
"If your daughter . . ." (Quayle)
"If your granddaughter . . ." (Bush)
Sister Souljah (Clinton)

A candidate's blunder gives the press an opportunity to seize control of his campaign. The political scientist Christopher Arterton sees the campaign as a power struggle between the press and the candidates in which each side has a major source of influence: the press through its control of what gets reported and the candidates through their control of what is said.[65] Hence, when a candidate makes a mistake, the press takes over.

The press does not always wait for gaffes to occur—the Miami *Herald*, for example, got its story of Gary Hart's weekend tryst with Donna Rice by staking out Hart's Washington townhouse. But such spying is rare. Other kinds of entrapment, however, are not. During the 1976 Democratic race, Jimmy Carter invited Sam Roberts of the New York *Daily News* to interview him as they flew from Buffalo to New York City. Carter was asked a list of prepared questions, including whether "a black central city can survive surrounded by all-white neighborhoods." Carter replied, "I see nothing wrong with ethnic purity being maintained. I would not force racial integration of a neighborhood by governmental action. But I would not permit discrimination against a family moving into the neighborhood." "Ethnic purity" became a headline issue. Was the southerner Carter a closet racist? "His roots run deep in Georgia redneck country," said *Time*.[66] Carter had a progressive record on race relations in his hometown of Plains and as governor of Georgia, and was backed by many African-American leaders, including Martin Luther ("Daddy") King, Sr., and Coretta Scott King. These factors, however, took second place to his remark. The furor began to subside only after Carter held a news conference and apologized for his "careless" and "improper" use of terms.[67]

The candidate usually has no choice but to respond to the press's demands for a *mea culpa*. The price of silence is crippling news coverage for days on end. In 1976, Ford's blundering statement about Eastern Europe stayed in the headlines until, a week into the story, he called a press conference to admit his "mistake." By then Ford (whom reporters considered slow-witted) had lost his ability to claim an edge in international affairs over the inexperienced Jimmy Carter.[68] The press got a *mea maxima culpa* from Hart in 1987. Five days after the Miami *Herald's* exposé, Hart withdrew from the race; a threat of new revelations by the Washington *Post* sealed the decision.

Although gaffe-driven news can kill or cripple a candidacy, this destructive effect stems mainly from news values. Some partisan bias may be involved; as will be shown later in this chapter, reporters apparently make distinctions between candidates they like and dislike when interpreting mistakes. Nevertheless, any candidate who stumbles can expect bad news; such stories are far too enticing for the press to ignore. Essentially, gaffes combine with news values to introduce into the campaign an element of random partisanship.[69] A mistake is likely to get the candidate's campaign off track for a time, and perhaps permanently. George Romney's quest for the 1968 Republican nomination collapsed from the feeding frenzy that resulted when he claimed to have been "brainwashed" by U.S. generals during a trip to Vietnam.

That Romney might have been telling the truth about the military briefing he got when he went to Vietnam was largely irrelevant. Gaffes result in vigilante justice. The incident itself is so prominent in the reporters' handling of the issue that it overwhelms all else. The question is not whether a candidate was or was not brainwashed; it is whether he said he was brainwashed, and what that might imply about the man's character. The candidate's protests or attempts to place the incident in a larger context get into the story, but they are not integral to it. They may even be portrayed as attempts to divert attention from the incident's real meaning. "Truth" in this case is often measured by the slide in the candidate's popular support. If the public begins to pull away from the candidate, he is guilty as charged. Since bad news nearly always results in some loss of public support, the verdict is predictable.

The fracas that accompanies gaffes contributes to voter cynicism. The voters may punish the candidate, but they resent the type of politics that makes mountains out of molehills. The effect is much like that associated with the candidates' attack ads. Says Kathleen Hall Jamieson, "Both are driven by the same deconstructionist dynamic: Find the wart; make the wart stand for the whole. Both are products of a culture of disbelief."[70]

According to the press, the lack of focus on issues in the modern campaign is primarily the fault of the candidates.[71] They speak in sound bites. They dwell on trivia. They evade the issues.

The problem with this claim is that it does not square with the facts. Certainly, candidates are reluctant to tackle difficult issues. In 1988, Bush sidestepped the problem of the budget deficit because it had developed during the Reagan years, while Dukakis avoided it because he felt the solution required a tax increase. *The New York Times*'s E. J. Dionne said that "there is a limit to how much the press can force [Bush and Dukakis] to behave against their own interests."[72] George Will was less charitable: "Dukakis didn't dare utter his ideas, and Bush has no ideas to utter."[73] There is nothing new, however, about candidates' hesitancy to speak out on given issues. If anything, because of the intense scrutiny they receive, they are more forthcoming today than in the past. Franklin Roosevelt promised a "new deal" during the 1932 campaign but provided few details. His economic recovery program was developed after the election. Abraham Lincoln spoke in 1860 of the country's "great racial divide" and had the support of the abolitionists, but he did not advocate full and immediate emancipation until two years into the Civil War.

Candidates risk "suicide," as one campaign consultant put it, if they stick their necks out on tough issues.[74] In 1984, Walter Mondale said flatly that he would raise taxes in order to trim the deficit. Reporters did not applaud Mondale's gutsy stance. While no other policy issue got more attention in the next few days, the coverage was mainly directed from Reagan's viewpoint. Reporters spoke of Reagan's countering strategy: "He is attempting to characterize Mr. Mondale as a long-time big spender who lacks credentials to talk about reducing the deficit."[75] They carried Reagan's denials that he, too, would have to raise taxes: "I have no plans for a tax increase."[76] And they gave voice to Reagan's description of Mondale's proposal as a "fairy tale" that would hurt working people: "They seek to reduce deficits but the futile way—by raising tax rates on American families."[77] *The New York Times* ran the headlines "President Denies Plan to Increase Tax in New Year: Mondale Stand Assailed,"[78] "Reagan Ridicules Mondale 'Realism,' "[79] "Presidential Aide Scoffs at Mondale Tax Pledge."[80]

The press, not by partisan design but owing to its predilection for controversy, helps the opposition to exploit a candidate's willingness to address a tough issue. In June 1972, George McGovern proposed to solve "the welfare mess" by offering an income redistribution plan that would guarantee "$1,000 for every American man, woman, and child." The payments would replace existing welfare programs and be phased out as income rose, so that only the poor would actually receive federal assistance. McGovern's proposal was similar to the Family Assistance Plan that Nixon had tried unsuccessfully to get Congress to adopt in 1969. The plan also contained elements of the conservative economist Milton Friedman's concept of a negative income tax—a measure advocated as a means to eliminate the large bureaucracy that is required to administer case-based welfare programs.

McGovern never got a chance to explain his version, which was labeled the "$1,000 giveaway." Herbert Stein, chairman of President Nixon's Council of Economic Advisers, received front-page coverage when he said that McGovern's plan would "polarize society."[81] In the ensuing controversy, McGovern was portrayed as a wild-eyed radical. *Time* described McGovern's plan as aiming at a "vast redistribution of income, not just from rich to poor, but also from the upper-middle class to the lower-middle class." The magazine also challenged McGovern's estimates of the program's costs: "fuzzed arithmetic," "dubious calculations," "[the] figures just do not add up."[82] According to the Gallup poll, McGovern never recovered the popular following he had achieved before his guaranteed-income plan was announced.

So much for responding to the press's demands for precise proposals on tough issues. As Michael Robinson states it, "Fresh ideas come out [in the news] sounding less like new and more like dumb."[83] The press is the Lorelei of election politics.

Sound bites are another source of press complaints about the way candidates conduct themselves. "The candidates rarely discussed the issues, preferring a sound-bite approach to their campaigning," concluded an evaluation of the 1988 election.[84] But if candidates increasingly speak in sound bites, they do so because it is the only way to get heard on the nightly newscasts. The sound bite is not unique to campaigns. It characterizes television news in general. The sound bite is part of a fast-paced format that broadcasters developed as a means of attracting and holding large audiences. Dan Hallin quotes NBC's John Chancellor as saying that "the politicians started it," referring to Nixon telecasts in 1968 that were built around short answers. The better explanation, however, lies in the competitive commercial pressures first evident in local news, which then made their way to the networks.[85] Now everyone speaks in sound bites on network news, whether they are presidential candidates, foreign leaders, military officers, business executives, or the pope.

According to a Harvard study, the average length of a television sound bite shrank from 42 seconds in the 1968 election to under 10 seconds in 1988.[86] This finding, and the resulting criticisms, encouraged the networks to promise longer sound bites in 1992. During the nominating period, however, the sound bites were actually *shorter*—by 2 seconds. In response to renewed criticism, CBS announced that its sound bites would be at least 30 seconds long for the rest of the campaign. The network quickly retreated to a 20-second policy; before long, the length of its sound bites dropped below even this level. The 1992 campaign ended where the previous campaign had left off: the sound bites on ABC, CBS, and NBC averaged less than 10 seconds.[87]

Although sound bites are synonymous with television, the one-liner is also attractive to the print media.[88] The length of the candidates' quoted statements in newspapers has shrunk by half since 1960.

But the problem of sound bites is not simply, or even primarily, one of length. Sound bites serve the press's need for controversy. Dukakis's "Good jobs at good wages" had no chance of competing with Bush's "Read my lips." The candidate who can deliver the barbed one-liner gets the media's attention. The candidates comply. "Where's the beef?" "You're no Jack Kennedy." "The L-word." "There you go again."

Candidates deliver the lines, but the press dictates their length and concentrates on the candidate who attacks. In a Times Mirror poll of journalists during the 1992 primaries, 85 percent claimed that the Pat Buchanan candidacy made the campaign more interesting for them to cover. Said one respondent, "He gives good sound bites. He's very quotable. Whether you're a print journalist or a broadcast reporter, he's a joy to cover."[89]

In the 1992 general election campaign, Bush provided most of the sound bites ("the failed governor of a small state," "those two bozos," "Ozone Man," "Not right for Arkansas, and not right for America"). He was searching—unsuccessfully—for a crushing one-liner that would serve him as well as "Read my lips" had four years earlier. Bill Clinton usually refrained from sharp attacks on Bush. He was more comfortable and effective when saying what he was for than what he was against. Reporters did not get many pithy sound bites from Clinton, and he received less television coverage than Bush, even though he campaigned more extensively.[90]

While candidates can be faulted for caving in to the press's demand for sound bites, they have no incentive to change if the press does not cover their longer statements. No less a sound-bite specialist than the late Lee Atwater said, "I guarantee you . . . we would tailor our speeches to three to five minutes, or certainly to 20 minutes, if we were guaranteed we would get them on the news."[91] The chances of the networks doing so are remote. Even if they had the time, they do not have the inclination. The candidates' policy statements lack the controversy and novelty the press seeks. In 1988, when Dukakis proposed a program that would allow college students to repay loans by having a fixed percentage of their income withheld once they had a job, which meant those earning less would pay less than those earning more, CBS's Bruce Morton labeled it "boring" and "complicated."[92]

The press likes to portray candidates as experts in the art of media manipulation. Some of them are. But most of them are not prepared to perform for the national press.

At a news conference two days after his 1984 defeat, Walter Mondale announced his retirement from politics and advised his party never again to nominate a candidate who could not dance to the media's tune. He had tried to run on the issues but had been unable to get his ideas across. During the general-election campaign, he had prepared a message for each day, which his campaign sought to get in the news. He also held two or three press sessions daily, giving reporters a chance to pursue their own concerns. They got their stories through these meetings; Mondale's messages were seldom reported.[93]

If Mondale's advice to his party was correct, they chose the wrong nominee again in 1988. Governor Dukakis was determined to run on economic issues and his Massachusetts experience, and he looked to the press for assistance. He stubbornly insisted on sticking to his agenda, even when it was clear that the issues of crime and patriotism were undermining his effort. The press criticized his failure to realize that the strategic significance of an issue could outweigh its policy significance.

In a speech two years after the election, Dukakis acknowledged "a failure to understand" the degree to which news values drive the campaign: "I said in my acceptance speech in Atlanta that the 1988 campaign was not about ideology but about competence. . . . I was wrong. It was about phraseology. It was about 10-second sound bites. And made-for-TV backdrops. And going negative."[94]

Senator Bob Kerrey said much the same thing in 1992. *Newsweek*'s Howard Fineman asked Kerrey why he had floundered in his presidential bid. Kerrey acknowledged that he had expected the presidential campaign to be "vast and different," but he had not imagined the press to be so jaded. "It's my first trip through the tunnel of unlove," he said.[95]

When challenged about the hazing process to which they subject presidential candidates, journalists claim that the campaign is a test of a candidate's ability to handle the tough demands of the Oval Office. If a candidate wilts under their gaze, he would have made a lousy president anyway. If this is so, it is remarkable that the nation got along for nearly two centuries without the hazing process, and it is truly astonishing that the candidates who survived it—Nixon, Carter, Reagan, and Bush —turned out to have presidencies that were less than great.

The ethicist Sissela Bok describes the interplay of the press and the politician as a "vicious circle."[96] Each has its own goals, and the other stands in its way. The potential for destructive behavior on each side is high.

Bush's 1988 campaign brought out the worst in both the press and the politician. Unlike most presidential candidates, Bush understood the ways of the national press and turned his ideas over to consultants. When the *Time* cover story "The Year of the Handlers" spoke of campaign consultants who manipulate symbols and know how to use "hot button" issues, it described the Bush campaign precisely.[97]

"Willie Horton" came to signify the Bush style. William Horton (he did not become "Willie" until the campaign) was a convicted murderer who while on a weekend furlough from a Massachusetts prison brutally raped a Maryland woman and assaulted her husband. The incident was described in a commercial prepared by Americans for Bush, an independent organization headed by Larry McCarthy. Since McCarthy did not have the money to air the commercial widely, he gave it to "The McLaughlin Group," which sensationalized it in its trademark indiscriminate manner.

The Bush campaign produced a derivative commercial featuring a revolving prison door. "As governor, Michael Dukakis vetoed mandatory sentences for drug dealers. He vetoed the death penalty. His revolving door prison policy gave weekend furloughs for first-degree murderers not eligible for parole. While out, many committed other crimes like kidnapping and rape. And many are still at large. Now Michael Dukakis says he wants to do for America what he's done for Massachusetts. America can't afford that risk." As the commercial concluded, the words "268 Escaped, Many Are Still at Large," were scrolled across the television screen.

The press jumped on the Horton issue. ABC quoted a Boston policeman: "Governor Dukakis . . . is no friend of police. . . . He has provided a revolving-door criminal justice system."[98] Horton's name was mentioned so often in the news that nearly two-thirds of the American public came to recognize it (nearly the same fraction who could recall without help the names of the two vice-presidential candidates). The devastating effect of

Horton on the Dukakis campaign was captured by an ABC "World News Tonight" story. Sam Donaldson, aboard Dukakis's campaign bus, turned to the candidate and said, "Did you see in the paper that Willie Horton said if he could vote he would vote for you?" Dukakis struggled to close a window, then finally replied, "He can't vote, Sam."[99]

The press did not make a forceful effort to tell the full Horton story.[100] The media could have emphasized that the Massachusetts furlough policy had begun under a Republican governor, not Dukakis, and that other states had similar programs (including California, whose program was initiated when Reagan was governor). It might have stressed that the 268 escapees represented less than 1 percent of those furloughed.[101] It could also have underscored the relatively small part that law enforcement plays in the full range of a president's policy responsibilities.

The press did none of these things. Instead, it played up the controversy, thereby acting as the Bush campaign's surrogate. Having established the rules of the game, it could do no less. Controversies are the real issues of election journalism. Each day, the Bush campaign held a carefully staged appearance, complete with a sound bite—usually an attack on Dukakis. The campaign also circulated two hundred speeches and papers containing specific proposals. The press focused on the attacks; at times it even contributed to them.[102] The Pledge of Allegiance, Boston Harbor, and "Read my lips" joined Willie Horton as issues that would contribute to Dukakis's defeat.

The press regretted what was happening—it accused Bush of conducting a deceptive, mean-spirited campaign—but was caught in its game-centered paradigm. When Dukakis was slow to respond to Bush's attacks and refused to go negative, the press portrayed him as a weakling. In an interview that took place as the campaign was drawing to a close, NBC's Tom Brokaw asked Dukakis: "You said this is a campaign not about ideology. It's about competence. What about the competence of the campaign?"[103]

The campaign turned off the voters. In a CBS/New York

Times poll conducted in late October, 64 percent of the respondents indicated they wished other candidates were on the ballot.[104] In a Times Mirror postelection survey, the public gave the press a C— for its reporting on the campaign and awarded Bush a grade nearly as low (C+) for the way in which he had conducted himself.

The sordid 1988 campaign persuaded the press that changes were required in election reporting. The strategic game had accounted for as much as three-fourths of the 1988 coverage.[105] It would get less attention in 1992, while policy issues would receive more mileage. "The key consideration," said the *Wall Street Journal*'s Al Hunt, "is not to get totally obsessed with the passions of the moment and the horse race."[106] The candidates' staged photo-ops would be ignored unless they had significance in themselves; the candidates' claims about their opponents would be subject to "truth-tests"; and the candidates' "character" would be carefully analyzed.[107]

For a time in 1992, the press held to its promise. There were a few breakdowns, as when Kerrey's lesbian joke upstaged news of Clinton's speech on the economy. Still, the press provided significant coverage of the issues in the period before the New Hampshire primary. Led by articles on the economy and taxes, policy discussions were three times more prominent than they had been during the same period in 1988, and horse-race coverage was reduced sharply.[108] Part of the change was circumstantial: because of Iowa senator Tom Harkin's candidacy, there were only 11 network stories about the Iowa caucuses, compared with 137 in 1988. Since Harkin had no competition in his home state, election coverage in the campaign's pre–New Hampshire phase was down by 50 percent from its 1988 level.[109] Nevertheless, top news organizations systematically described the candidates' positions on major national problems and profiled their political records.

In late January, the press's game plan unraveled when Gennifer Flowers claimed to have had a twelve-year extramarital affair with Bill Clinton. "We were forced off our coverage plan," CNN's political director, Tom Hannon, said later. "Maybe there is a Gresham's law of media coverage, namely, that more sensational information will drive out the more substantive"[110]

The Flowers story entered the news stream on January 23 through a supermarket tabloid, *The Star*, which paid her an undisclosed sum (later revealed to be $125,000) to describe her alleged twelve-year relationship with Clinton. The story's tabloid origins made some news editors hesitant to carry it. However, as Clinton made a public appearance the same day, more than one hundred reporters arrived to shout questions about Flowers's allegations. That evening on "Nightline," ABC's Ted Koppel questioned Mandy Gruenwald, Clinton's media adviser, about Flowers, giving the story further legitimacy. When Clinton appeared on CBS's "60 Minutes" three days later in an attempt to save his faltering candidacy, all barriers had collapsed. A Gennifer Flowers press conference conducted the next day at the Waldorf-Astoria drew more than five hundred reporters and was carried live on CNN. The feeding frenzy was in full swing.[111]

Top journalists would later claim to have had misgivings about the tabloid origins of the Flowers story, and argue they had acted more responsibly than in the case of the Gary Hart–Donna Rice story in 1988.[112] A Times Mirror poll of reporters indicated that 55 percent felt they had covered the Flowers story "fairly responsibly," and another 7 percent "very responsibly." Journalists cited each other as the reason why Flowers got attention. "Once the story began to appear in the *Washington Post* and the *Los Angeles Times*," one journalist said, "my ability to decide the issue was gone."[113]

The Flowers story was less frenzied than the Rice story had been. Partly this had to do with reporters' personal feelings. Many of them loathed Hart, but most liked Clinton. "Truth is," said one journalist two weeks into the Flowers story, "the press is willing to cut Clinton some slack because they like him —and what he has to say."[114] With Hart, the issue had been "credibility," while in the case of Clinton it became "privacy," which limited the extent of the press's inquiry, and hence the damage to Clinton's candidacy.[115] Despite the scandal and opening losses to Tsongas (New Hampshire), Harkin (Iowa), and Kerrey (South Dakota), the press continued to treat Clinton as the Democratic frontrunner.

The Flowers incident was a big story nonetheless. It received by far the highest coverage of any issue in the month preceding the New Hampshire primary; in fact, because of it, Clinton got as much coverage as all of his Democratic rivals combined.[116] When four hundred members of the campaign press corps were surveyed in May in a Times Mirror poll, 46 percent said that Clinton's character was the campaign's top issue, and 20 percent identified Flowers's press conference as the campaign's "most important moment."[117]

The voters thought otherwise. A CNN survey taken a week into the story asked, "Does the press pay too much attention, too little attention, or the right amount of attention to a candidate's personal life?" More than 80 percent of the respondents said "too much," while only 3 percent said "too little."[118] There was a touch of idealism in their response. Many voters had in fact been drawn to news of the campaign for the first time by Flowers's revelations—in a Time Mirror poll, 43 percent of the respondents said they had been following the Flowers story "very" or "fairly" closely. Nevertheless, the public's attention was focused more on the issues than on the candidates' personal failings. "Everybody in the press seemed to be interested in Gennifer Flowers," ABC's Peter Jennings said, "and everybody in New Hampshire wanted to know about the economy."[119] On April 1, Clinton appeared on "Donahue," where the host peppered him with personal questions. "Have you ever had an affair?" "Have you and Hillary ever separated?" Clinton told Donahue that he would not answer such questions, and a member of the audience declared, "Given the pathetic state of the

United States at this point—Medicare, education, everything else—I can't believe you spent half an hour of air time attacking this man's character. I'm not even a Bill Clinton supporter, but I think this is ridiculous." The studio audience burst into loud applause. Donahue then turned the microphone over to his audience, not one of whom asked Clinton about his private life.[120]

The press gradually backed away from the adultery issue, even to the point of all but ignoring new allegations about Clinton that surfaced later in the campaign.

There were other developments that indicated the press had changed somewhat from 1988. The leading newspapers, such as *The New York Times* and the Washington *Post*, carried issue stories regularly. If most of them were not featured on the front page, they were nonetheless serious and substantial.[121] The Public Broadcasting System had an extraordinary package of programs, led by Bill Moyers's "Listening to America," which examined public attitudes toward the issues and candidates. CNN and ABC had innovative coverage, as did, to a lesser degree, NBC and CBS.

Yet election news did not change fundamentally in 1992. With the New Hampshire primary, the press turned from issues to the horse race, and it stayed there until the nominating contests were settled. At this point, issues got renewed attention, but the election itself declined in "newsworthiness." The political scientist Matthew Kerbel found that horse-race stories were at the top of television newscasts, while issue articles were placed nearer the bottom.[122] In the summer, the Clinton-Gore bus caravan got extensive coverage, particularly on network television. It was a staged photo-op that exceeded anything Bush had produced in 1988, but the press went for it without hesitation.

By the time of the fall campaign, the press's normal tendencies were fully evident. Horse-race coverage in October exceeded its 1988 level, while issue coverage was lower than it had been four years earlier.[123] There was more context to the 1992 coverage, but that was not always saying a lot. The nation's weak economy was blamed squarely on George Bush. More than 80 percent of the network references to Bush's handling of the economy were negative.[124] The press never tried to reconcile its claim of Bush's incompetence regarding the economy with the more severe recession experienced by Japan and Western Europe.

The media also let unsubstantiated charges slip through its filter. Allegations that Clinton had acted unpatriotically while at Oxford in the late 1960s started with Representative Robert Dornan's accusations on the House floor. The press ignored the right-wing congressman's charges, not reacting when the story appeared in the conservative Washington *Times.* But it responded when Bush himself questioned Clinton's visit to Moscow on "Larry King Live." It was the lead story for a few days in mid-October, although the allegations were never anything more than rumor.[125]

Election news was thus not greatly different in 1992. "The media had organized all these conferences and white papers about how they were going to do better," said Darrell West, a media researcher at Brown University, "but as the campaign wore on, the sound bites got shorter, the coverage seemed to degenerate into the horse race, and all the other old tendencies came out. It's almost as if the media got hijacked by Gennifer Flowers and never recovered."[126]

Eric Sevareid once compared election reporters to alcoholics, saying that their good intentions are all but forgotten when the wine of a new campaign touches their lips. Like other professionals, reporters learn to see things in a particular way and have a "trained incapacity" to see them differently. This is why the press in 1992, having declared its determination to redesign its coverage, reverted to old habits.

The Flowers story contributed to a change in the candidates' media campaigns. The candidates turned increasingly to the "new media"—talk shows, morning shows, and "soft" news programs like "20/20." Perot announced on "Larry King Live" that he might seek the presidency, Clinton appeared on the Arsenio Hall show wearing Blues Brothers dark glasses and playing the saxophone. President Bush initially disdained the new media but later joined in.

Presidential candidates had appeared on such shows before (Larry King has hosted presidential candidates in every election since 1968), but the extensive use of these outlets was unprecedented. During a three-week stretch in June, Clinton relied almost entirely on the new media; he did not hold any scheduled news conferences.[127] The candidates had an eager audience; their appearances on morning television increased the programs' ratings.[128] The public clearly desired a more direct look at the candidates than they were receiving through the traditional press.[129]

Arguably, the new media, in combination with the debates and the return of Ross Perot to the race, "saved" the 1992 campaign. Until these developments, voter disillusionment was higher even than it had been at the same stage in 1988. The new media helped to energize the campaign, give the public a sense of greater participation, and improve people's opinions of the candidates.

The press was at first hostile to the new media's intrusion on its role. One editorial claimed that campaigning had "descended to the talk-show level, which specializes in trivialization. Are you ready for presidential debate on Geraldo Rivera?"[130] Tim Russert, the moderator of NBC's "Meet the Press," said: "The candidates have decided they prefer to communicate in an unfiltered way, more their personality than their position on the issues. But in the long run, there is no substitute for discussing the tough issues they're going to have to handle as President."[131]

In fact, the questions asked of the candidates on the talk shows were at least as pertinent to the nation's problems as the questions asked by the reporters. If, as some journalists complained, Larry King and the others did not address the "tough" questions, they asked more issue-oriented ones. They also let the candidates do most of the talking, unlike the news shows, where journalists monopolize the discussion. And the talk-show hosts gave the contenders a chance to talk without ripping apart their every response.

The press soon took a different view of the new media. The emphasis on issues and the public response convinced most journalists that talk shows could enhance the campaign. "I think the more you get to see these guys on television the better," said Bill Hamilton, the Washington *Post*'s political editor.[132]

Although novel in certain ways, the new media were somewhat of a throwback to the days when the press gave the candidates a chance to speak, more or less on their own terms, to the voters. Daily news once had this quality, as did shows like "Meet the Press." Candidates have since become wary of these venues, knowing they can get trapped into costly misstatements. In May, Ross Perot made a contentious appearance on "Meet the Press," where he accused Tim Russert of trying to show him up. "This is an interesting game we're playing today," Perot said. "It would have been nice if you'd told me you wanted to talk about this and I'd had all my facts with me, but you didn't, right?"[133] When the show was over, the switchboard at his Dallas headquarters was swamped with calls from new volunteers. "For two days," Perot related, "people called in and said, they really tried to trap you, Perot, and you didn't let them."[134]

The candidates would have discovered the new media even if the press had not been adversarial. If anything, presidential hopefuls were slow in adapting to the opportunities provided by cable television. The new media gave the candidates access to a lot of people who otherwise were not very attentive to election politics. That they also allowed the candidates a chance to circumvent the traditional press was a bonus.

The new media did not represent the first time candidates had bypassed the press. In 1984, applying a model used earlier by Richard Nixon,[135] President Reagan based his re-election campaign primarily on televised political advertising. Reagan's reluctance to communicate through the press was based on experience. In response to a reporter's question during the 1976 Republican primary, he said he would "not rule out" sending a U.S. peacekeeping force to Rhodesia. The San Francisco *Chronicle* headlined its story "Reagan Would Send GI's to Avert Rhodesian War." The resulting news flurry sent the Reagan campaign into what *Time* called a "full retreat." Reagan observed, "I made the mistake of trying to answer hypothetical questions with hypothetical answers."[136]

In 1980, Reagan was burned again, for what his campaign called the Four Blunders: a press conference statement that he favored an "official government relationship" with Taiwan; his line in a speech that said Vietnam should be "recognized [as] a noble cause"; a news-conference remark after a speech to fundamentalist Christians that "creationism might be taught" as an alternative to evolutionary theory; and his claim in a speech that the country's "recession" should be regarded as a "severe depression."[137] These incidents created enough controversy to persuade Reagan to cut back on news conferences and speak only from prepared texts. He continued to do the same in 1984, relying on television advertising and presidential pronouncements to communicate his message.

Bush adopted a similar strategy in 1988 after he gained the lead from Dukakis. The "revolving door" and "tank" ads kept Dukakis on the defensive, and staged photo-ops without accompanying news conferences helped Bush to control his press coverage.

There is danger to democracy in both the unrelenting negativism of the press and the increased ability of candidates to avoid the press's scrutiny. These tendencies are related; the first fosters the second. And neither is healthy.

The bad press that accompanies a run for the presidency weakens the candidates' ability to lead. They have to communicate with an electorate that is continuously warned by the press to mistrust them. A wall of suspicion is thus created, and disbelief sets in. The people may still vote (although many do not), but they have doubts as to whether the candidates can be entrusted with their future.

It is this climate of suspicion that allows a candidacy like Ross Perot's to surface and thrive. The press is not the chief cause of this political malaise, but it bears primary responsibility for creating the campaign environment that encourages the malaise. When the campaign is portrayed as not much more than a manipulative game, the public becomes receptive to someone who promises, as Perot himself did so often, that he "will fix it." Said one voter, "Bush, Clinton are politicians. They talk out of both sides of their mouths. Mr. Perot gets things done."[138] Brookings Institution scholar Thomas Mann said that Perot's success was due partly to "the naïve hope that if only we can get the politics out of it, everything will be fine."[139]

The significance of Perot's candidacy should not be underestimated. Comparisons with Theodore Roosevelt in 1912, the only third-party or independent candidate whose percentage of the vote exceeded Perot's, are facile. Roosevelt had been a popular president and represented the Progressive movement, whose principles had been a driving force in American politics for more than a decade. His platform, the "New Nationalism," called upon Washington to use its power to achieve economic justice for the urban and backwater poor.[140] Perot has never held high office and did not emerge out of any social movement. Perot was the candidate representing a deep rejection of politics. He was the proverbial man on the white horse who rides out of nowhere to save the country from itself. He knew little of the issues and had no experience that would recommend him for the most powerful job in the world.

Some members of the press have said that Perot's candidacy may portend the "scary future" of an electoral system "open to manipulation by the super-rich."[141] But it was deep popular discontent, not money, that was the basis of Perot's appeal; he was a *tabula rasa* for an electorate yearning for politics without the politicians. Although journalists did not seem to realize it, Perot, in this sense, personified the model of leadership that they uphold: He vilified politics, resisted compromise, and refused to be bought. He was a down-home old-time Progressive reformer who would rescue politics from the parties, interest groups, and bureaucrats and return it to the people.

Perot was not the demagogue—"a bully, a tyrant, a paranoid"[142]—that some in the press suggested (though he was a product of the kind of forces that allow demagogues to thrive). If Perot truly were a demagogue, the warnings of the press might have been taken more seriously. Instead, the press's attacks gained him new followers, indicating the dissatisfaction of many Americans with the press's cynicism. Through its relentless criticism of almost everything political, the press has compromised its watchdog role, which is an essential part of a properly functioning electoral process. Candidates should be subject to tough questioning, but when every question is a potential trap and every response is ripped apart, the voters become inured to the press's admonitions. And when the media do make an allegation worthy of the public's concern, people only half-listen and half-believe. Like the boy who cried wolf, the press has an audience that no longer responds to its warnings.

The irony is apparent. The means that the press uses to block the candidates from communicating effectively with the public have now damaged the press's own credibility.

The length of the modern campaign intensifies the "vicious circle" that characterizes the relationship of press and politician. The campaign lasts for ten months, and journalists are expected to produce stories about it daily. The media's appetite for news exceeds the candidates' ability to supply it. There are not enough major issues for the candidates to keep their policy priorities at the top of the news for nearly a year. After they take a stand on the major issues, all they can do is repeat and refine their positions or turn to lesser issues, neither of which is considered very newsworthy. An ABC News characterization of a Jimmy Carter speech in the fall of 1976 as "old familiar lines" was as much an observation that its news value had been undermined through endless repetition as a judgment that Carter's ideas were insignificant.[143]

As candidates repeat their ideas and the press asserts its needs, the tensions between them mount. The candidate becomes more wary, and the press gets more skeptical. A potentially constructive, if necessarily guarded, relationship between press and politicians gives way to hostility. Thus, a principal effect of the long campaign is to heighten the conflict that is inherent in the press-candidate relationship.

A second consequence is that a relatively fixed amount of substantive information is spread over a greater period of time. The shorter campaigns of the past worked to focus the election on the candidates' agenda. What they had to say held its news value for much of the campaign. Given the length of the present campaign, the substance of the election undoubtedly gets more news coverage in absolute terms than in the past. Still, there are not enough fresh policy and leadership issues to satisfy the media's appetite for news during the full period of the campaign. The press hence has abundant opportunities to base news selection on its own values, which means that campaign controversies will stand out.

A presidential campaign is necessarily a long campaign. Unlike European elections, which are based on strong parties, parliamentary systems, and prime-ministers-in-waiting, the U.S. presidential election takes place in the context of federalism, weak parties, and an independently elected executive. America's presidential hopefuls must address themselves to 250 million people through a nominating process that takes their campaigns across fifty states. They need time to get their ideas across. It is ironic that it is the length of the campaign which eventually buries their ideas in a press-driven avalanche of controversy.

CHAPTER FIVE

News, Truth, and That State of Nature We Call Election Coverage

News and truth are not the same thing, and must be clearly distinguished.

WALTER LIPPMANN[1]

If reporters had flipped coins, their attempts to predict the outcome of the 1976 Republican presidential race would have been just as accurate.[2] In March, the Los Angeles *Times* named Gerald Ford "a solid favorite" in North Carolina a week before Ronald Reagan easily won that state's primary. *Time* wrote in the same month that Reagan had been "practically eliminated . . . from the running" by Ford's Florida win and that his candidacy had "died" after his fifth straight loss in Illinois. Reagan exceeded Ford in total number of delegates won a few weeks later.

In April, NBC News asserted that Ford was the heavy favorite to win the Republican nomination. Shortly thereafter, Reagan ran off a string of five primary victories in eleven days. Perhaps this prompted *Newsweek* to write in early May that Ford faced a stiff test in his native Michigan and that "a defeat there would leave his candidacy tapped out and might even force his withdrawal from the race." Yet Ford won 65 percent of the Michigan vote and led Reagan within a week by more than a hundred delegates.

When their predictions went awry, journalists responded with surprise, speaking in their postprimary analyses about "shocking wins," "stunning turn-abouts," and "eleventh-hour reprieves." The day after Reagan's North Carolina win, ABC's Herb Kaplow said: "Aside from foreign policy and inflation maybe turning the voters towards Reagan, there's talk that maybe local politics helped him to win; and maybe sympathy for the underdog, particularly when the President's men tried to pressure Reagan to quit, but so far it's just maybes, just speculation. And so nobody knows just what happened here yesterday. . . ."

Reviewing the Republican primaries, *Time* magazine concluded that the voters had upset "many an expert forecast." The Washington *Post*'s David Broder echoed that sentiment when he wrote: "A weary reporter, unpacking his suitcase and sorting through his jumbled impressions of the last five months, is struck by the paradoxes of the primary season. Almost any generalization that springs to mind is immediately contradicted . . . there were so many surprises."

In fact, there was a relatively straightforward pattern to the 1976 Republican contest. The outcome reflected an enduring ideological split between moderate and conservative rank-and-file Republicans that surfaced each time there were strong contenders to represent each wing of the party. The division was apparent in 1952, when Republican voters had to choose between the conservative Robert Taft and the moderate Dwight D. Eisenhower; in 1964, when the contest pitted the conservative Barry Goldwater against the moderates Nelson Rockefeller and William Scranton; and again in 1976, as the conservative Reagan and the moderate Ford vied for the Republican nomination.

The persistence of this split is evident in a comparison of the 1976 and 1964 Republican races. In 1964, Goldwater received the most solid support from Republicans in the following twenty-five states: Alabama, Arizona, California, Georgia, Idaho, Illinois, Indiana, Kansas, Louisiana, Mississippi, Missouri, Montana, Nebraska, Nevada, New Mexico, North Carolina, Oklahoma, South Carolina, South Dakota, Tennessee, Texas, Utah, Virginia, Washington, and Wyoming. All but three of these states also produced wins for Reagan in 1976. Only in Kansas, Mississippi, and Illinois did Reagan win fewer delegates than Ford. All told, Reagan acquired 833 delegates from these states, while Ford received only 276.

On the other hand, Ford received 881 delegates to Reagan's 237 in the twenty-five states that had provided Goldwater his least solid support in 1964; Alaska, Arkansas, Colorado, Connecticut, Delaware, Florida, Hawaii, Iowa, Kentucky, Maine, Maryland, Massachusetts, Michigan, Minnesota, New Hampshire, New Jersey, New York, North Dakota, Ohio, Oregon, Pennsylvania, Rhode Island, Vermont, West Virginia, and Wisconsin. With the exceptions of Arkansas and Colorado, each state gave Ford a delegate edge.

Although the conservative Reagan's victories in North Carolina, Indiana, Idaho, and Nebraska were labeled surprising by the press, these states had also been dominated by Goldwater in 1964 and by Taft in 1952. Ford's surprising wins were in New Hampshire, Florida, Kentucky, and West Virginia, but these states had not strongly supported either Goldwater or Taft. Primary results presented by the press as voter upsets were in reality parts of a recurring pattern.

The 1976 GOP race was not an aberration. Reporters often misjudge the course of presidential campaigns. During the 1992 nominating period, the press wrote off Bill Clinton several times, was surprised by Bush's weak support, and was puzzled by Ross Perot's strong appeal. The shift of one-fourth of the electorate into the Clinton column when Perot dropped from the race caught the press by surprise. "This year, the political world has changed so quickly, so many times, that even the pundits have grown wary of punditry," wrote *The New York Times*'s Robin Toner. "No one was quite sure of the impact of Mr. Perot's withdrawal."[3]

If the press had adjusted its focus, it might have seen more clearly some of the clues to what the voters were thinking. Perot's money, Clinton's womanizing, and Bush's diffidence had influenced the journalists' outlook and affected their predictions. A Times Mirror poll in May asked journalists to estimate the Democrats' chances of winning the presidency. Only 13 percent said "good" or "excellent," compared with 84 percent who said "fair" or "poor." Six of every seven journalists thought the Democrats were likely to lose the November election—and this at a time when the economy was sluggish and public anger with government was high. Such conditions foreshadow a likely shift in control of the presidency to the out-party,[4] even if the voters have doubts about its nominee. In 1980, voters put Reagan in the White House despite misgivings about his bellicosity and economic proposals. If reporters in May 1992 had been looking more directly at conditions in America, they might have seen the combination of circumstances that gave the Democrats at least an even chance of victory.

If the campaign is to be a time for the voters to exercise *their* discretion, they need help in discovering what their choices represent. Their persistent problem is to find clues that do not lead them down blind alleys or on wild-goose chases. The political parties were once their mapmakers, and to a degree they still are. But a presidential election is no longer party-centered, and people look to the news for help. While they get some guidance from it, they also receive a lot of misinformation.

In his essay "News, Truth, and a Conclusion," Walter Lippmann warned against a tendency to look to the press for guidance. He distinguished news from truth, saying the two coincide only at those few points where the instruments of record and the subjects of news coincide. When Clinton received his unprecedented 27-point bounce in the polls during the week of the Democratic convention, and it did not disappear overnight, the press cemented him in the favorite's role. This judgment was an easy one to make. The difficult task is to provide direction in situations characterized by complexity and interruptions. The press is particularly ill-equipped to help out in these cases.[5]

Lippmann gave several reasons why the news does not provide a reliable basis for judgment. By tradition, news is found in particular events rather than the underlying forces in society that create them. The event is the tip of the iceberg—a small and unrepresentative manifestation of a vastly more intricate reality. The news is also what is new and out of the ordinary. But novelty, however interesting or compelling it may be, is by definition atypical and thus is a weak basis for judging trends that are powerful and lasting. And then there is the unrelenting pressure of the news cycle. The press must re-create reality every twenty-four hours, giving the journalist little time to reflect back or think ahead.

Lippmann was writing in 1922, but these limitations of the press still exist. Journalists today are more highly educated and linked to better and swifter sources of information, but they still labor at a hectic job, looking at the world in all its bewildering complexity through the narrow lens of events, leaders, and fast-breaking developments.

Yet the press presents the news in an authoritative manner. During the 1992 campaign, a leading journalist claimed that the reporting had been "what good reporting has always been: the best obtainable version of the truth."[6] It is only after the fact, when predictions have gone haywire, and then only if they choose to look back, that journalists admit to great uncertainty.

The interpretive style of reporting that has come to dominate election coverage is a version of truth-telling. It requires the journalist to give shape to things that cannot be seen and to understand things that are not easily grasped. The older, descriptive model of reporting was more modest in its aims. The journalist sought to tell the reader or listener what had happened; the larger meaning was left to the audience to determine. While descriptive journalism was subject to errors of observation and inference, its goal was accuracy rather than truth.[7] Descriptive reporting suggests that the news *reflects* reality, and interpretive reporting implies that the news *is* reality, in narrative form.

Even at its best, however, the news is filled with unreliable "truths." The journalists' perspective on politics and the constraints under which they operate combine to make their observations fleeting and inexact. While Republicans in 1976 were waging a longstanding intraparty feud, the press was busy finding significance in facile differences. After Reagan's poor showing in New Hampshire, *Time* suggested that he might have won had he not declined an appearance on NBC's "Today" show on the morning of the primary. When Ford won in Florida, the Associated Press gave credit to a switch in his state campaign manager just before the election. NBC News attributed the size of one of Ford's wins to his presidential demeanor, and the margin of another to "the fire in his belly." His defeat in North Carolina was attributed by *Time* to a failure to recognize "how soft his support was." Reagan's victory in Nebraska was associated with "his Hollywood glamour—still a factor in the rural Midwest." A UPI story indicated that Ford's victory margin in Michigan was due to his "whistle-stopping across the state by train in the style of his political hero, Harry Truman." In mid-May, the Los Angeles *Times* said that "Ford had the strongest organization in Maryland, with telephone banks and mass mailings, and it showed in the election results."

The press was certainly not entirely unmindful of either the split within Republican ranks or the regional concentration of the split. In late May, *Time* said of a Ford victory: "The President needed that lift because the fight now moves to Reagan's friendly southern and western turf." But the press used these elements only occasionally to interpret primary results. Journalists skimmed the surface of campaign events to find explanations. My own study of the 1976 campaign found that over 80 percent of the news media's explanations for outcomes of Republican primaries were based on personality or events; fewer than 20 percent referred to ideological or regional patterns within the GOP.[8]

Lippmann reasoned that the flimsy foundation of the news

makes it an unsuitable basis for political action. And the news is not, as some would have it, a corrective for defective political institutions. Some people, both in and out of the press, assume that the combination of an attentive public and a truth-telling press can surmount the challenges of democracy. Research and experience have shown us that the public's attention to politics is sporadic at best, and now we also need to recognize that the press's capacity to communicate reliable truths is limited. The media's usual effect is not to correct problems but to exacerbate them. The press, Lippmann concluded, "necessarily and inevitably reflect[s], and therefore, in greater or lesser measure, intensif[ies], the defective organization of [politics]."[9]

Primaries and caucuses are the critical events of a presidential campaign. The McGovern-Fraser reforms instituted after the 1968 election were premised on the idea that popular participation is the legitimate method of selecting nominees. Indeed, the current system makes sense only when put in this context. Otherwise it is a cumbersome, drawn-out process that has little to recommend it.

In theory, the nominating process consists of fifty separate contests. No one state is decisive; its votes are but a single indicator of the candidates' popular support. The states differ in population, so they contribute in unequal proportions to the total number of delegates. But the preferences of voters in one state can never substitute for the opinions of voters elsewhere, and there is no presumption that the result in one state is somehow superior to the result in others. Moreover, primaries and caucuses lack the finality of a general election; each has a relative rather than an absolute outcome. A presidential primary or caucus does not elect anybody to office; it is an expression of how one state's voters divide their support among the various contenders. The difference between a candidate who gets 51 percent of the vote and another who gets 49 percent is theoretically insignificant; each is the preferred nominee of half the state's voters.

In reporting the primaries and caucuses, the press honors virtually none of these distinctions, but is governed by an entirely different set of principles. Some states are regarded as nearly irrelevant to the selection of the nominees, while others get greater attention. And a few are treated as microcosms of the nation as a whole, within which something resembling a winner-take-all rule applies. "With 88 percent of Iowa's caucuses in, no amount of bad-mouthing by the others can lessen the importance of Jimmy Carter's finish," CBS News concluded in a report direct from the 1976 Iowa caucuses.

When the press decides that a contest is a crucial test of the candidates' strength, the buildup can be extraordinary. In 1976 during the preprimary period, the New Hampshire primary was the subject of 34 percent of newspaper articles and 54 percent of television stories about the campaign.[10] In 1980, Iowa and New Hampshire received more than a fourth of the total news coverage devoted to the fifty state contests.[11] In 1984, New Hampshire's coverage exceeded that of all the Southern and Border states combined.[12] In 1988, there were 84 network news stories on New Hampshire and 53 stories on all the Super Tuesday states combined.[13] This type of singular attention was devoted to a state which accounts for less than 1 percent of the delegates to the national conventions.*

The winner in a contest that has been declared crucial by the press gets a windfall of publicity. Studies indicate that the first-place finisher in such a primary or caucus averages three to four times the news coverage of his rivals in the week that follows.[14] In allocating coverage according to a "winner-take-all" formulation, the press is conforming to traditional news values. The real story is the winner. To submerge a victory in the intricacies of the nominating process would lessen its dramatic quality.

The press's game schema also prompts it to ignore the in-

---

* A 1976 survey asked voters what percentage of the national convention delegates were from New Hampshire. The average guess was 10 percent—an obvious reflection of the extraordinary media attention this tiny state's primary receives.

tended purpose of the nominating process. The voters in a single state may not be representative of voters elsewhere, but the candidates' role there is the same as their role elsewhere: they must raise money, build support, create an organization, gain press coverage, plan and execute a strategy. Since the game schema holds that these activities are critical to the candidates' success, the press regards a single state like New Hampshire as a valid test of their electability. "The fact is that the reality in the early going of a presidential campaign is not the delegate count at all," according to Jules Witcover. "The reality at the beginning stage is the psychological impact of the results—the perception by press, public, and contending politicians of what has happened."[15]

The press's bias toward hard-news events also contributes to this pattern of coverage. Until a state's vote is counted, the press relies on softer indicators of the competition, such as the candidates' poll standings and finances. Given its traditional emphasis on events, the press prefers to focus on actual outcomes, even if they involve few voters or narrow margins, and have a questionable relationship to the preferences of the electorate as a whole. "The early caucuses and primaries are seen as the first 'hard news' stories of the presidential race, a perception which almost guarantees an inflated value placed on the results of these events," writes Christopher Arterton. "The unrepresentative nature of the early contests is neglected because finally the contest has begun."[16]

Of course, the candidates also target these states, campaigning longer and spending more money there than elsewhere.[17] To a large extent, however, it is the press's game they are playing. The New Hampshire primary has a long history as the opening contest but a shorter one as a pivotal encounter. In *America in Search of Itself*, Theodore H. White describes a quiet scene in New Hampshire with Estes Kefauver, who minutes earlier had been declared the winner of the state's 1956 Democratic primary. "I recall sitting in Senator Kefauver's uncrowded hotel room, each of us on a bed, with a bottle of bourbon between us, our only communication relay to the outside world the local radio."[18]

New Hampshire got increased attention in the 1960s, but the decisive change came in 1972, when the press decided that the state was a critical test of Edmund Muskie's position as Democratic frontrunner. "[Muskie] must not only win, but win with a large enough percentage of the vote that the press acknowledges it to be a victory," the Washington *Post*'s David Broder wrote two months before the primary.[19] The press increased its New Hampshire coverage, and Muskie intensified his efforts, saying, "New Hampshire is important to me, in part, because you gentlemen of the press have undertaken to make it important. . . ."[20] He won, but by less than the press's "magic figure" of 50 percent; he was thus declared the loser, and his campaign faltered. When news coverage of New Hampshire's primary increased again in 1976, the state's crucial position in presidential nominating politics was secured.[21]

The overwhelming importance of Iowa's caucuses as a critical test is even more a creation of the press. Iowa drew few reporters and barely any notice until *The New York Times*'s R. W. Apple, Jr., and other key journalists claimed late in 1975 that Iowa might play a key role in the 1976 Democratic race. Though Iowa had only 47 of the 3,008 delegates at the Democratic convention, the campaign press corps descended en masse on Iowa, forcing Morris Udall to reconsider his decision not to contest the caucuses. He shifted ten campaign days and $80,000 to Iowa in a belated effort to overtake Jimmy Carter, who had been campaigning for a year in the state.[22] The networks originated their newscasts from Iowa on the evening of the caucuses. When Carter came out ahead among the actual candidates (the largest proportion of the votes was cast for "undecided"), CBS declared him "the clear winner in this psychologically crucial event." CBS then singled him out for extra coverage through a live interview: "So the candidate with the highly prized political momentum tonight is Jimmy Carter, covered now by Ed Rable in New Hampshire."[23] *The New York Times*'s R. W. Apple said

Carter had "burst from the pack," trumpeting his win with the front-page headline, "Carter Is Regarded As Getting Big Gain from Iowa Results."[24]

The media's coverage of Iowa increased again in 1980, which worked primarily to George Bush's advantage. He had returned to private life in 1978 "after years of transient and uneventful service in a succession of [government] jobs," and was hence able to spend vast amounts of time "in Iowa and New Hampshire, running for president."[25] When he won Iowa's Republican caucuses by 2,000 votes, he received a publicity windfall; in *Newsweek*, for example, he had 675 lines of coverage compared with the 125 lines allotted to his six Republican rivals combined.[26] Within a few days the percentage of Republicans favoring Bush in national polls rose from less than 10 percent to nearly 30 percent.

People are just beginning to pay attention to the campaign when the press highlights an early winner. "So Carter emerges from New Hampshire as the man to beat," declared NBC's Tom Pettit after Carter won narrowly in New Hampshire's crowded Democratic field in 1976. The voters are affected by the press's focus on the frontrunner. George McGovern in 1972, Jimmy Carter in 1976, George Bush in 1980, Gary Hart in 1984, Michael Dukakis in 1988, and Paul Tsongas in 1992 gained substantial support when the press singled them out early in the campaign as frontrunners. When Hart won the New Hampshire primary in 1984, he rose within a few days from 7 percent to 34 percent as the choice of Democrats in nationwide Gallup polls. Dukakis's national poll standing jumped from 14 percent to 36 percent with his New Hampshire victory in 1988.

These surges, however, were not accompanied by a significant change in the information voters had about the candidates. Studies indicate that voters are not appreciably more aware of the winning candidate's political position a few days after Iowa or New Hampshire than they were previously. They are simply more aware of the candidate's existence.[27]

The press's attention to early winners is not designed to boost their candidacies, but it inevitably does so. A halo effect is evident in the media's focus.[28] The sociologists Paul Lazarsfeld and Robert Merton noted that mass audiences subscribe to the circular belief: "If you really matter, you will be at the focus of mass attention, and if you are at the focus of mass attention, then you must really matter."[29] Voters have a tendency to judge the suitability of candidates for nomination at least partially in the context of their electability.[30] "Stories about election victory, accordingly, were processed as evidence that the winners were qualified," Doris Graber concluded on the basis of her election study.[31]

After the nominating process was changed in 1970, candidates did not immediately get a grip on the press's rules. Senator Henry Jackson did not enter the 1976 New Hampshire primary, choosing to make his first stand in the Massachusetts primary, scheduled a week later. He won handily in Massachusetts, which has a population ten times that of New Hampshire, but the press had its spotlight on New Hampshire's winner, Carter, and his showdown with George Wallace in the coming week's Florida primary.

In 1980, Ronald Reagan miscalculated when he decided to skip the Republican debate in Iowa. The press played up Reagan's decision, claiming the debate was not the "farce" he predicted it would be. "Televised debates are more often lost than won, and last night in Des Moines the clear loser was 1,447 miles away," concluded *The New York Times*.[32] Reagan was subsequently defeated in the Iowa caucuses, after having led by more than 20 points. Afterward, in a straw poll at the National Press Club, more than 80 percent of the participating journalists picked someone other than Reagan as the likely GOP nominee.

Leading candidates have since learned to play within the media's rules. They downplay a contest only if the press allows it, which it did in 1992 with Iowa, because Tom Harkin was in the race.

When Super Tuesday was created in 1984, the press's role changed somewhat. The multiple contests that take place on Super Tuesday present a more complex outcome, defying the simple winner-take-all interpretation that the media imposes on a single state like New Hampshire. While Super Tuesday has reduced the press's influence in this sense, it has given the media more freedom to interpret the result. In 1984, Gary Hart won six states on Super Tuesday, but he "lost" when the press interpreted Mondale's wins in Alabama and Georgia, the latter by 3 percentage points, as a "psychological victory" in that he had prevented a Hart sweep. In 1988, Dukakis acquired momentum by winning fewer than half the Super Tuesday contests, because he did better than expected for a Northeastern governor.

The press also determines "electability," giving rapt attention to a candidate who it believes has a chance of gaining nomination. Clinton had "electability" in 1992, which gave him a news advantage in the early stages. He appeared on the covers of *Time*, *New York* magazine, and *The New Republic* before the first primary had been held. Along with the publicity surrounding Gennifer Flowers, Clinton's "electability" earned him as much news coverage in the early phase of the nominating campaign as all of his Democratic rivals combined.[33] Bob Kerrey complained about the press's tilt toward Clinton. "In Nebraska we don't do horserace stuff," he said. "Never in my life have I experienced someone moving ahead because they were 'electable.' "[34]

The nominating game that the press helped create has become institutionalized.[35] It fails to distribute power evenly across the electorate.[36] Voters in states judged insignificant by the press (Vermont ranks almost as low as New Hampshire ranks high), or scheduled for the latter part of the process, have exercised little influence on nominations, even though they constitute a population majority.

The intricacies of the race are nearly completely lost in the press's narratives. Any special advantage or disadvantage that a candidate might have possessed in a particular state or from the makeup of the contending field is acknowledged but not portrayed as a critical factor. Clinton succeeded in 1992 where his fellow Southerner Gore had failed in 1988 partly because Clinton did not face on Super Tuesday what Gore had—Jesse Jackson. Jackson cut deeply into Gore's potential Southern support, helping Dukakis to win pluralities in several key states.

Morris Udall compared the press's winner-take-all version of nominating politics to a bizarre sports event. "It's like a football game, in which you say to the first team that makes a first down with ten yards, 'Hereafter your team has a special rule. Your first downs are five yards. And if you make three of those you get a two-yard first down. And we're going to let your first touchdown count twenty-one points. Now the rest of you bastards play catch-up under the normal rules."[37]

However, the effect of news coverage is not as decisive as Udall claims. Although he was unable to catch up with Carter in 1976, the momentum a candidate receives from early victories is not always sustained. Bush in 1980, Dole in 1984, and Tsongas in 1992 are examples of candidates who could not maintain a fast start. Nevertheless, the press's attention provides a significant boost. It means a sudden burst of favorable news and a surge in the polls; it also makes it easier for the winner to raise funds, attract volunteers, garner endorsements, and acquire additional news coverage.

Sudden shifts in preference cannot be attributed solely to news coverage. Hart's sharp rise in the polls in 1984 was due in part to voters who were looking for an alternative to frontrunner Walter Mondale.[38] When Hart broke from the pack, many voters embraced him without knowing much about his politics. Moreover, momentum is not the whole story of nominating politics.[39] In the 1976 GOP race, Ford and Reagan were well known to Republican voters before the campaign began, and each had hardcore support. In 1972, the Vietnam conflict provided antiwar Democrat George McGovern with a steadfast following. Jesse Jackson's 1984 and 1988 candidacies were sustained with the backing of African-Americans.

But presidential primaries are not like a general election. Voters are not anchored by party loyalties, and most of them are feebly motivated and poorly informed. In these circumstances, the press's interpretations of what is happening in the race, and the glare of its spotlight, can significantly influence the vote.[40]

This type of decision might be called the "whimsical vote." The process of persuasion resembles what Herbert Krugman describes as "learning without involvement." In this situation, attitudes and motivation are weak, but people do absorb some information. People "learn" the message, and since they are "uninvolved," they do not resist it. Thus, when required to make a choice, they make a decision compatible with their new understanding. This process contrasts with the situation where people have strong attitudes. In such instances, their psychological defenses are at work; new information is tested against existing beliefs, and affected by those beliefs. Their decisions depend more on their prior opinions than on the new information. In this case, the individual is largely in control. Whereas in the case of "learning without involvement," power rests primarily with the communicator.[41]

Krugman's model describes with some accuracy the manner in which many voters reach their decisions during the nominating process. They are not totally uninformed, but their information is meager and their motivation weak. Large numbers of them base their decisions on idiosyncratic considerations, often of the last-minute variety. In 1984, on Super Tuesday, two out of three voters chose their candidate in the week before they cast their ballot.[42]

Voters do acquire information during the primary election phase. The problem, as the political scientist Henry Brady notes, is that "primaries force people to choose before they are ready to do so." They learn, but they learn "too late."[43] By the time they acquire a reasonable understanding of their choices, the race, for all practical purposes, is over. One or another candidate has probably already accumulated the number of delegates required to establish an insurmountable lead.

When the Democratic party set out to reform the nominating process after the 1968 election, it could hardly have sought the resulting system. The Democrats wanted a process that would express the will of rank-and-file voters. And for this reason, the party abolished winner-take-all allocations of a state's delegates; they now had to be divided in proportion to each candidate's support. Above all, the party could not have wanted a process that gives the voters so little of a real say in the choice of nominees. It envisioned a truly democratic process in which the principle of "one person, one vote" would govern the choice of a nominee. The Democrats did not foresee a system driven by journalistic values, momentum, and the decisions of voters in a few key states.

The Democratic party should have had more foresight. The process established in the early 1970s inevitably gives added influence to voters in states holding the initial contests. What the party did not anticipate, but as Lippmann foresaw, is that the press would magnify the bias. The press's influence does not serve any discernible public purpose. It is not routinely motivated by considerations of which candidate might be more representative of his party or better for the country. The press is driven primarily by news values, which make winners and decisive encounters the name of the game, and it does not allow for an appreciable recognition of the purposes the nominating process was designed to serve.

In the world of politics, issues flow from societal problems and values and are thus well embedded in the social fabric. In the world of news, issues are less deeply rooted; they flow from candidates, events, and information. Although the news has been compared to a mirror held up to society,[44] it is actually a highly selective account of obtruding events.[45] There are always critical problems facing the nation, but whether they play a large or small part in the campaign, and do so in a true or distorted form, depends significantly on journalistic values.

Earlier chapters described some of the ways in which journalistic values affect the presentation of issues. The press treats issues as tokens in a strategic game and prefers issues that are lively and controversial. The press refracts society's problems and the candidates' agendas in other ways as well.

Issues get attention in rough proportion to the degree to which they personify a candidacy.[46] This tendency, as noted in Chapter Two, accounted for the press's uneven treatment of the issue of voter alienation in 1992. Although the signs of an angry public were apparent even at the beginning of the campaign, alienation was not a correspondingly important election topic until Ross Perot shot ahead of Bush and Clinton in the polls in the late spring. The media scrambled to correct the oversight. "We didn't have a great deal of that in our blueprint six months ago, but now we are hard at it," said the Associated Press's John Wolman.[47] Nevertheless, when Perot withdrew from the race, the issue lost favor with the news media once more. Philip Wander and David McNeil note, "The problem with personification . . . is that analysis pivots on an individual. Personifying social, political, and moral issues means that they will be resolved by definition. The issues vanish when the figure for whom the problem is named leaves the political stage."[48]

On the other hand, some issues get exaggerated attention because of personification. From the time that Iranian fundamentalists stormed the U.S. embassy and seized its fifty-two occupants in November 1979, the hostage crisis had the defining qualities of a top news story: it was a dramatic, riveting event that could be told in terms of its leading characters, Jimmy Carter and the Ayatollah Khomeini. No incident in recent decades has been more intensely reported. A television program, ABC's "Nightline," was born of the crisis; Ted Koppel began each night's report by noting the number of days that the hostages had been held in captivity. By the time Koppel presented "America Held Hostage: Day 365," only days before the November election, Jimmy Carter's foreign-policy record had been framed primarily in terms of this one issue. In a desperate final effort at re-election, Carter suspended his campaign for three days to personally oversee negotiations for release of the hostages. When the talks collapsed, so did his chances of winning a second term.

The attention that issues receive is also affected by whether they take the form of an event. Few developments have made a bigger impact on the nation's politics than the northward trek of Southern blacks, but it was seldom on the front pages or emblazoned in headlines. As African-Americans moved into Northern cities by the hundreds each day, white people, pushed by racial fears and pulled by the charms of suburban life, moved out in equal numbers. Within a few decades, the political, social, and economic landscape of urban America had been radically altered—a dramatic transformation that went largely unheralded. The columnist George Will jokingly said that a ribbon should have been stretched across the Mason-Dixon Line to give the press an event to cover as the one-millionth African-American crossed it on the way north.[49]

The changing face of urban America was not a big election story until 1968, after pent-up frustration and anger in the black community took on the shape of events. The burning of America's cities fostered the "law and order" issue that became a central theme of Richard Nixon's campaign. In 1992, when the Rodney King verdict sparked the Los Angeles riots, the conditions in the inner city again became a central focus of election coverage. In a three-week period, discussions of urban policy appeared in 35 percent of all election stories on network television.[50] Thereafter the issue virtually disappeared.

The 1947 Hutchins Commission on Freedom of the Press concluded that the media's chief failing is an inability to provide a proper context for the conduct of public affairs, and that its values result in a form of news that lacks any reasonable sense of proportion.[51] Lippmann's judgment was harsher. The limits on news, he said, quoting from Isocrates, cause it "to make of moles mountains, and of mountains moles."[52]

"Of moles mountains" aptly describes the press's handling of the so-called character issue. Journalists have come to regard character as a primary subject of presidential politics.[53] "It may not matter what Bill Clinton's 26-point health plan is all about by the time he might get to the White House," said one journalist. "What will matter is whether we see in the man elected to the highest office in the land the leadership capabilities to respond intelligently and quickly to problems."[54] Another said, "Voters don't believe . . . that the party labels are much help in determining how [candidates are] going to act, so what are we left with? What is our politics based on? Well, we're looking for clues to what kind of a person this man or woman is. What will they do in office? Well, if they cheat on their wife, maybe they're going to cheat on us. That becomes one of the few straws of information that we have left to judge our candidates by. . . . The public really is looking for clues to character, having been left with nothing else."[55]

The proposition that character is the basic issue of presidential politics is dubious. It makes sense only in the context of a personality-centered conception of politics. The voters do not accept the proposition. A Times Mirror poll in October 1991 asked, "In reporting on a presidential candidate, what one factor do you think news organizations should pay more attention to: a candidate's personal character, a candidate's stand on issues, or a candidate's experiences and qualifications?" Only 7 percent of the respondents chose character.

Reduced to its simplest terms, the character issue asserts that moral fiber is the key presidential attribute, while political ideology and partisanship are far less relevant. Yet it is policy, not character, that distributes costs and benefits in a society, and Republicans conduct policy differently than Democrats. Abortion, social welfare, economics, and civil rights are but a few of the policy areas in which it makes a difference which party is in power. Furthermore, the presidency extends beyond the president to several thousand high-ranking executive and judicial appointees who also influence public policy. In comparison with the Democrat Carter's appointees to the federal bench, for instance, the Republican Bush's nominees were six times more supportive of antiabortion rulings and five times less supportive of the rights of the accused in criminal cases.[56]

This is not to say that character is irrelevant. In *The Presidential Character*, James David Barber argues that a president's capacity to lead is central to his success in office.[57] The presidency is the focal point of leadership in the American political system, and the incumbent's performance as leader critically affects the performance of other institutions and the public at large.

The press sets up character as a question of leadership, but in practice it reports on character in terms of personal failings. "I've been a journalist longer than I've been anything else in my life, and I still believe that there are no bad questions, there are only bad answers," said an editor. "Everyone should be prepared in public life to have the key questions asked, such as, 'Did you cheat on your wife?' "[58] According to the findings of the Center for Media and Public Affairs, there was relatively little attention given to the character issue in 1992 except in the case of one candidate, Bill Clinton. He received more than 90 percent of the networks' character coverage during the primaries, most of it centering on his alleged sexual relationship with Gennifer Flowers.[59] Between January 1 and March 15, one in every six campaign stories included at least a brief reference to allegations about Clinton; most of the allegations were made by reporters without attributing the source, or were attributed to other news organizations.[60] In the general election, with the Flowers controversy out of the way, character accounted for only 2 percent of Clinton's coverage (mostly in the context of the draft issue) and 1 percent of Bush's coverage.[61] The pattern was similar in 1988, when character was largely an issue based on Gary Hart's relationship with Donna Rice.[62]

The press's focus on character during the primaries does have an impact. It drove Hart out of the 1988 race, and it almost ended Clinton's quest for the presidency. The effect is what media researchers call "priming," which is "the capacity of the press to isolate particular issues, events, or themes in the news, as criteria for evaluating politicians."[63] Research indicates that, when primed by news stories to judge a candidate in the context of governmental performance, voters do tend to assess the candidate largely within this framework. On the other hand, when primed to judge a candidate by his private behavior, many voters will do just that.[64] A Times Mirror poll in May showed that half of the public believed Clinton was not trustworthy. There was only one way they could have come to this conclusion; the media, in effect, had said so. Clinton had been unknown to the general public a few months earlier.

Candidates' private lives can offer some insights regarding their trustworthiness and similar personal traits. The difficulty is that such insights are by no means a reliable guide to a person's character. The broad assertion that Hart's philandering was a sign he could not be trusted on women's issues is difficult to defend for very long without encountering inconvenient facts, such as the 95 percent approval rating that *Ms.* magazine gave Hart for his Senate votes on legislation affecting women.

The Clinton situation was much the same. There were some good, tough investigative reports early in the campaign on Clinton's tenure as governor of Arkansas,[65] but these articles, giving him a relatively clean bill of health, dropped by the wayside in the feeding frenzy that followed Flowers's allegations. Did his alleged relationship with Flowers represent a disqualifying defect of character? As the communications theorist Judith Lichtenberg notes, there are no logical rules that accurately link patterns of private behavior to patterns of public leadership, while there are countless historical examples, including George Washington, Thomas Jefferson, and Franklin D. Roosevelt, that suggest the two patterns are largely unrelated.[66]

The press asserts a public-private connection by shifting ground from the sexual behavior to the candidate's response to the allegations. "The Issue Is Not Morality, It's Candor," was the headline of a Tom Wicker column in *The New York Times* on the Hart-Rice controversy.[67] NBC's Tory Beilinson said it was "a double standard" for George Bush to promote "family values and then say it is sleazy when you are asked about one of those values, which is marital fidelity."[68] But these rationalizations still do not address the issue of what sexual behavior has to do with presidential leadership.[69]

Lurking behind the press's difficulty in keeping issues in perspective is its commitment to impartiality. American journalists do not easily deal with the values inherent in issues, since this would require them to take sides. Martin Walker, the Washington bureau chief of the London newspaper the *Guardian*, said of campaign coverage in 1992: "European journalists are puzzled by this idea of objectivity, this intellectual apartheid. Like farting into a keyhole, it's clever but not worth the effort."[70]

Whether worth the effort or not, it does wring the politics out of issues. The rules of American journalism require the journalist to distinguish facts from values. Facts can be reported and evaluated; partisan values can be reported but not evaluated. If this "intellectual apartheid" is not always maintained in practice, it still exercises a severe constraint on journalists' actions.

It helps explain why they quickly reach a dead end in their character analysis. When leadership is removed from the context of partisan values, it becomes an abstraction that is difficult to define in a meaningful fashion. Great leaders are those who take up important causes, have the skill to see them through, and are able to carry others along. Character in public life is dedication to a vision of the public good. Concern with marital infidelity is petty puritanism by comparison.[71]

Journalists' commitment to impartiality also helps explain why they define issues in terms of controversies, events, and persons—these are factual. It is also a reason why journalists do not make a serious effort to probe the candidates' position on issues. Thus, the irony in 1992 was the press's preoccupation with the stances of the one candidate who had the least to say on the issues, Ross Perot. He was contemptuous of reporters for wanting to know his position "on everything from mosquitoes to ants," as he described it. In contrast, Bill Clinton had trouble getting reporters to ask him about his views on the issues. Since he had an answer to nearly every issue-related question, the press was not very interested in his responses.

When issues are abstracted from the context of partisan values, they become sterile, which is why side-by-side summaries of the candidates' positions in newspapers are so lifeless in comparison with the candidates' stump speeches. Reporters were surprised by the wildly enthusiastic response of delegates and the television audience to Edward Kennedy's speech at the 1980 Democratic convention. They had heard the speech many times over on the campaign trail and, having thoroughly dissected it, had concluded that it contained few fresh ideas. As a source of new information, it was unimpressive. As an expression of values, it was electrifying. It evoked the vision of a more equal and just society that was the driving force of the New Deal, the civil rights movement, and the war on poverty.

In recent decades, as the journalist's voice has pushed the candidate's voice out of the news, much of this kind of advocacy has been lost to the public. In the 1960s, when the candidates were given the opportunity in the newspapers and on network news shows to speak at length, audiences were regularly exposed to issues presented in the context of partisan values. Today, issues are presented as just another type of information. The information culture of the journalist has supplanted the political culture of the candidate.

The communication of information is important to elections, but its significance is often misunderstood. A common assumption is that if voters are fed enough information, they will have all they need to act responsibly. "Democracy," Alexander Heard writes, "requires a voluminous exchange of information among its diverse participants, including 'rulers' and 'ruled,' voters and candidates, competing interests and cooperating interests."[72] While the claim has some truth to it, people do not have the capacity to absorb great quantities of information. Studies have found that most people forget the details of political messages within a relatively short time.[73] What they retain is the lasting impression left by a message. Ronald Reagan's strength as a communicator was not an ability to impart information but a capacity to deliver a powerful message in a few words ("Ask yourself this one question, are you better off today than you were four years ago?") and to frame issues within a set of values that appealed to a great many people's vision of America. This is why most Americans ignored the press's complaints that Reagan could not keep his facts straight.

Reagan's ideas, like Kennedy's, came out of a party tradition. Parties and candidates are carriers of values and are thus a powerful source of cues for their followers.[74] In one of my election studies, I compared people's news exposure with their perceptions of the parties' positions as predictors of whether they were aware of the candidates' positions on a series of issues. Party perceptions were the better predictor. Voters often assumed—correctly in most instances—that a candidate held the same position as his party. Even when the candidate held an aberrant position, people's party perceptions were the better predictor of whether they knew his actual position. An awareness of the party's positions gave them a reference point that helped them to place the candidate's position.[75] Partisanship helps voters to map information.

Dependent as the press is on providing context solely through information, it struggles in its attempt to guide the public. News space is limited, politics is complicated, people's memory is short, their attention is inconstant.

When reporters set out in 1992 to act as "character cops" and "truth squads" in order to broaden the public's understanding of the candidates and their positions, they were choosing one of the few options available to them. Forbidden by their norms to judge partisan values, they were left with the task of acting on behalf of "good government," as opposed to "bad government," which in practice meant comparing a candidate's claims against facts they could gather. If a candidate exaggerated his accomplishments, the press pointed out the discrepancy between his words and his actions. When a candidate called forth statistics to buttress his position or attack his opponent, reporters produced their own statistics to show how well or badly the candidate's figures matched theirs. Some of this reporting took the form of high-sounding regular features: "ad watches," "Reality Check" ("CBS Evening News"), and "Fact or Fiction" ("The MacNeil-Lehrer News Hour") are examples.

This type of reporting is potentially useful, but in practice becomes problematic. For one thing, labels such as "Fact or Fiction" falsely imply that the press has a firm handle on truth. Second, when it becomes a regular feature of coverage, this form of reporting compels the journalist to search continually for suitable material; if there are no major problems, the reporter has almost no choice but to focus on minor problems or to stretch the evidence (the "Reality Check" described in the Prologue is an example).

Nevertheless, in an era of high-powered media campaigns with their glut of images and issues, the press has the opportunity and a responsibility to help the voters gauge the accuracy of the messages aimed at them. When this type of reporting rises above the level of nitpicking and is careful in making its claims, it can help the voters better understand their choices. But it is also reflective of how far removed from real politics journalism can be. When the test of a candidate's positions is the precision of the statistics that he uses to illustrate them, politics resembles a subfield of accounting rather than what it is meant to be—a struggle over society's values.

Success for a presidential candidate is easy to measure. Candidates are in the campaign to win and to promote the policy goals of themselves and their followers. They succeed fully when they are victorious and gain the opportunity to pursue their advocated aims. Even if candidates lose the election, they can succeed in part by creating support for their ideas and forcing their opponents to take them into account.

Success for the journalist is more elusive. As the scholar Jay Rosen notes, journalists have no "clear [idea] about what success means for them." They are not advocates of a particular cause, nor do they win in any significant sense when the election turns out one way rather than another. Reporters are skeptics. "Typically, they define themselves *against* others; they're watchdogs, critics, adversaries of [those] who try to manipulate the news. This is a reasonable conception, but also a negative one. It leaves no room for constructive communication. So when the press 'wins' during the campaign, it's usually because the negative functions of journalism—critique, exposé—have won out."[76]

It was the view that they had "won" which led many journalists to claim that the 1992 coverage was the best ever, and a portent of future elections. "Perhaps the best news about this campaign," Carl Bernstein wrote in an article titled "It's Press vs. Bush," "is that the next president stands forewarned. The press may feel empowered and self-confident enough to keep on the business of real reporting. . . ."[77]

Some negativity is no doubt a good thing. The political scientist W. Lance Bennett talks about "degradation rituals" in campaigns. These rituals take place primarily as a part of testing candidates against their fabricated images. Electoral norms ought to allow the candidates considerable freedom to define their campaigns and force them to defend their positions. The counterclaims of opponents and the press and the candidate's response can provide the voters with insights into the candidate. Criticism also affirms the principle of accountability—that candidates have a responsibility to level with the voters.[78]

But when criticism is synonymous with being "against" the politician, and negativity overwhelms the positive aspects of election politics, the degradation ritual becomes an acid bath. According to a content analysis of television coverage of the 1992 general election, on-the-air sources were deeply critical of the election: 100 percent of those quoted said the choices were bad, and 93 percent said the quality of the campaign was bad.[79]

No reasonable standard of what is good or bad in candidates and elections could justify this one-sided refrain. And journalists' portrayal of the 1992 campaign was no exception in this respect:

1988: "The real winner is clear: Congress. It will fill the vacuum created by the election of whichever of these guys gets preferred because he is not the other guy."[80]

1984: "I write at a time when the results of some of the lesser contests are not known, such as that for President of the U.S., for instance."[81]

1980: "Angry, frustrated and discouraged, Americans are heading into the 1980 election unhappy with the choices for president and convinced that—whatever the outcome—it will do little to rekindle the nation's spirits."[82]

1976: "It is now the fall of '76 and once again people tell me that neither candidate merits a vote."[83]

1972: "A choice between the lesser of two evils."[84]

If this pattern were found in another institution, it would be described by the press as an abuse of power. It *is* an abuse of power—and it goes largely unchecked. The press has become more assertive and judgmental, and yet it has no real accountability.[85] News organizations are reluctant to monitor one another, and complaints from politicians are dismissed as self-serving.

Politicians are not saints, but when the balance of coverage tilts so strongly in the negative direction, the election cannot serve as it should to raise the quality of public life. The voters blame both the candidates and the press for the situation, but assign a greater share of the blame to the media. A November 1988 Gallup poll indicated that five out of seven voters thought the problem of negativity was primarily caused by the press. A Harvard report suggested that the reason for this might be the fact that the press is "closer to the electorate," while the candidates "more and more hide behind the camera and distance themselves from the voters."[86] Perhaps so, but the voters may simply have it right. When the public sees the unmediated images of the candidates in debates and convention speeches, they like what they see. The images conveyed through news have the opposite effect.

Every presidential campaign is somewhat Janus-faced. It is certainly a time for candidates to offer the voters a choice about national policy and leadership, but it is also a game of strategy and manipulation. The challenge for the press is to provide a balanced perspective on both sides of an election. Even strategy is not a one-sided issue. Although strategy can reflect a calculated effort to fool the public, it is also part of the bargaining process that goes on between the candidate and the electorate. When a candidate makes a promise in hopes of attracting support, he is also making a commitment to a particular group.

The public should be kept informed about the manipulative aspects of electoral politics. And in this era of candidate-centered campaigns, the press has a greater responsibility than ever to warn the public about inept and venal politicians. However, when manipulation is the primary context within which the electorate's choices are repeatedly framed, the trust that should bind candidates and voters is undermined. Candidates are more than tacticians. They represent real and significant alternatives. It was not the public but the press who defined the 1988 Democratic race as a choice among the "seven dwarfs," and who characterized the 1992 campaign as a choice between "Slick Willy," an inept president, and a paranoid billionaire.

Given its traditional watchdog role, the press has great difficulty in handling the positive side of election politics. The purpose of watchdog journalism is to expose flaws; it makes no provision for constructive commentary. Moreover, journalists suffer from a fear of flacking; they worry about looking foolish if their praise of a candidate is contradicted by subsequent developments.[87] Accordingly, as the press's influence on the campaign agenda has increased, a principal effect has been to tilt this agenda toward the darker side of politics. Candidates are seldom portrayed as leaders and representatives; they are routinely made to appear deceptive, hypocritical, and manipulative.[88]

The candidates have certainly contributed to this tendency. But negative campaigning is as old as politics itself. Negative news is the new element. When Watergate and Vietnam turned the press against the politicians, negative reporting became the norm. The political scientist Dan Hallin found that positive and negative stories were equally prominent in 1968, but by the 1980s "negative stories clearly predominate[d]."[89]

It is ironic that Vietnam also led to electoral reforms that require the press to play the constructive role of bringing the candidates and the voters together. However, the critical perspective of the watchdog asks the press to question the words and the actions of the candidates. Journalists have not been able to balance these schizophrenic demands; the more familiar watchdog role dominates. As a result, the press's bitter narrative contributes to an electorate soured with its choices. As was noted in the Prologue, half or more of the voters have had an unfavorable image of one or both major party nominees in all but one election since 1968.

The rise of the press-centered campaign has coincided with a decline in voter turnout combined with an increase in voter cynicism. There are many reasons apart from the reporting of the campaign for this tendency. However, negative news surely adds to it. When turnout rose in 1992, there was no evidence that news was a cause of this increase, but there were clear indications that alternative media such as debates and talk shows were a contributing factor. These forms of communication were all that the news was not—upbeat, earnest, and packed with issues presented in the context of values.

In searching for a situation that parallels today's media campaign, my thoughts are drawn to the late V. O. Key's classic study *Southern Politics*. It was the late 1940s, before the civil-rights movement, when the South was racially segregated by law and practiced a form of politics based on loose factions rather than two-party competition. "Although it is the custom to belittle the contributions of [political] parties," Key wrote, "their performance seems heroic alongside that of pulverized factionalism."[90]

Key described a type of politics in the South that was based on "transient squabbling." Issues came and went with lightning speed as and when they served a faction's needs. There was "no discussion," only "attacks" and "disassociation." At times within this framework, campaigns were "but personal rivalries uncomplicated by substantial social and economic issues." The issue becomes one of who is the " 'best man' or the 'most competent' man." Campaigns were "often the emptiest sorts of debates over personalities."[91]

The carriers of these messages had "not a semblance of . . . responsibility." Free of accountability for the actions of government (there were no identifiable "ins" and "outs," since the factions re-formed with each election), they could serve "as critic." The attacks were "erratic" and "chaotic," characterized more by "disorganization" than any identifiable sense of "collective interest" or clear notion of "public choice."[92]

Within this framework of competition the voters were "whipped from position to position by appeals irrelevant to any fundamental interest." They were allowed "fitful rebellions," but no real "voice." They were forced to keep up with "a loose, catch-as-catch-can politics" in which there was "a high premium on demagogic qualities of personality" and a low premium on "general-policy orientations." And, in the end, the voters were the losers. They were "confused" over their choices and forced to function "in a sort of state of nature."[93]

The press-centered campaign established by the electoral reforms of the early 1970s is a poor substitute for the kind of campaign that properly functioning political parties can offer. The great virtue of effective two-party competition is not that it always produces the best leadership and provides a full discussion of the issues, for it does not, but that it offers a steady and relatively coherent set of ideas and traditions for the voters to choose from. The discontinuous, fluid, and transient form of politics that the press generates can at times defy the grasp of even the more attentive citizens. It is a politics of shifting standards and fleeting controversies, with no identifiable core.

Americans express impatience with parties, sometimes for good reasons. They impute virtue to a politics that centers on the individual candidate and takes place through direct communication with the voters. This type of politics is not altogether unhealthy, but it necessarily takes place through the medium of the press. The media, while playing an important role in the campaign, are not designed to serve as a political broker. They have a powerful drive toward skepticism, a persistent need for novelty, and a weakness for personality. These are not the desired characteristics for an *electoral* intermediary. Like the "pulverized" factions of the one-party South, the news media "fail by far to meet the standards of permanence, cohesiveness, and responsibility that characterize the political party."[94]

The nature of news exposes the foolhardiness of the idea that the press, if it would only handle things a little better, could make a presidential election into a sensible affair. The press is in the news business, and the news is simply not an adequate guide to political choice. The state of nature that we call the media campaign is, to rephrase the philosopher Thomas Hobbes, nasty, brutish, and long—much too long.

CHAPTER SIX

How to Fix the Campaign: Shorten It

The press is no substitute for institutions. It is like the beam of a searchlight that moves restlessly about, bringing one episode and then another out of darkness into vision. Men cannot do the work of the world by this light alone. They cannot govern society by episodes, incidents, and interruptions.

WALTER LIPPMANN[1]

After every presidential election, scholars and pundits, along with many journalists, say that campaigns would be better if only the press would report them differently. The assumption underlying this conclusion is that the press has the ability to organize the choices facing the voters. The burden on the media is particularly severe during the nominating phase. Within the limited time it has to communicate with the voters, the press is expected to create an electorate that can understand what a half-dozen previously unfamiliar candidates represent and can calculate the possible outcomes of a multiple-candidate race.

It is an impossible task. The press is far less effective as a linking mechanism than is commonly believed. The problem is that the press is not a political institution. Its business is news, and the values of news are not those of politics. Election news carries scenes of action, not commentary on the values reflected in those scenes. Election news emphasizes what is controversial about events of the previous twenty-four hours rather than that which is stable and enduring. The coverage is framed within the context of a competitive game rather than being concerned with basic issues of policy and leadership. It projects images that fit story lines rather than political lines. Election news highlights what is unappetizing about politics rather than providing a well-rounded picture of the political scene.

This is not to say that election news is unimportant. It can enlist the voters' interest in the campaign, keep them abreast of new developments, and make them aware of facts that may otherwise stay hidden. But the news is not an adequate guide to making political choices. Insofar as we depend on the media to formulate our mental image of the campaign, we get a picture that is not value-neutral but is instead embedded with the values of journalism and its particular biases and refractions.[2] Some of these pictures inform our judgment, but more of them mislead us about what is at issue in campaign politics.

And yet we are stuck with a press-centered version of the campaign. When the McGovern-Fraser reforms changed the nominating process two decades ago, the press was handed the political party's job of providing voters with a version of the campaign upon which to act.

It is an unmanageable role. The situation can be likened to the failure of Soviet economic planning. Some fifty years ago the economist Oskar Lange argued that it was impossible for central planners to handle the computational complexity of demand, supply, and price decisions for a national economy. A marketplace system does not depend on such a mechanism: the uncoordinated decisions of individual firms and consumers serve to bring demand, supply, and price into workable relationships. Lange predicted the Soviet system would someday collapse unassisted, leaving the economy in a state of complete disrepair.[3]

With its assigned task of creating political coalitions out of the voters' interests, the press is in a similar situation. The media have neither the means nor the incentives to bring these interests together in a coherent fashion. They lack the where-withal to determine the public's demand for particular policies on a continuing basis, or to formulate these policies, or to deliver them to the people in a timely and workable way.

There is an institution capable of performing all of these functions: the political party. The party system is to a democracy what the free-market system is to a marketplace economy. The job of parties is to aggregate society's interests and offer voters a choice between coherent competing alternatives. The party's incentive is power: if it can build the larger coalition, it gets to rule. Similarly, if it fails in office, it can be rejected by the voters in the next election—just as consumers can stop buying from a firm that sells them shoddy goods.

The press is not equipped to play a comparable role. The media's incentive lies in attracting and holding the audience's attention, and thus it endeavors to deliver the news in a form that will do so. This is why, despite the sincerity of the press's intentions to the contrary, news of the campaign is consistently melodramatic.[4]

As long as the press is entrusted with the job of political intermediary it will flounder, and so will the campaign. In this sense, the problem of today's campaign lies deeper than the press's shortcomings. No reform of the press can equip it for this mediating role. This is not to say that the press cannot improve its campaign coverage. It should recognize more fully how some of its tendencies distort the campaign. Must the candidates' small mistakes be among the major news stories of the campaign? Must the first primary or caucus be inflated beyond all reason? Must bad news so completely overwhelm good? But even if the press were to respond to all these problems, it would still not be able to do the job expected of it. The press is necessarily guided by its own conventions and organizational imperatives, and these are certain to dominate its decisions. Hence, it cannot be expected to organize political choice in a coherent way.

If the campaign is to be fixed, and it needs fixing, one must look beyond the shortcomings of the press. If the campaign is going to work, it must be organized for the press, not by the press. The campaign must be made more coherent, so that communication during the campaign is more instructive.

The campaign could be improved by shortening the nominating phase. The challenge is to abridge the nominating process and at the same time to slow it down. As things stand now, the weeding-out process occurs too quickly, while the campaign lasts too long. Both are detrimental to effective communication between candidates and voters.

The usual arguments made against a lengthy campaign are that it disrupts the policy process, discourages the candidacies of responsible officeholders, and wears out the voters. On the other hand, it has been claimed that a lengthy campaign enables the voters to learn about the choices they face. As previously indicated, the evidence does not support this contention. The public acquires very little information about the candidates' politics during the nominating phase, and over the course of a long campaign, the voters get distracted from the performance of government, as lesser issues compete for their attention. A lengthy campaign also makes it difficult for the candidates to establish their agendas; their pledges quickly become "old news." Ironically, today's nearly year-long campaign actually makes the candidates' politics less intelligible to voters than would a shorter one.

A lengthy campaign has another degenerative effect on election communication. As Figure 6.1 indicates, the tone of news coverage becomes increasingly negative as the campaign progresses through the primary election, convention, and general election phases. As the campaign wears on, the press becomes increasingly critical of the candidates. The reasons are several, including a tendency for negative themes to become embedded in journalists' narratives of the campaign.

Electoral reform is a tricky business. There is good reason to be skeptical of claims that changes will make things better. The

Figure 6.1   "Bad News" Coverage of Presidential Candidates by Stage of the Campaign

As the campaign progresses, news coverage of presidential candidates becomes increasingly negative.

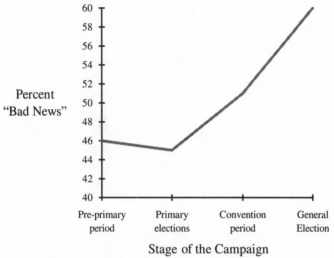

Stage of the Campaign

Note: Figure is based on favorable and unfavorable references to the major-party nominees in 4,263 *Time* and *Newsweek* paragraphs during the 1972–1992 period. "Horse-race" references are excluded; all other evaluative references are included.

problems often remain, and the reform may have unforeseen and unintended consequences that produce new problems. The McGovern-Fraser Commission, for example, assumed that the voters would control a presidential nominating process opened to their full participation. In a technical sense, they do control it. Their votes for a particular candidate result in the selection of delegates pledged to the candidate who gains nomination on obtaining a majority. Yet, as discussed earlier, these votes in many cases do not conform to any reasonable conception of informed choice.

Such experiences suggest that reform should not be undertaken lightly.[5] A need for order and predictability in governing structures is also a recommendation against reform. James Madison warned that if institutional change were undertaken in response to every perceived defect in government, the one predictable result would be chaos. This view is widely shared by political scientists. "Electoral reform," Everett Carll Ladd writes, "should be approached from a perspective that recognizes how important it is in this area to settle on something and stick with it."[6]

Reform in response to a single episode is nearly always ill-advised. The McGovern-Fraser reforms changed a presidential selection system that went haywire in 1968 but had otherwise worked well. Implemented by Progressive reformers after the election of 1900, the process had regularly produced strong leaders. Theodore Roosevelt, Wilson, Franklin D. Roosevelt, Truman, Eisenhower, Kennedy, and Johnson—all ranked by historians as good or great presidents—were selected under this system. It balanced peer review by party leaders with popular opinion as expressed through primary elections. Candidates had the opportunity in primaries to demonstrate their popular appeal, but the final judgment was made in the deliberative setting of a national convention.

I have attempted to show that the problems besetting post-1968 campaigns are systemic; they are not the result of particular candidates or issues. They surface in every campaign and have become more pronounced with the increasing influence of the press on the agenda. In claiming that the game has overtaken substance, bad news overshadows good, controversies outrank policy matters, news images prevail over issues of leadership, and news attention is distributed unfairly, I am identifying problems that have characterized all recent campaigns, and a situation that will not cure itself.

The pitfalls of reform are substantial enough to make modifications of the existing system the preferred approach to reform. A shortening of the campaign by truncating the nominating process is a change of this type.

Before I describe what a shorter campaign would accomplish, it will be helpful to specify the goals of a nominating process.

Nominations are a critical choice in the presidential selection process—perhaps as important as the final selection in November. The legendary Boss Tweed of Tammany Hall said, "Elect who you will, just let me do the nominating." Of course, Tweed was in a city where his party's nomination was tantamount to election; but nominating decisions are still vitally important. A large field of candidates is narrowed to the major-party nominees, one of whom is almost certain to become president.

It is imperative that the nominating process produce good candidates. In the past, the strength of a nominee was measured largely by his presumed ability to fulfill the requirements of the presidential office. Today, the ability to campaign effectively is also a critical consideration. Austin Ranney notes that nominees "must have the qualities of personality, achievement, and good campaigning skills that make them good votegetters. And they must also have the qualities of character, judgment, experience, and ability to work with other public officials that will enable them to be effective presidents."[7]

Though victory in today's campaign is heavily dependent on a candidate's campaign skills, these should not be allowed to outweigh governing ability as a determining factor in presidential selection. The system should be biased toward candidates who have the background and talents to serve effectively as president. Nominees should possess sufficient experience in government to understand how the political process operates and to make it work to achieve their goals. And they should have the required knowledge of national and international affairs to assume the full policy duties of the presidency when they take office.[8]

Legitimacy is the second goal of a nominating system. The people must believe that the process is fair, serves their interests, and is responsive to their opinions.[9] This may mean that rank-and-file voters must have a direct voice in the process. Given the American political tradition, a European-style system of nomination, wherein control rests fully with party leaders, would probably lack legitimacy in the United States. Such a system would also not provide what a popularly based system, at its best, can offer: protection against unresponsive party elites.

In practice, legitimacy may require the continued use of primary elections as a means of choosing some of the convention delegates. This assumption, however, is perhaps unwarranted; a Harris Poll in 1992 found that a 51-to-38 percent majority of those who voted in the primaries favored abolishing them as a means of choosing presidential nominees.[10] And there is a good alternative. More than one-fifth of the states select their delegates through caucuses that are open to participation by rank-and-file voters. The Iowa caucuses are the best known. In a caucus state, voters have the opportunity to discuss the candidates among themselves before expressing their preferences, making the process more deliberative than in a primary. And as the caucuses move up to district and state levels, the participants may reconsider initial preferences, which adds a further element of deliberation to the process.

The McGovern-Fraser Commission thought—wrongly, as it turned out—that most states would use the caucus system as the means of choosing their convention delegates. The caucuses have their proponents, some of whom believe they should be universally adopted. "Let's abolish the primaries," says the political scientist Charles O. Jones. "They mistakenly assume that voters are prepared to participate at a very early stage in the presidential nominating process. Turnout is low, candidates race around the nation insulting one another, the sequence is irrational, and it is all too expensive. Let's get political parties back into this process by having caucuses and party conventions select delegates to the national convention. Why not? They work perfectly well in those states that use this process."[11]

If the selection of good nominees and legitimacy are widely acknowledged requirements of a proper nominating system, there is a third requirement that is less often recognized: the process should strengthen the political party as an instrument of governance. Nominating contests are inherently divisive in that they pit elements within a party against each other. However, a nominating process makes no sense as an instrument of party destruction. The McGovern-Fraser Commission recognized that the nominating process must allow for competition while also furnishing a basis for cohesion. Its solution was to establish rules that all factions could agree on as being fair. When antiwar candidate Eugene McCarthy won the Pennsylvania primary in 1968, he received only 20 percent of the state's delegates; the rest were controlled by party leaders who opposed him. The new rules allocated delegates in closer proportion to the candidates' strength in a state, giving contending sides a sense they were in a fair fight, and thereby increasing the likelihood they would accept the outcome if they lost. The problem with the McGovern-Fraser Commission's reforms was that they were so skewed toward plebiscitary democracy that the party, as traditionally defined, was effectively placed outside the system. Subsequent reforms set aside delegate positions for party officials, but the rules of the game continue to favor a candidate-centered and press-centered contest that does not provide substantial opportunities for party influence.

A presidential election cannot work effectively if it does not provide a firm basis for party influence. For all their shortcomings, parties are the best instrument of democratic politics.[12] The Committee on the Constitutional System, chaired jointly by Nancy Kastenbaum, C. Douglas Dillon, and Lloyd Cutler, identified the decline of political parties as one of the two leading causes* of America's governance problems.[13] Thomas Jefferson's view of the American states—"we would have to invent them if they did not already exist"—applies just as well to parties in late-twentieth-century America.

In arguing that the nominating process should include a strong voice for the party, I do not have in mind a return to the

---

* Divided government was the other, and it was resolved, temporarily at least, by the election of a Democratic president and Democratic Congress in 1992.

era of smoke-filled rooms of party bosses. The modern political party is an organization whose members are thousands of active citizens with a passionate commitment to politics. They represent the best among us in their willingness to invest time and energy toward making elections function effectively.

The current system of selecting presidential candidates fails to meet the requirements of a sound nomination process: to produce good nominees, legitimize their selection, and buttress the parties.

The system encourages candidates to act on their own.[14] They can assemble a personal staff, raise funds, and set up shop in Iowa and New Hampshire with the hope of gaining an early victory that will propel them into national prominence. If they are able to capture the news, they may be able to secure the nomination without ever having to undergo peer review. The extreme case was Jimmy Carter, who at the end of his campaign claimed he was beholden to "no one."

Sheer campaign effort and media-generated momentum often outweigh governing experience and support by prominent leaders. Of course, a candidate can bring to the campaign a reputation built on governing experience, but this in itself does not carry him or her very far. In 1980, Senate minority leader Howard Baker was no match for George Bush in the contest to become chief rival to Ronald Reagan in the Republican nomination race. Bush held no public office and had no natural constituency, but he was free to campaign for months in Iowa and New Hampshire while Baker was tied down with Senate business. When he won in Iowa, Bush's campaign coverage quadrupled, which within a few days pushed him far ahead of Baker in the polls.[15] Bush was following the road to the presidency paved by Jimmy Carter, who spent more than 30 days campaigning in Iowa in 1976. Richard Gephardt set a new record in 1988, when he spent 148 days campaigning in Iowa.[16]

The system also encourages candidates to make an endless number of commitments, often without much consultation or foresight. The promises are sometimes made on a whim, and sometimes under momentary pressure. Candidates tend to keep the promises they make, but they overpromise, at the expense of their leadership, and, if elected, at the cost of their presidency. The floundering early months of the Clinton presidency are a textbook example of the dilemma.

The legitimacy of the current system is also weak. Of course, Americans vote—or, at least, some of them do—and they accept the outcome without rioting in the streets. But in several post-1968 elections, after a nomination has been decided, a majority of a party's rank-and-file voters have indicated in polls a dissatisfaction with its nominee.

Opinion polls have repeatedly shown that Americans are less than enamored of the present system. In a 1988 CNN poll, two out of three voters said the process keeps the best people out of the race; half said they did not like the way we choose our president; nearly two out of three said the early contests have too much power in picking the nominees; only one in four said the voters have the most influence; and three out of four said the media have too much say in picking the candidates.[17] Several years ago, urging against jettisoning the current system, the political scientist Michael Nelson suggested that the public would come to like the process over time.[18] As it happens, they have become increasingly disgruntled. Turnout in the primaries is dropping, and rank-and-file voters increasingly say the nominating process is controlled not by them but by the candidates and the press.

The level of public interest in the nominating races is low. The campaign is too long and too remote to hold people's attention. There are frequent lulls, and the action is too often concentrated in a few states. The dulling effect is so pronounced that voters do not respond even when the campaign gives them an unexpected chance to play kingmakers. The 1992 New York Democratic primary was hotly contested and closely watched, as it represented the last realistic chance to stop Bill Clinton's nomination. Yet only a fourth of the state's eligible Democrats participated in the primary.

Nor does the current system do anything to strengthen the parties. Candidates have no great incentive to build links to other party leaders before the contests begin. In fact, since their time is better spent on fundraising, meeting with reporters, and gladhanding in states holding early contests, they have a definite inducement not to do so. "It is now possible to become president without a stable constituency or set of allies even within one's own party," Alan Ehrenhalt observes. "It is very difficult to govern this way."[19]

A simple reform that would help redress these deficiencies would be to hold the first contests not in late February or early March but in late May or, better yet, June. The nominating phase would end with the last contests, six to eight weeks later. States could choose either the primary or the caucus method as the means of selecting their delegates. They would also be free within this time period to select the Tuesday on which their contest would be held, although it would probably be advisable to leave every other Tuesday open. This would give candidates more time to campaign in the next set of states and would slow down the process by providing the public and party leaders time to consider the implications of the most recent contests.

States would probably distribute themselves somewhat evenly across the available Tuesdays. If a large number appeared likely to hold their contests on the same Tuesday, a state would have the required incentive to select a different date in order to maximize its possible influence on the outcome.

Under this reform, Iowa and New Hampshire would not be allowed to hold their contests outside the specified time frame. Iowa and New Hampshire are unrepresentative states, and their positioning at the start of the campaign inevitably gives their voters disproportionate influence. The big winner in these states nearly always ends up on the covers of *Time* and *Newsweek* and dominates television and newspaper coverage for days on end, producing momentum that can continue through the entire nominating process. This kind of undue influence of a single state makes no sense in a national campaign.

A more complex beginning to the campaign would help: if it has to start somewhere, as it must, let it start in several states at once, thus providing a better test of the candidates' strength. The contenders should be required to demonstrate that they have broad support, rather than a following built on months of handshaking in a single state. If a candidate were to win all, or nearly all, of the first Tuesday's contests, as would happen frequently, the press's inevitable declaration of a clear winner and frontrunner would at least be based on a broader stratum of the American electorate. On the other hand, if several candidates were each to place first in one or two contests, or if two candidates were to win an equal number of contests, the press's interpretation would have to take into account the voters' divided preferences. As it stands now, a close vote in Iowa or New Hampshire is treated by the media as an unqualified victory, actual or "psychological." There would still be momentum under the new system, and the press would continue to play the "electability" game, but these would occur in a larger and more representative context.

Any system of nomination has its biases. The current system favors aspiring politicians who are willing to organize quickly and campaign relentlessly in the states with the early contests. A truncated system with state contests stacked together within a shorter time span would be biased toward candidates with established political reputations. Without the opportunity of using a victory in Iowa or New Hampshire as a springboard to prominence, little-known contenders would have difficulty succeeding.

Evidence for this point is provided by opinion polls in the year before the Iowa caucuses and New Hampshire primary. In most cases, there has been very little aggregate change in the candidate preferences of voters during this period.[20] In 1984, for example, the leading Democratic contender, Walter Mondale, had an 18 percent lead over his nearest rival a year before the Iowa caucuses, and a 16 percent lead a month before they were held.[21] The pre-campaign frontrunner has, like Mondale, nearly always been a politician with a reputation built upon a lengthy political career, including several years as a prominent national figure.[22] Because they are known widely, such candidates would have an inherent advantage in attracting votes in a system that required them to compete in several states at once.

Of course, the outcome of the first round of state contests would not exactly mirror the national polls, and the top vote-getter would gain momentum from his or her success and its accompanying news coverage. But in most cases this momentum would in fact favor the initially more prominent candidate, since he or she would likely fare the best in the opening contests. If this momentum helped carry the candidate to nomination, the system would behave more as it did before the McGovern-Fraser reforms than afterward. In elections before 1972, most of the nominees in races without an incumbent president were candidates who led in the opinion polls in the year before the first primary. Since 1972, most such nominees have been candidates who were not ahead in the pre-campaign polls.

Much ink has been spilled in recent years on the merits of a system which allows a little-known politician to run successfully for the nation's highest office.[23] For myself, I see no advantage to such a system. I agree with Alexander Hamilton that "the little arts of popularity" should not determine who becomes President of the United States. An overnight reputation built on the basis of nonstop campaigning in Iowa and New Hampshire is a poor substitute for a substantial reputation built on years of high-level governmental service.

A critic might argue that the proposed system would not make much difference in practice and that the same candidate, as in Mondale's case, would win nomination in most cases anyway. If this is so, it provides a further reason for the reform: Why occupy the nation's attention for five months when two months will do? If this is not so, then the argument for reform is still strengthened: a campaign whose dynamics are fed by the preferences of voters in several states is surely preferable to one influenced by the choices of those in Iowa or New Hampshire alone. If the "one person, one vote" ideal can never be attained in practice, a broader sampling of preferences in the early stage is certain to improve the representativeness of the outcome. As things stand now, the winnowing process can take place so quickly and decisively that most voters are, in effect, left out of the process. When Jimmy Carter all-but-clinched the 1976 Democratic nomination by winning that year's ninth primary, in Pennsylvania, only two-fifths of the eventual number of primary votes had been cast, and Carter had won less than a third of the delegates selected to that point.[24] Less than 5 percent of the nation's Democrats had cast a vote for Carter.[25]

There is no good reason to hold the country hostage to a year-long presidential campaign every quadrennium. If the nature of the American political system rules out a European-style month-long campaign, it does not dictate a marathon. Of course, the proposed reform would not prevent candidates from positioning themselves for a run at the presidency far in advance of the first contests. In this sense, "the permanent campaign" would remain a feature of the nation's politics. But the new system would confine the frenetic phase of the campaign to six months or less. Not only would the voters welcome the change, they would benefit from it.

The national electorate nearly ignores the nominating process until the first primary or caucus takes place.[26] Even then, voters do not pay a lot of attention, particularly if their state contest is weeks or months away. A truncated campaign would close the space between the first and last contests, and heighten the sense of voters across the country of participating in the same campaign. The change would also encourage party leaders in all states to organize early and activate the local press, thus serving to mobilize the electorate. The magnitude of events on the first Tuesday would further help to get the public more fully involved. The campaign would begin with a rousing start in states around the country, rather than, as now, with a single contest in Iowa or New Hampshire.

If voters are to make better-informed choices, they must be drawn more fully into the campaign. A compressed campaign with multiple contests on the first Tuesday would not provide a magical cure. Many citizens would continue to ignore what was happening. But an abbreviated contest would have a better prospect of catching their attention, and a much higher chance of retaining it. Oregon citizens cannot be expected to take a deep interest in what happens in New Hampshire several months in advance of their own vote, but they might be persuaded to note a multistate campaign that coincides with theirs or precedes it by only a few weeks.

The choice of a candidate should not be something that pops into a voter's head on primary morning. A *New York Times* poll of likely voters on "junior" Tuesday in 1992 found that no fewer than half of them in any state, and as many as three-fourths in one state, had "no opinion" about the five Democratic contenders among whom they were expected to choose a few days hence. It was not because they had carefully narrowed their alternatives and were having difficulty deciding between the final two. The voters literally had no opinion; they had not thought enough about the election to have made a decision about a vote they would soon cast.[27] In this situation, there is a substantial possibility that news values will override political values as an influence on their decision.

In a truncated campaign, nationally televised debates would be an important means of getting the voters' attention. In 1992, ABC, CNN, NBC, and PBS each broadcast a national debate before March 15. Ratings ranged from 2.1 to 5.5 (each rating point represents nearly a million households), which placed these debates in the bottom ninth of network programming in the weeks they were held. In contrast, a debate in Georgia at the time of its primary achieved a local audience rating of 10.2, while a Chicago debate at the time of the Illinois primary attracted an 8.3 audience share.[28] Clearly, the proximity of their state's contest affects the voters' willingness to pay attention to it. If the nominating process had more of a national character, as it would if it were abbreviated, audience ratings for national debates would rise significantly. Debates could also be staged for states holding their contests at the same time.

In the present situation, televised debates in the nominating phase are as much fodder for news stories as they are a stimulus for public involvement. The most publicized moment of the 1992 nominating debates might have been Jerry Brown holding up his 800 number in a New Hampshire debate, despite the protests of his opponents. Other high points were Paul Tsongas's remark to Clinton in the Denver debate that while he was not "perfect," he was at least "honest"; Clinton's response to Brown in the Dallas debate that he should "chill out"; and Brown's charge in the Chicago debate that Clinton had "funneled" state business to his wife's law firm.[29] These remarks became the sound bites for news stories, thereby constituting most people's information about the debates. Unless the public can be persuaded to actually watch the nominating debates, their principal effect may be to heighten the voters' suspicion that candidates spend their time insulting each other.

A shortened campaign with multiple contests on the first Tuesday would encourage presidential hopefuls to build closer ties with their peers in Congress and the states.

Candidates would find it harder to go it alone in this system. Forcing the contenders to spread themselves thinly across several states would encourage them to look for surrogates able to make their case in their absence. The organizational resources of party chairs would be a potentially important factor, as would the support and endorsements of local and state elected officials—members of Congress, governors, mayors of major cities, and other political leaders. It would not be like the old days, when presidential aspirants spent their time and energy building bridges to other leaders. Candidates would still have a greater incentive to raise funds and attract the press's attention; money and media would play a large role in the process. But the endless politicking in Iowa and New Hampshire would likely be replaced by meetings with party leaders, who could act in the candidate's stead when he or she was campaigning elsewhere.

In the effort to enlist the support of peers, a candidate with a substantial public record and a knowledge of policy issues would have an advantage over an outsider. The type of exchange that takes place between political peers is very different from the barter with powerful groups, which is where candidates now look for support. Party leaders are concerned with whether presidential candidates share their general policy beliefs and can be entrusted to lead the party as president. They are also inclined to support a candidate whom they know or who has a record of solid achievement.

Of course, party leaders are also concerned with a candidate's electability, inducing them to weigh the campaign skills of potential nominees. But in evaluating a candidate, these skills are relatively less important to peers than to interest groups. Such groups seek to make a narrowly defined bargain: they look to exchange their backing for a pledge of policy support. Although not altogether a bad thing, such bargains carried to the extreme create a long list of promises that makes it difficult for a president to exercise proper leadership. The presidency becomes a seamless extension of the campaign, at the cost of what the writers of the Constitution called presidential "temperament" —the detachment that is necessary if a president is to keep the national interest in focus when formulating positions.

By comparison, closer ties to party leaders can promote effective government. They are the individuals with whom a president must work most directly in order to accomplish national policy goals. Ties to Congress are particularly important, because of the constitutional separation between the executive and legislative branches. A strengthening of party in the nominating process would fortify the bonds of cooperation, which have been weakened by the extraordinary emphasis in the current system on self-promotion and competition.[30]

A truncated nominating system would be particularly beneficial to a president seeking re-election. In half of the elections since the McGovern-Fraser reforms, the incumbent has faced a well-known challenger. The confrontation is irresistible to the press, which builds it up as part of its New Hampshire story, making it nearly impossible for the incumbent to stay off the campaign trail in the early months. If the campaign was shorter and began with multiple contests, the president could depend more heavily on the powers of his office and ties to party leaders to underpin his drive for renomination. In the case of a president widely unpopular even within his own party, this feature would be of little help. However, the change would make it difficult for a nuisance challenger to force the president into a campaign that in some instances is a disservice to the party and the country.

The Bush re-election campaign is an example of the problems inherent in an electoral system that regularly places a president at risk within his own party. Important presidential decisions were put on hold and others were made in response to the pressures exerted by Patrick Buchanan's challenge. The continuity of policy that is essential to effective governance was disrupted by Bush's short-term need to respond to Buchanan's attacks and physical presence in the primary states. It is not that such voices should be muzzled—democracy is often untidy —but to have intraparty competition driving the presidency for a substantial period is detrimental to effective conduct of the nation's affairs. Some analysts see a single six-year presidential term as a solution, but this measure would also deny voters the opportunity to hold presidents directly accountable within the context of competition between the parties.

An abridged campaign would strengthen the relationship between the parties and the people.

Although parties in the United States are sometimes portrayed as dying, if not dead, there are signs that they are very much alive, and in some respects they are more vital than ever. The number of individuals now active in party politics is higher than it was several decades ago; the percentage of voters contacted during elections through a party canvass is higher today than at any time on record (although the ease of telephone canvassing has more than a little to do with this); and the state and national party organizations are far better organized and more active than at any time in the past.[31]

However, the public's image of parties is less favorable than in the past. Americans today perceive fewer significant differences between the parties and are more likely to express neutrality or indifference toward them.[32] A 1992 Washington Post/ABC News poll indicated that 82 percent of Americans believe the parties "are pretty much out of touch" with the people. It also indicated that most people think the parties are playing "a smaller role" than in the past.[33]

Parties have always provoked somewhat ambivalent feelings in Americans. This ambivalence at best, antagonism at worst, has grown stronger in recent years, and it poses a severe threat to the parties. "In the last analysis, [the public's support] is *the* test of viability of any particular party and of any particular party system," notes the political scientist Samuel Eldersveld. "If there is a continuous decline in the public's positive evaluation of parties, rooted in disaffection over party capability and performance, a withdrawal of public support will occur which is meaningful and difficult to reverse."[34]

Scholars who study parties are somewhat puzzled by the contradictory tendencies demonstrated in the strength of party organizations and the public's negative attitude toward parties. However, there is no necessary connection between the two. The public's judgment of the relevance of parties is not made on the basis of whether they are contacted in a telephone canvass every two to four years. Their perceptions derive from more substantial influences, one of which is the way the parties are presented in the news.

The press has no time for parties. Michael Robinson's research indicates that television's portrayal of parties is overwhelmingly negative, which he concludes contributes to the "continuous decay of the American party system."[35] Americans, says Robinson, suffer from "videomalaise," a consequence of the "negativistic, contentious or anti-institutional bias" of television news.[36] A 1979 study of 94 newspapers conducted by Arthur Miller, Edie Goldenberg, and Lutz Erbring provides related evidence. They discovered that 70 percent of newspaper stories about parties were unfavorable, and that persons exposed to newspapers which had a "higher degree of negative criticism directed at politicians and political institutions were more distrustful of government and [had] higher levels of cynicism."[37]

The style of modern campaigns also contributes to the public's perception of the irrelevance of parties. Congressional campaigns are dominated by incumbents promoting a personal relationship with the public through mailings and constituent service. Presidential campaigns are characterized by self-starting candidates who rarely talk about their party during the primaries and do so during the general election only when it is advantageous. The national conventions stand alone during the campaign as something resembling a true party affair.

The presidential nominating process may be more important to the public's attitude toward parties than is commonly assumed. Although no convention since 1952 has gone past the first ballot, there were suspenseful conventions in the 1950s and 1960s, when nominations were still in the control of party leaders. Even if a candidate had gone into the convention with a lead, it was not safe to take the nomination for granted: the delegates could always change their minds. As a result, the viewing audience saw the party at work in the caucusing of state delegations, the deliberations of party leaders, and television interviews with undecided delegates and party officials. The party mattered, and every four years the public had a chance to see it at work.

No American has witnessed such a scene for more than two decades. The balloting is pro forma, and the nominee-to-be is the center of attention throughout. There is only the barest suggestion that the party truly matters.

A shortened campaign with the stacking of the primaries would highlight the conventions and in some cases award them a deliberative role, because the winnowing process would not take place as quickly or decisively in one candidate's favor. A brokered convention is no threat to the public's interest. Although individual voters in separate state primaries cannot easily sort through a crowded field to make an optimal and informed choice, party leaders in the context of a deliberative convention can perform this task. Moreover, these leaders are at least as adept as the voters themselves in selecting nominees who have the voters' acceptance. In the twenty years before the McGovern-Fraser reforms, only one nominee was perceived more negatively than positively by the electorate. In the twenty years since, almost half of the nominees have been viewed in this way. "The parties," E. E. Schattschneider wrote, "do not need laws to make them sensitive to the wishes of the voters any more than we need laws compelling merchants to please their customers."[38]

A reform that shortens the campaign by several months and forces Iowa and New Hampshire to have the same status as other state contests can be implemented without action by Congress. It is the type of policy the courts have judged to fall within the power of the parties. The parties currently allow

Iowa (no official caucus can precede Iowa's) and New Hampshire (no state primary can precede New Hampshire's) to hold their contests first; other states (excluding Maine and South Dakota) are prohibited from holding their contests except in the period of early March to early June.

These rules respect the federal character of the American political system. The states are given some discretion in selecting the scheduling and type of their nominating contests. They can decide when during the allowable period their contest will be held, and whether the delegates will be chosen by the primary or caucus method.

Other proposals for reforming the selection process, such as regional primaries, would require congressional action, making them more difficult to implement. Such schemes also involve a significant departure from the present system, which increases the likelihood of unforeseen and unintended consequences. However, they would correct some of the defects in the current system, and hence deserve consideration.

Regional primaries are an option that has received significant attention from policymakers. According to a common formulation of this idea, the country would be divided into four regions —the Southeast, the Northeast, the Southwest, and the Northwest—with all states in each region required to hold their nominating contest on the same Tuesday. The regional primaries would be scheduled two weeks apart, which means that the voting would be compressed into a period of six weeks.

The advantages of regional primaries are similar to those already described for a truncated version of the present system. The chief disadvantage of regional primaries is that they would favor a candidate who was strong in the region that held its balloting on the first Tuesday. Proponents have suggested rotating the order of the regional primary as a means of addressing this built-in bias. But rotation does not eliminate the problem; it simply shifts it from one region to another in succeeding elections.

Advocates of the regional-primary idea advance the notion

that it would ease the burden of a national campaign. Since all of the state contests on a given Tuesday would be located in the same region, candidates could concentrate their efforts in this area. This justification, however, must be considered in the light of the bias introduced by regional primaries. Like New Hampshire or Iowa, regions have special political characteristics and problems, making them favorable to particular types of candidacies.

An alternative form of regional primaries was proposed in Congress in 1991. It sought to "equitably disburse influence [over nominating decisions] throughout the states." The Senate memorandum that was circulated with the bill said, "The combination of the Iowa caucuses and New Hampshire primary with the huge number of primaries held on Super Tuesday have perpetuated a front-loaded, chaotic and inequitable system."[39] The bill proposed to divide the country into eight regions, with the first regional primary taking place in early March and subsequent primaries every two weeks thereafter until June. The regions would be approximately equal in population and divided roughly along the following lines (my labels): New England (including New York), Mideast, Southern Atlantic Seaboard, Deep South, Midwest, Great Plains (including Texas), West (less California), and California Plus (including Nevada and the Pacific Islands).

This form of regional primaries would not appreciably shorten the campaign. Nor would it eliminate the bias inherent in any regional-primary plan. Indeed, by making the regions smaller and more homogeneous, it would exaggerate this form of inequity.

If the proposal is reintroduced in Congress, it could be strengthened by pairing the regions, with two holding their contests on the same Tuesday. Subsequent pairs would hold their contests two weeks apart. This would result in a shorter campaign; six weeks, as compared with fourteen. And by basing the pairings on the principle of diversity, the effect of regional bias would be diminished. For example, New England

and the Deep South could be scheduled simultaneously, as could the West and the Midwest, the Atlantic Seaboard and California Plus, and the Great Plains and the Mideast. The pairings would test the candidates' strength in different areas of the country and still allow them to concentrate their efforts to some degree.

A national primary is yet another approach to reform of the presidential selection process. Opinion polls have consistently indicated that most Americans would prefer a national primary to the present system—a response that stems as much from a desire for a shorter campaign as from an understanding of the implications of a national primary.

Advocates of a national primary have put forward some compelling arguments. It would reduce the length of the campaign significantly, diminish the importance of campaigning as an influence on presidential choice, simplify the process, and increase the level of popular participation.

Despite these advantages, political scientists have cautioned against the adoption of a national primary. They see such a contest as potentially dangerous and effectively marking the end of the party's role in the campaign. A plebiscite would be substituted for a process that still possesses some deliberative elements. A national primary would work to the advantage of well-known candidates who possessed the large amount of money required for a nationwide campaign. While such aspirants would in most cases be highly respected public officials, they could also be political mavericks or celebrities without any significant political experience. Although candidates of the second type would normally have difficulty persuading voters that they have the requisite qualifications for the presidency, they might have a special appeal to certain voters during hard times.

Such candidates might also appeal to a sufficient number of voters in normal times that a victory would be possible if the rest of the electorate were divided somewhat evenly among a crowded field. This problem could be corrected by holding a runoff primary if no candidate received 50 percent, or some other specified percentage, of the vote, but this would entail the time and expense of an additional national election. Even if the threat of an outsider is not so great, a runoff provision would probably be a necessary part of a sensible national primary system. In a crowded field of contenders, the advantage would often rest (as it does in the current system) with a candidate who appeals to a hardcore minority within the party. Its vote would constitute a firm bloc of support, while the rest of the vote would be distributed among candidates more acceptable to the majority.

A national primary would also deprive the national convention of some of its purpose, as the nominee would already have been officially chosen. The exception would be if the convention were used in place of a runoff primary to resolve the nomination in those cases in which no candidate received the specified percentage of the vote. In such situations, however, the party would risk a backlash if it nominated someone other than the candidate who had come in first in the national vote.

An innovative solution to the problems associated with a national primary would be to hold the party convention *before* the primary. Similar systems are in effect in a few states, including New York and Colorado. The purpose of the convention would be to write a platform and to endorse (not nominate) a national ticket. The endorsed presidential and vice-presidential candidates would get the publicity attendant upon a national convention and would have the party's backing in a national primary, should they be challenged for nomination. If unchallenged, they would automatically become the party's ticket. The right to challenge the convention's decision would be permitted to any candidate who received a specified percentage (say, 20 percent) of the delegate votes at the convention or who could gather enough petitions nationwide to force a runoff. It is assumed that a challenge would not ordinarily materialize, but it would always be a possibility, encouraging party regulars to keep in touch with public opinion.*

This reform would have several advantages, chief of which would be to re-establish the party as the central force in presidential nominations. Those who seek the presidency would be required to spend their time meeting with party chairs, governors, members of Congress, and other party leaders, persuading them of their electability and their ability to handle the country's problems. The process would discourage candidates who were unable to withstand review by their peers and would, in the words of one advocate, "allow the hard questions to be asked outside of the media-induced circus atmosphere that currently dominates."[40] The reform would also have the safeguard of a national primary when it was necessary, and it would significantly reduce the length of the presidential campaign, with all of the benefits that this entails.

A chief objection to this system is that the reform would be a radical departure from the current arrangement, creating the possibility of unforeseen problems. Similar systems at the state level, however, have worked effectively. In New York, while there have been instances in which a state convention's decision was reversed in the primary that followed, the decision has usually gone unchallenged, and the state's voters have not expressed any reservations about the system. If the parties should decide that a truly major change in the nominating process is advisable, the party convention with a national-primary contingency might well be the preferred solution.

This system would blend popular and elite influences and

---

* A thoughtful variation on this system has been proposed by former Virginia governor Gerald L. Baliles. He suggests that the national convention nominate two slates, each with a presidential and a vice-presidential candidate, who would then compete in a national primary two months later to decide which slate would represent the party in the general election. With a two-thirds vote, the convention could decide to nominate a single slate—an option that the party would likely exercise when the incumbent president was running for re-election.

furnish both deliberative and plebiscitary opportunities. The state caucuses that kick off the process would provide indications of the candidates' initial strength, weeding out lesser challengers. The convention would supply the deliberative element, resulting in the endorsement of a candidate supported by a majority of the delegates, who would include a substantial portion of the party's leadership. The primary, when necessary, would give rank-and-file voters the final say in the choice of a nominee.

Although the presidential selection process cannot be made more sensible without structural reform, no systemic change can absorb all of the forces that lend disorganization to the modern campaign. The politics of today is candidate- and press-centered. Any attempt to improve the election process requires direct attention to communication factors.

In a report that I wrote several years ago for the Alfred P. Sloan Foundation Commission on Presidential Selection,[41] I argued that the presidential campaign should provide the candidates with adequate broadcast opportunities to present themselves and their policies as they wished them to be seen. Candidates are responsible for their campaigns. Furthermore, one of them will eventually become president. It is imperative in the television age that they have significant opportunities to offer their plans to the American people.

Before 1992, this imperative was not fully met. News coverage distorted the candidates' agendas, and although the televised conventions and debates offered significant opportunities for communication, they were not a sufficient forum in themselves. In my report to the Sloan Foundation Commission, I proposed a series of general-election broadcasts that included televised debates, speeches, and discussions. In 1991, the Joan Shorenstein Barone Center on the Press, Politics and Public Policy at Harvard's John F. Kennedy School of Government advanced a similar idea in the "Nine Sundays" proposal, written by John Ellis.[42]

This proposal recommended that the nine Sunday evenings between Labor Day and Election Day be devoted to candidate telecasts. There would be at least two debates between the presidential candidates and one vice-presidential debate. The final Sunday before Election Day would be devoted to back-to-back speeches by the candidates. The other Sunday evenings would be used for "conversations" with the candidates. Each conversation would be on a different issue, and the candidates, in back-to-back appearances, would be questioned by panelists. The telecasts, possibly excepting the debates and speeches, would be carried on a rotating basis by the major broadcast and cable networks.

As it happened, the 1992 campaign fulfilled the candidates' imperative without the need for a television series of the "Nine Sundays" format. The four debates and the "new media" gave the candidates unprecedented opportunities to communicate directly with the voters. There is no guarantee, however, that what happened in 1992 will become the norm. There was even a time in the 1992 campaign when the debates seemed in jeopardy. President Bush held back on participating, and at one point his staff signaled that he was leaning strongly in the direction of forgoing debates altogether. In 1980, President Carter refused to participate in any debate involving John Anderson. Then the Reagan camp held back. When the opposing sides finally agreed to debate, there was time only for a single encounter. Televised debates are a potential hostage to the candidate who needs them least.

Debates in any case are no panacea, and in a close election can attain altogether too much importance. In recent campaigns, some undecided voters adopted a "wait-and-see" attitude once the debates were scheduled. By some accounts, the single 1980 debate between Jimmy Carter and Ronald Reagan turned a heretofore close election decidedly in Reagan's favor. Debates, moreover, tend to reward certain talents, such as style and quick wit, that do not have much to do with successful presidencies.

Nevertheless, it would be wise to institutionalize a series of general-election candidate telecasts that included debates and perhaps other candidate forums. This series would provide a fixed amount of time for the candidates to get their ideas across to the voters, and give the voters regular access to the candidates over a substantial period. This arrangement would not preclude additional forums, such as call-in and morning TV shows. However, the series, if it were on the scale of the "Nine Sundays" proposal, would include enough telecasts to give the nominees adequate opportunities to speak directly with the American people.* At the very least, institutionalized debates would end the squabbling that has in past years characterized arrangements for debates, and would exert pressure on any candidate who wanted to avoid them.

The basic principle underlying the series is that the telecasts should be designed to allow the candidates to speak directly to the people, yet under conditions in which they can be held accountable for their remarks. Scrutiny must be a part of any television series that is intended as a serious forum for bringing candidates and voters together. When the candidates' statements are subject to immediate scrutiny by journalists or others, the candidates are more likely to address the issues directly; and the electorate, in turn, is more likely to take an interest in what they are saying.

Such scrutiny would ensure that all of the telecasts, not just the debates, would feed into the news process. The telecasts would "make" news, because the candidates would be required to account for the positions they take and for their past behavior in relation to these positions. In this way, the series would help the press to present the campaign and what the candidates represent more fully and accurately.

---

* A similar broadcast series might be advisable during the campaign's nominating phase. Any set policy for this period, however, is confounded by questions of when the broadcasts should be held, who should participate, and whether they should be required of an incumbent president running for renomination. An ad hoc policy may be more advisable in the nominating phase.

If candidates are more likely to act responsibly when under direct scrutiny, so too are journalists. Participation in a debate imposes on journalists a restraint that day-to-day news coverage does not. In news stories, journalists are more or less free to make claims about the candidates. In a debate, the candidates have the opportunity to respond, challenging or redirecting reporters' questions. If debates expose inconsistencies in the candidates' portrayals of themselves, they also reveal weaknesses in the way others portray them.

The inclusion of scrutiny is one reason why a series of telecasts of the "Nine Sundays" variety is preferable to the alternative of providing free broadcast time. Most European political systems grant this to parties and candidates, but such a policy makes less sense in our weak-party, presidential system than in a strong-party, parliamentary system. Moreover, free time may not serve the public interest as fully as is commonly assumed. In Britain, a few elections after the free-time policy had begun, 60 percent of the voters said they were dissatisfied with the programs, and a majority deliberately avoided watching them. The most common complaint was that the broadcasts were nothing but out-and-out attempts by the parties to sell their wares.[43]

A series of telecasts is also preferable to Paul Taylor's well-publicized idea of "a five-minute fix." He suggests that during the final five weeks of the campaign each major candidate, on alternating nights, should receive five minutes of free broadcast time simultaneously on every television station in the country. The only restriction would be that the candidate would have to appear on the air alone for the entire five minutes.[44] Compared with a series, the five-minute plan has several disadvantages: it would disrupt broadcasting, give the candidates insufficient time to develop some of their arguments, and take place without the immediate screening of the candidates' statements.

Would Americans pay attention to a series of candidate telecasts? Critics who insisted that the public is not interested in lengthy discussions of the issues were proved wrong by the huge audiences that tuned in to the 1992 debates, the call-in shows, and Ross Perot's "infomercials." These critics would not have made the claim in the first place if they had paid close attention to the audiences for past debates. Since 1960 there have been more than a dozen televised presidential debates during the general election, and each had an audience well in excess of 50 million viewers. The single Reagan-Carter debate in 1980 had an estimated audience of 120 million. The Clinton-Bush-Perot debates in 1992 drew equally large audiences. When candidates appear together and are subject to scrutiny, the American people are more than willing to listen and to learn.

The reforms suggested to this point are designed to organize the campaign *for* the press, rather than to have it organized *by* the press. The goal is to bring the version of the campaign that Americans see and hear through the news media closer to what the campaign actually represents. Changes in election journalism could also facilitate this process, although most of what I recommend asks the press to do less, not more, in its campaign coverage.

To reiterate Walter Lippmann's argument, news and truth coincide at only a few points, and all else is the journalist's opinion. This distinction provides a basis for deciding which tendencies in election coverage should be encouraged, and which must be avoided. News reflecting the journalist's opinion, particularly when it results in partisan consequences, should be avoided. As election news slides into the realm of opinion and works to the disadvantage of either one candidate or the other, or both, it becomes less acceptable.

One news area in which the journalists' opinions prevail is in their evaluation of the candidates' policy stances. Journalists presume that the candidates do not stand for anything, but will instead say whatever is needed to win the election and then act as they please while in office. This view, as indicated earlier, is not supported by the evidence. Candidates do, in fact, tend to keep their promises.

The attribution of motives is a risky enterprise under the best of circumstances. The person engaged in the behavior himself often cannot untangle the complex web of motives that led to a particular action. How, then, can the press, viewing the candidates from the outside, know that their promises are calculated deceptions?

Reporters get away with such charges because the campaign runs on promises rather than performance. In this respect, the campaign setting is different from the governing context. If reporters accuse an elected official of acting improperly in a particular instance, past or present evidence can be summoned. Did the official do so, or not? The campaign presents a different situation. The candidates are unable to prove their good intentions. They can only reiterate their promises, leaving the press free to dismiss them as false pledges.

This behavior on the part of the press needlessly weakens the capacity of the candidates to mobilize the electorate. News that incessantly labels candidates' promises as insincere fosters cynicism and mistrust on the part of the voters. Of course, the press should not always take the candidates at their word, either. Candidates sometimes make statements that cannot possibly be supported by the facts. The press can challenge the candidate if it can conclusively demonstrate that a candidate's promise is irreconcilable with his past performance or with other reliable indicators.

But the burden of proof should remain on the press. It is mere opinion when the journalist makes an unsubstantiated claim that a candidate cannot be trusted to keep his word or is acting solely out of self-interest.

If in the pre-Watergate era the press was too willing to take candidates at their word, it has since become too eager to undermine their every statement. Some members of the press justify the change by claiming that the public interest is better served by an overly critical perspective than by uncritical acceptance.

This argument is disingenuous. The press's responsibility is to tell it as it is. When the press claims the candidate is not telling the truth, it should substantiate the charge. There is no concept of the public interest that would justify a blanket assumption that candidates for the presidency cannot be taken at their word. In its tendency to make just that assumption, the press abdicates the responsibility that attends its freedom under the First Amendment and, in the process, undermines the relationship between the candidates and the voters.

The press should also beware of speaking for the candidate. The trend in journalism toward interpretive reporting emphasizes the journalist's version of what the candidate is saying over the candidate's view of what he is proposing. The candidate's words become noteworthy largely insofar as they illustrate the way the journalist sees things. The candidate may appear to be the source of the message, but he is in fact only the actor, while the journalist becomes the dramatist.

This type of reporting makes the campaign look more chaotic, more manipulative, and more combative than it actually is. It highlights the disorganization of the campaign and wrenches the candidates out of the context provided by their roles as leaders of electoral coalitions. In addition, it misrepresents the candidates' positions and priorities. Of all the issues they address, only those suited to the press's story lines have a reasonable chance of regularly making the news.

Some of the developments in election journalism over the past two decades have represented an improvement. However, the trend that elevated the journalist's voice to a position above that of the candidate is not among them. It presumes that the press, rather than the candidate, should be charged with defining the public's choices. The media are in no position to act as the voters' representative. They can serve as the voters' watchdog, but not as their trustee. The press has no constituency and bears no responsibility for the consequences of its influence on policy. In fact, the voters have made it clear that they would prefer to have the press move over and allow them to see and hear the candidates, their real representatives, directly.

Some observers have recommended that the press give less attention to the candidates' statements and place more emphasis on analysis.[45] I would disagree. Although there is a need for insightful analysis in campaign coverage, it should not supplant the candidates' messages. In their coverage of the party conventions, for example, the networks perform a disservice by making their reporters rather than the politicians the center of attention. Since the 1960s, convention air time has increasingly consisted of journalists talking with other journalists. If the politicians' statements are, as the networks complain, predictable and partisan, they are nonetheless closer to what the campaign is actually about than the banter that takes place between reporters.

The trend toward interpretive reporting has diminished the press's role as a common carrier of the messages of political leaders. This role is not a glamorous one, and it is subject to abuse by leaders, as demonstrated by the Nixon and Johnson presidencies. Nevertheless, it is a vital function in a democratic society; it is the foundation for effective mass communication between the leaders and the people.

What the electorate needs from the press, in addition to a clear channel of communication that provides connection to its leadership, is a watchdog with the judgment to distinguish real abuse from normal political activity. Politics is the art of compromise. To criticize politicians for "playing politics" is to fault a process that is necessary to reconcile society's competing interests. What politicians should be held accountable for are the dirty tricks, special favors, and other acts that carry them beyond the law or recognized standards of public morality. The distinction between such acts and the play of politics can be hard to maintain, which is one reason why otherwise decent public officials sometimes get themselves in trouble. Whether it is the product of carelessness or design, such behavior should not be tolerated in public life, and the press is better equipped than any other institution to blow the whistle on wrongdoing. But campaign promises are not misdemeanors. They may be wise or foolish, may represent signs of a healthy or a defective electoral system, but campaign pledges are not crimes against the body politic.

In 1890, the Englishman James Bryce wrote an essay titled "Why Great Men Are Not Chosen Presidents." He compared America's first presidents—Washington, Adams, Jefferson, Madison—with its more recent ones—Grant, Hayes, Harrison, Arthur, Cleveland—and concluded that the later group were vastly inferior. Bryce laid much of the blame on a change in the 1830s in the system of presidential selection, saying that the newer method rewarded candidates more for "safe" mediocrity than for political courage and eminence.[46]

Of course, no method of leadership selection is foolproof. The same system in Great Britain that produced Winston Churchill also produced Neville Chamberlain. The same system in the United States put both Franklin D. Roosevelt and Warren G. Harding in the White House. But some are more prone to failure than others.

An effective electoral system must take into account what the press, the parties, and the voters can and cannot do. However alluring the idea of a campaign in which candidates and voters find common ground through the intermediation of journalists, it cannot provide the basis for a sound electoral process. A well-functioning system should strengthen presidential leadership, give force to voters' opinions, and set the stage for effective governance. The present system does none of these things. Its weaknesses are substantial and painfully apparent: self-selected candidates, overloaded voters, a miscast press.

NOTES

PROLOGUE

1. Walter Lippmann, *Public Opinion* (1922; reprint, New York: Free Press, 1965), p. 19.
2. "CBS Evening News," September 25, 1992.
3. "Clinton's the One," *Media Monitor* (Center for Media and Public Affairs, Washington, D.C.), November 1992, p. 3.
4. Ibid.
5. C. Richard Hofstetter, *Bias in the News: Network Television Coverage of the 1972 Election Campaign* (Columbus: Ohio State University Press, 1976).
6. See Ann Crigler, Marion R. Just, and Timothy E. Cook, "Local News, Network News and the 1992 Presidential Campaign" (Paper presented at the annual meeting of the American Political Science Association, Chicago, September 3–6, 1992), p. 11.
7. Michael Robinson and Margaret Sheehan, *Over the Wire and on TV* (New York: Russell Sage Foundation, 1983), pp. 92–95.
8. Ibid, p. 302.
9. Quoted in Thomas E. Patterson, "More Style than Substance: Television News in U.S. National Elections," *Political Communication and Persuasion* 8 (1991): 157.
10. See Michael Robinson, "Improving Election Information in the Media" (Paper presented at the Voting for Democracy Forum, Washington, D.C., September 11, 1983), p. 2.
11. Twentieth Century Fund Task Force on Presidential Campaign Communication Conference, New York, November 23, 1992.
12. This section was informed and inspired by Paul Gray's "Lies, Lies, Lies," *Time*, October 5, 1992, pp. 32–38.
13. "The Press and the Presidential Campaign, 1988" (Seminar proceedings of the American Press Institute, Reston, Va., December 6, 1988), pp. 11–12.
14. David Friedman, "Winning Ugly?" New York *Newsday*, October 1, 1992, p. 56.

15. *The New York Times*, July 20, 1984, p. A12.

16. Gwen Ifill, "Clinton Defends His Privacy and Says the Press Intruded," *The New York Times*, January 27, 1992, p. A14.

17. Gray, "Lies, Lies, Lies," p. 37.

18. V. O. Key, Jr., *Public Opinion and American Democracy* (New York: Knopf, 1961), p. 538.

19. Michael Schudson, *What Time Means in a News Story*, Gannett Center for Media Studies Occasional Paper no. 4 (Columbia University, New York, 1986), p. 3.

20. Gerald Pomper with Susan Lederman, *Elections in America* (New York: Dodd, Mead, 1976), pp. 162-63.

21. Michael G. Krukones, *Promises and Performance: Presidential Campaigns as Policy Predictors* (Lanham, Md.: University Press of America, 1984).

22. Ian Budge and Richard I. Hofferbert, "Mandates and Policy Outputs: U.S. Party Platforms and Federal Expenditures," *American Political Science Review* 84 (1990): 111–32.

23. Jeff Fishel, *Presidents and Promises* (Washington, D.C.: Congressional Quarterly Press, 1985), pp. 38, 42–43.

24. Benjamin I. Page, "The Theory of Political Ambiguity," *American Political Science Review* 70 (1976): 742–52, and Kenneth A. Shepsle, "The Strategy of Ambiguity: Uncertainty and Electoral Competition," *American Political Science Review* 66 (1972): 555–68.

25. Editorial, "13 New Taxes," Washington *Post*, October 26, 1992, p. A20.

26. Stephen J. Wayne, *The Road to the White House 1992* (New York: St. Martin's Press, 1992), p. 267.

27. Donald Wittman, "Candidate Motivation: A Synthesis of Alternative Theories," *American Political Science Review* 77 (1983): 142–57, and Randall L. Calvert, "Robustness of the Multidimensional Voting Model: Candidate Motivations, Uncertainty, and Convergence," *American Journal of Political Science* 29 (1985): 69–95.

28. "MacNeil-Lehrer News Hour," PBS, October 5, 1992.

29. "Week in Review," CNN, January 10, 1993.

30. Figure provided by the U.S. Government Printing Office.

31. "Clinton's the One," *Media Monitor*, p. 2.

32. Austin Ranney, *Channels of Power* (New York: Basic Books, 1983), pp. 52–55.

33. See, for example, Max Kampelman, "The Power of the Press,"

Policy Review, Fall 1978, pp. 7–41, and Irving Kristol, "Crisis over Journalism," in *Press, Politics, and Popular Government*, ed. George Will (Washington, D.C.: American Enterprise Institute, 1972), p. 50.

34. Quoted in Kampelman, "Power of the Press," p. 18.

35. James Reston, "End of the Tunnel," *The New York Times*, April 30, 1975, p. 41.

36. Paul Taylor, *See How They Run* (New York: Knopf, 1990), p. 23.

37. Robin Toner, "Bush and Clinton Sag in Survey; Perot's Negative Rating Doubles," *The New York Times*, June 23, 1992, p. A1.

38. Peter Goldman, "John Anderson on the Verge," *Newsweek*, April 28, 1980, p. 26.

39. Thomas E. Patterson, *The American Democracy* (New York: McGraw-Hill, 1990), p. 227.

40. Ernest K. Lindley, "How Old—How Good," *Newsweek*, July 18, 1960, p. 32.

41. Michael Kelly, "Being Whatever It Takes to Win Election," *The New York Times*, Sunday, August 27, 1992, sec. 4, p. 1.

42. V. O. Key, Jr., *The Responsible Electorate* (Cambridge, Mass.: Belknap Press, 1966), p. 2.

43. See Scott Keeter and Cliff Zukin, *Uninformed Choice* (New York: Praeger, 1983), pp. 63–88.

44. NBC/Wall Street Journal poll, "NBC Evening News," October 22, 1992.

45. Meg Greenfield, "The Anxiety of Choosing Sides," *Newsweek*, October 20, 1980, p. 108.

46. George Will, "Debates Keep Them off the Streets," syndicated column, as reprinted in the Syracuse *Post-Standard*, October 15, 1992, p. A10.

47. Marvin Kalb, "Too Much Talk and Not Enough Action," *Washington Journalism Review*, September 1992, p. 33.

48. N. R. Kleinfield, "In All Corners, Volunteers for Perot Set Up Camp," *The New York Times*, June 1, 1992, p. A15.

49. Cited in "Clinton's the One," *Media Monitor*, p. 5.

50. "NBC Nightly News," October 22, 1992.

51. Taylor, *See How They Run*, p. 252.

CHAPTER ONE

1. Walter Lippmann, *Public Opinion* (1922; reprint, New York: Free Press, 1965), p. 229.
2. Carl Bernstein, "It's Press vs. Bush: A Bruising Fight," Los Angeles *Times*, October 25, 1992, p. M1.
3. Lippmann, *Public Opinion*, p. 226.
4. "Clinton's the One," *Media Monitor* (Center for Media and Public Affairs, Washington, D.C.), November 1992, p. 2.
5. Jonathan Alter, "The Smear Heard 'Round the World," *Newsweek*, October 19, 1992, p. 27.
6. Lippmann, *Public Opinion*, p. 229.
7. William R. Keech and Donald R. Matthews, *The Party's Choice* (Washington, D.C.: Brookings Institution, 1976), pp. 103–5.
8. Terry Sanford. *A Danger of Democracy* (Boulder, Co.: Westview Press, 1981), p. 19.
9. Quoted in Austin Ranney, *Participation in American Presidential Nominations 1976* (Washington, D.C.: American Enterprise Institute, 1977), p. 6.
10. William Crotty and John S. Jackson III, *Presidential Primaries and Nominations* (Washington, D.C.: American Enterprise Institute, 1977), pp. 44–49.
11. See Howard L. Reiter, *Selecting the President: The Nominating Process in Transition* (Philadelphia; University of Pennsylvania Press, 1985); Richard Rubin, *Press, Party, and President* (New York: Norton, 1981), pp. 147-80.
12. Alan Ehrenhalt, *The United States of Ambition* (New York: Times Books, 1991), p. 265.
13. James David Barber, *The Pulse of Politics: Electing Presidents in the Media Age* (New York: Norton, 1980), pp. 157–58.
14. *Mandate for Reform* (Washington, D.C.: Democratic National Committee, 1970), p. 49.
15. This statement is based on an examination of *New York Times* and Washington *Post* stories at the time the McGovern-Fraser Commission's guidelines were made public.
16. Timothy Crouse, *The Boys on the Bus* (New York: Ballantine, 1974).
17. See Max Kampelman, "The Power of the Press," *Policy Review*, Fall 1978, pp. 11-14.

18. Michael J. Robinson, "Television and American Politics: 1956–1976," in *Reader in Public Opinion and Communication*, 3rd ed., ed. Morris Janowitz and Paul Hirsch (New York: Free Press, 1981) p. 109.

19. See "The Press and the Presidential Campaign, 1988," (Seminar proceedings of the American Press Institute, Reston, Va., December 6, 1988).

20. Ibid.

21. See Everett Carll Ladd, *American Political Parties* (New York: Norton, 1970), p. 2.

22. Lippmann, *Public Opinion*, p. 229.

23. Richard Davis, *The Press and American Politics* (New York: Longman, 1992), pp. 21-27.

24. James David Barber, "Characters in the Campaign: The Literary Problem," in *Race for the Presidency*, ed. James David Barber (Englewood Cliffs, N.J.: Prentice-Hall, 1978), pp. 114–17.

25. Quoted in Edward Jay Epstein, *News from Nowhere* (New York: Random House, 1973), p. ix.

26. Holli Semetko, Jay G. Blumler, Michael Gurevitch, and David H. Weaver, with Steve Barkin and G. Cleveland Wilhoit, *The Formation of Campaign Agendas* (Hillsdale, N.J.: Lawrence Erlbaum, 1991), pp. 3, 4.

27. Charles S. Hyneman, "Republican Government in America," in *Founding Principles of American Government*, ed. George J. Graham, Jr., and Scarlett H. Graham (Chatham, N.J.: Chatham House, 1984), pp. 3–28.

28. Robin Toner, "While Others Shrank from Race, Clinton Clung to Dream of Presidency," *The New York Times*, Sunday, July 12, 1992, sec. 1, p. 18.

29. Paul F. Boller, Jr., *Presidential Campaigns* (New York: Oxford University Press, 1984), pp. 149–50.

30. "The McLaughlin Group," CNN, February 13, 1988.

31. Hedrick Smith, "Mondale Lead over Nearest Rival in Poll Sets Nonincumbent Record," *The New York Times*, February 28, 1984, p. A1.

32. Alan Mayer, "Bush Breaks Out of the Pack." *Newsweek*, February 4, 1980, p. 30.

33. "Reagan's Rousing Return," *Time*, March 10, 1980, p. 14.

34. Thomas E. Patterson, *The Mass Media Election* (New York: Praeger, 1980), pp. 125–30.

35. "The Making of a Front Runner," *Newsweek*, January 10, 1972, pp. 11–13.

36. Crouse, *The Boys on the Bus*, p. 47.

37. Frank Morgan, "The New Hampshire Story," *Newsweek*, February 21, 1972, p. 31.

38. David Moore, "The *Manchester Union Leader* in the New Hampshire Primary," in *Media and Momentum*, ed. Gary R. Orren and Nelson Polsby (Chatham, N.J.: Chatham House Publishers, 1987), p. 107.

39. See "Campaign Teardrops," *Time*, March 13, 1972, pp. 20, 22.

40. See, for example, "Ed Muskie's Underwhelming Victory," *Newsweek*, March 20, 1972, pp. 20, 22.

41. Jonathan Alter, "Voters to Press: Move Over," *Newsweek*, October 14, 1991, p. 29.

42. See, for example, Patterson, *Mass Media Election*, p. 167, and Paul Taylor, *See How They Run* (New York: Knopf, 1990), pp. 202–03.

43. Scott Keeter and Cliff Zukin, *Uninformed Choice: The Failure of the New Presidential Nominating System* (New York: Praeger, 1983), pp. 110, 136.

44. Austin Ranney, *Channels of Power* (New York: Basic Books, 1983), p. 93.

45. V. O. Key, Jr., *Southern Politics* (New York: Vintage, 1949), p. 303.

46. These results were related to the author by one of the designers of the poll, which was conducted for a leading newspaper. The newspaper did not do a story on the results, ostensibly on the grounds that they were too complicated to explain. A survey that I conducted measured candidate support differently, but provides evidence of the same phenomenon.

47. Quoted in Paul Taylor, *See How They Run*, p. 117.

48. National Public Radio, December 20, 1991.

49. Quoted in "A Statement of Purpose for Political Parties," Institute of Policy Sciences and Public Affairs report, Duke University (Durham, N.C., 1981), p. 4.

50. Ehrenhalt, *The United States of Ambition*, p. 266.

51. Ibid., p. 265.

52. Theodore Lowi, *The Personal President: Power Invested, Promise Unfulfilled* (Ithaca, N.Y.: Cornell University Press, 1985), p. 11.

53. Michael Duffy, "That Sinking Feeling," *Time*, June 7, 1993, p. 24.

54. James W. Ceaser, *Presidential Selection: Theory and Development* (Princeton, N.J.: Princeton University Press, 1979), p. 11.

55. "Jimmy Carter: Not Just Peanuts," *Time*, March 8, 1976, p. 15.

56. An exception was *Time*, from which the Gore example was taken. Charles Krauthammer, "The Pornography of Self-Revelation," *Time*, August 10, 1992, p. 72.

57. Ehrenhalt, *The United States of Ambition*, p. 265.

58. Quoted in "Perspectives," *Newsweek*, January 13, 1992, p. 17.

59. Ceaser, *Presidential Selection*, p. 310.

60. Ibid., pp. 82–83.

61. Donald L. Horowitz, *The Courts and Social Policy* (Washington, D.C.: Brookings Institution, 1977), p. 23.

CHAPTER TWO

1. Walter Lippmann, *Public Opinion* (1922; reprint, New York: Free Press, 1965), p. 223.

2. "World News Tonight," ABC, April 6, 1992, in *Television News Index and Abstracts* (Vanderbilt Television News Archive, Nashville, Tenn., April 1992), p. 578.

3. "Clinton Makes Final Plea as Brown Closes Gap in Tight Race," news services compilation, reprinted in Syracuse *Herald-Journal*, April 7, 1992, p. A1.

4. "Brown and Clinton Trade Charges," Associated Press, as reprinted in Syracuse *Herald-Journal*, April 5, 1992, p. A2.

5. Richard L. Berke, "Why Candidates Like Public's Questions," *The New York Times*, August 15, 1992, p. A7.

6. "Excerpts from President's News Conference at White House," *The New York Times*, June 5, 1992, p. A16.

7. Doris Graber, *Processing the News* (New York: Longman, 1988), p. 28.

8. Susan T. Fiske and Donald R. Kinder, "Involvement, Expertise, and Schema Use: Evidence from Political Cognition," in *Personality, Cognition, and Social Interaction*, ed. Nancy Kantor and John F. Kihlstrom (Hillsdale, N.J.: Lawrence Erlbaum, 1981), p. 173.

9. Graber, *Processing the News*, p. 29.

10. Larry J. Sabato, *Feeding Frenzy: How Attack Journalism Has Transformed American Politics* (New York: Free Press, 1991), pp. 109, 127.

11. Ibid., p. 127. See also Frederick T. Steeper, "Public Response to Gerald Ford's Statements on Eastern Europe in the Second Debate," in *The Presidential Debates: Media, Electoral, and Policy Perspectives*, ed. George F. Bishop, Robert G. Meadow, and Marilyn Jackson-Beeck (New York: Praeger, 1978), pp. 84–87.

12. Graber, *Processing the News*, p. 264.

13. Sabato, *Feeding Frenzy*, p. 109.

14. Paul Weaver, "Is Television News Biased?" *The Public Interest* 27 (1972): 69.

15. Robin Toner, "Arkansas' Clinton Enters the '92 Race for President," *The New York Times*, October 4, 1991, p. A10.

16. Ken Auletta, untitled paper delivered at Twentieth Century Fund Conference, New York, September 3, 1992, p. 3.

17. W. Lance Bennett, "Perception and Cognition: An Information-Processing Framework for Politics," in *The Handbook of Political Behavior*, vol. 1, ed. Samuel L. Long (New York: Plenum Press, 1981), p. 168.

18. V. O. Key, Jr., *The Responsible Electorate: Rationality in Presidential Voting, 1936–1960* (Cambridge, Mass.: Belknap Press, 1966), p. vii.

19. Samuel L. Popkin, *The Reasoning Voter: Communication and Persuasion in Presidential Campaigns* (Chicago: University of Chicago Press, 1991), p. 7.

20. James David Barber, "Characters in the Campaign: The Literary Problem," in *Race for the Presidency*, ed. James David Barber (Englewood Cliffs, N.J.: Prentice-Hall, 1978), pp. 114–17.

21. Howard Kurtz, "Media Circus," *Washington Post Magazine*, July 12, 1992, p. 36.

22. Leon Sigal, *Reporters and Officials* (Lexington, Mass.: D. C. Heath, 1973), p. 102.

23. Quoted in Paul Taylor, *See How They Run* (New York: Knopf, 1990), p. 25.

24. Ann Devroy, Dan Balz, E. J. Dionne, Jr., and Edward Walsh, "Bush Makes Four-Debate Offer," *Washington Post*, September 30, 1992, p. A1.

25. Barber, "Characters in the Campaign," pp. 117–18.

26. "Meet the Press," NBC, April 8, 1984.

27. Timothy Crouse, *The Boys on the Bus* (New York: Ballantine, 1974), p. 24.

28. Ibid.

29. Kathleen Hall Jamieson, *Dirty Politics* (New York: Oxford University Press, 1992), p. 166.

30. Michael Robinson and Margaret Sheehan, *Over the Wire and on TV* (New York: Russell Sage Foundation, 1983), p. 148.

31. Richard Davis, *The Press and American Politics* (New York: Longman, 1992), p. 23.

32. "The Press and the Presidential Campaign, 1988" (Seminar proceedings of the American Press Institute, Reston, Va., December 6, 1988), p. 46.

33. Quoted in Barber, "Characters in the Campaign," p. 117.

34. Ranney, *Channels of Power*, p. 57.

35. Kurt Lang and Gladys Engel Lang, *Politics and Television* (Chicago: Quadrangle, 1968), pp. 199–203.

36. Kurtz, "Media Circus," p. 19.

37. Michael Kelly, "Seeking Better Image, Perot Shifts Campaign," *The New York Times*, July 8, 1992, p. A12.

38. Tom Wicker, "The Role of the Media—Informing or Influencing the Electorate?" (Paper presented at NBC Forum, Washington, D.C., March, 1977), pp. 1–2.

39. "Clinton's the One," *Media Monitor* (Center for Media and Public Affairs, Washington, D.C.), November 1992, p. 2.

40. Shanto Iyengar and Donald R. Kinder, *News That Matters* (Chicago: University of Chicago Press, 1987), p. 128.

41. Marvin Kalb, "Too Much Talk and Not Enough Action," *Washington Journalism Review*, September 1992, p. 33.

42. Cited in Gore Vidal, "Monotheism and Its Discontents," *Nation*, July 13, 1992, p. 37.

43. Quoted in R. W. Apple, Jr., "Wisconsin 'Snoozer' Stirring to Life," *The New York Times*, March 26, 1992, p. A21.

44. Editorial, "Listen to the Anger," *The New York Times*, March 26, 1992, p. A22.

45. Andrew Tyndall, *Tyndall Report* (ADT Research, New York), September 1992, pp. 1, 3.

46. Auletta, untitled paper, p. 12.

47. Andrew Tyndall, *Tyndall Report* (ADT Research, New York), December 1992, p. 6.

48. Elizabeth Kolbert, "Uh-Oh Perot," *The New York Times*, Sunday, October 25, 1992, sec. 4, p. 1.

49. Howard Kurtz, "Backlash: Can Perot Change the Rules?," *Washington Post Magazine*, July 12, 1992, pp. 21–22.

50. Quoted in Kristi Andersen and Stuart J. Thorson, "Public Discourse or Strategic Game? Changes in Our Conception of Elections," *Studies in American Political Development* 3 (1989): 264.

51. Alexis de Tocqueville, *Democracy in America* (New York: Vintage Books, 1945), p. 195. (Published originally in English in 1835.)

52. See Michael Schudson, *Discovering the News* (New York: Basic Books, 1978).

53. See V. O. Key, Jr., *Public Opinion and American Democracy* (1961; reprint, New York: Knopf, 1966), p. 392.

54. Weaver, "Is Television News Biased?" p. 69.

55. Andersen and Thorson, "Public Discourse or Strategic Game?" p. 270.

56. James Reston, "The Third Debate," *The New York Times*, October 14, 1960, p. 22.

57. Andersen and Thorson, "Public Discourse or Strategic Game?," pp. 271–73.

58. Ibid., p. 270.

59. Ibid., p. 271.

60. Quoted in ibid., p. 273.

61. Gwen Ifill, "On TV, Clinton Finds an Audience That Listens," *The New York Times*, June 6, 1992, p. A23.

62. W. H. Lawrence, "400,000 Expected to Ballot Today in West Virginia," *The New York Times*, May 10, 1960, p. 32.

63. Theodore White, *The Making of the President 1960* (New York: Atheneum, 1961), pp. 107, 299.

64. Leo Egan, "Candidates Term Religion Less of an Issue than in '28," *The New York Times*, October 20, 1960, p. 1.

65. Thomas L. Friedman, "Clinton Swipes at Bush for Lack of Jewish Aides," *The New York Times*, September 10, 1992, p. A20.

66. *Covering the Presidential Primaries*, Freedom Forum Media Studies Center report, Columbia University (New York, June 1992), p. 27.

67. Kurtz, "Media Circus," p. 23.

68. "The Parties Pick Their Candidates," *Media Monitor* (Center for Media and Public Affairs, Washington, D.C.), March 1992, p. 2.

69. "Clinton's the One," p. 2.

70. *Tyndall Report*, December 1992, p. 8.

71. Iyengar and Kinder, *News That Matters*, pp. 80–81.

72. Kiku Adatto, *Sound Bite Democracy: Network Evening News Presidential Campaign Coverage, 1968 and 1988*, Joan Shorenstein Barone Center on the Press, Politics and Public Policy, Research Paper R-2, John F. Kennedy School of Government, Harvard University (Cambridge, Mass., June 1990), p. 4.

73. Ibid.

74. Ibid.

75. "Clinton's the One," p. 2.

76. "Clinton's the One," p. 2.

77. These figures are based on the content analysis of the Center for Media and Public Affairs. It reports that George Bush had 66 minutes of combined speaking time on the ABC, CBS, and NBC nightly newscasts, while Clinton had 55 minutes and Perot, 23 minutes. Since a viewer would be able to watch only one of these newscasts on a given night, the average exposure would be 22 minutes to Bush, 18.3 minutes to Clinton, and 7.6 minutes to Perot. (See "Clinton's the One," p. 2.)

78. David von Drehle, "Clinton Walks Gingerly through a Day in L.A.," Washington *Post*, May 5, 1992, p. A9.

79. Holli Semetko, Jay G. Blumler, Michael Gurevitch, and David H. Weaver, with Steve Barkin and G. Cleveland Wilhoit, *The Formation of Campaign Agendas* (Hillsdale, N.J.: Lawrence Erlbaum, 1991), p. 60.

80. Jay G. Blumler and Holli A. Semetko, "Legislative Campaigns in Britain," *Legislative Studies Quarterly* 12 (1987): 426.

81. Ibid.

82. Semetko et al., *The Formation of Campaign Agendas*, pp. 68, 95.

83. Ibid., pp. 74, 98.

84. Quoted in Larry Meyer, "The Media's Role in Campaigns" (paper presented at the Conference on Campaign Reform, John F. Kennedy School of Government, Harvard University, Cambridge, Mass., November 19–20, 1991), p. 4.

85. See Jarol Manheim, *All the People, All the Time* (Armonk, N.Y.:

M. E. Sharpe, 1991), and Stephen Ansolabehere, Roy Behr, and Shanto Iyengar, *The Media Game* (New York: MacMillan, 1993), p. 3.

86. *Covering the Presidential Primaries*, p. 28.

87. John Lancaster, "Military Moves with Political Overtones," Washington *Post*, September 3, 1992, p. A1.

88. Key, *Public Opinion and American Democracy*, p. 393.

89. See, for example, Max Kampelman, "The Power of the Press," *Policy Review*, Fall 1978, pp. 11–14, and Irving Kristol, "Crisis over Journalism," in *Press, Politics, and Popular Government*, ed. George Will (Washington, D.C.: American Enterprise Institute, 1972), p. 50.

90. Robinson and Sheehan, *Over the Wire and on TV*, p. 8.

91. Ibid., p. 206.

92. Quoted in Taylor, *See How They Run*, p. 22.

93. Quoted in Robinson and Sheehan, *Over the Wire and on TV*, p. 226.

94. Weaver, "Is Television News Biased?," p. 69.

95. Ibid., pp. 67–68.

96. Dayton Duncan, *Press, Polls, and the 1988 Campaign: An Insider's Critique*, Joan Shorenstein Barone Center for the Press, Politics, and Public Policy, Discussion Paper D-1, John F. Kennedy School of Government, Harvard University (Cambridge, Mass., April 1989), pp. 5–6.

97. James Glen Stovall and Jacqueline H. Solomon, "The Poll as a News Event in the 1980 Presidential Campaign," *Public Opinion Quarterly* 48 (1984): 619.

98. Comment by Scott Razan, Conference on Polling, Joan Shorenstein Barone Center on the Press, Politics and Public Policy, John F. Kennedy School of Government, Harvard University (Cambridge, Mass., February 8, 1989), p. 28.

99. See Paul J. Lavrakas and Jack K. Holley, *Polling and Presidential Election Coverage* (Newbury Park, Calif.: Sage Publications, 1991).

100. C. Anthony Broh, "Horse-Race Journalism: Reporting the Polls in the 1976 Election," *Public Opinion Quarterly* 44 (1980): 514–29.

101. Kevin Keenan, "Polls in Network Newscasts in the 1984 Presidential Race," *Journalism Quarterly* 63 (Autumn 1986): 617.

102. Stovall and Solomon, "The Poll as a News Event," p. 621.

103. Duncan, *Press, Polls, and the 1988 Campaign*, p. 3.

104. Ibid., pp. 3, 5.

105. Barber, "Characters in the Campaign," pp. 126–32.

106. Crouse, *The Boys on the Bus*, p. 37.

107. W. Russell Neuman, *The Paradox of Mass Politics: Knowledge and Opinion in the American Electorate* (Cambridge, Mass.: Harvard University Press, 1986), pp. 134–48.

108. Quoted in Semetko et al., *The Formation of Campaign Agendas*, p. 130.

109. Michael Levy, "Disdaining the News," *Journal of Communication* 3 (1981): 24–31.

110. Semetko et al., *The Formation of Campaign Agendas*, p. 74.

111. See Adatto, *Sound Bite Democracy*, and Matthew R. Kerbel, "Cable and Network Television Coverage of the 1992 Presidential Primaries: Some Preliminary Findings" (paper presented at the annual meeting of the American Political Science Association, Chicago, September 3–6, 1992), p. 13.

112. Adatto, *Sound Bite Democracy*, p. 5.

113. Transcript of the "CBS Evening News with Walter Cronkite," October 7, 1980, pp. 8–9.

114. Deborah Tannen, *You Just Don't Understand: Women and Men in Conversation* (New York: Morrow, 1990).

115. Thomas E. Patterson, *The Mass Media Election* (New York: Praeger, 1980), p. 86.

116. Ibid., p. 89.

117. Graber, *Processing the News*, pp. 203, 206.

118. See Diana Owen, *Media Messages in American Presidential Campaigns* (Westport, Conn.: Greenwood Publishing, 1991).

119. Daniel Kahneman and Amos Tversky, "Choices, Values, and Frames," *American Psychologist* 39 (1984):343. Cited in Shanto Iyengar, *Is Anyone Responsible? How Television Frames Political Issues* (Chicago: University of Chicago Press, 1991), pp. 11–12.

120. Iyengar and Kinder, *News That Matters*, p. 4.

121. Ibid., p. 72.

122. Graber, *Processing the News*, p. 204.

123. Patterson, *The Mass Media Election*, p. 103.

124. Graber, *Processing the News*, p. 141.

125. Patterson, *The Mass Media Election*, p. 29.

126. Thomas E. Patterson, "The Press and Its Missed Assignment," in *The Elections of 1988*, ed. Michael Nelson (Washington, D.C.: Congressional Quarterly Press, 1989), p. 103.

127. Ibid., p. 104.

128. See Robinson and Sheehan, *Over the Wire and on TV*, p. 149.

129. S. Robert Lichter, Daniel Amundson, and Richard Noyes, *The Video Game: Network Coverage of the 1988 Primaries* (Washington, D.C.: American Enterprise Institute, 1988), p. 18.

130. See "Clinton's the One," p. 3, and "Battle of the Sound Bites," *Media Monitor* (Center for Media and Public Affairs, Washington, D.C.), August–September 1992, p. 2.

131. Theodore H. White, *The Making of the President 1972* (New York: Bantam, 1973), p. 327. For scholarly studies on agenda setting, see Bernard Cohen, *The Press, the Public and Foreign Policy* (Princeton, N.J.: Princeton University Press, 1963), p. 13, and Maxwell E. McCombs and Donald L. Shaw, "The Agenda-Setting Function of the Mass Media," *Public Opinion Quarterly* 36 (Summer 1972): 176–87.

132. Patterson, *The Mass Media Election*, p. 105.

133. Bernard Berelson, Paul Lazarsfeld, and William McPhee, *Voting* (Chicago: University of Chicago Press, 1954), p. 106.

CHAPTER THREE

1. Walter Lippmann, *Public Opinion* (1922; reprint, New York: Free Press, 1965), pp. 54–55.

2. "Seldom an Encouraging Word," *Newsweek*, November 1, 1948, p. 17.

3. "Prayer for a Chain Reaction," *Newsweek*, October 25, 1948, p. 27.

4. Ernest K. Lindley, "The Dewey Good-Will Tour," *Newsweek*, October 25, 1948, p. 40.

5. Anthony Leviero, "Truman Confident of a Groundswell," *The New York Times*, November 1, 1948, pp. 1, 19.

6. "Experts See Dewey Victory but Tight Race for Senate," *Newsweek*, November 1, 1948, p. 12.

7. "Democrats," *Time*, October 18, 1948, p. 24.

8. Edward Jay Epstein, "The Selection of Reality," in *What's News*, ed. Elie Abel (San Francisco: Institute for Contemporary Studies, 1981), p. 122.

9. James David Barber, "Characters in the Campaign: The Literary Problem," in *The Race for the Presidency*, ed. James David Barber (Englewood Cliffs, N.J.: Prentice-Hall, 1978), p. 114.

10. Lippmann, *Public Opinion*, p. 55.

11. Paul Weaver, "Is Television News Biased?," *The Public Interest* 27 (1972): 69.

12. Colin Seymour-Ure, *The Political Impact of Mass Media* (Beverly Hills, Calif.: Sage, 1974), pp. 175–76.

13. See Marjorie Randon Hershey, "The Campaign and the Media," in *The Election of 1988*, ed. Gerald Pomper (Chatham, N.J.: Chatham House, 1989), pp. 78–79.

14. James David Barber, *The Pulse of Politics* (New York: Norton, 1980), p. 11.

15. Hugh Heclo, "The Presidential Illusion," in *The Illusion of Presidential Government*, ed. Hugh Heclo and Lester M. Salamon (Boulder, Col.: Westview Press, 1981), p. 8.

16. James R. Dickenson, "Mondale's Image Is a Victim of Television's Eye," Washington *Post*, October 5, 1984, p. A4.

17. Howell Raines, "Chance of Revival Seen for Mondale After TV Debate," *The New York Times*, October 9, 1984, pp. A1, A28.

18. "Reagan Wins a Draw," *Newsweek*, October 29, 1984, p. 27.

19. Quoted in Kristi Andersen and Stuart J. Thorson, "Public Discourse or Strategic Game? Changes in Our Conception of Elections," *Studies in American Political Development* 3 (1989): 271.

20. Evan Thomas, "From the Bunker to the Hill," *Time*, September 10, 1984, p. 11.

21. Michael J. Robinson and Margaret A. Sheehan, *Over the Wire and on TV* (New York: Russell Sage Foundation, 1983), pp. 101–2.

22. Quoted in ibid., p. 101.

23. Adam Clymer, "Use 'Economic Warfare' on Iran, Bush Demands," *The New York Times*, March 15, 1980, p. 8.

24. Thomas Patterson, *The Mass Media Election* (New York: Praeger, 1980), p. 52.

25. Timothy Crouse, *The Boys on the Bus* (New York: Random House, 1973), pp. 7–8.

26. "CBS Evening News," January 24, 1980.

27. Jeff Greenfield, *The Real Campaign: How the Media Missed the Story of the 1980 Campaign* (New York: Summit, 1982), p. 12.

28. Howard Kurtz, "Are Reporters Letting Clinton Off Easy?," *Washington Post National Weekly Edition*, September 7–13, 1992, p. 13. Some of the examples that follow are taken from this article.

29. David Maraniss, "For Clinton, a Chance to Start Over," Washington *Post*, June 4, 1992, p. A1.

30. "Young Guns: The Generational Gamble," *Newsweek*, July 20, 1992, p. 3.

31. David Maraniss, "Bill Clinton: Born to Run . . . And Run . . . And Run," Washington *Post*, July 13, 1992, p. A1.

32. "Battle of the Sound Bites," *Media Monitor* (Center for Media and Public Affairs, Washington, D.C.), August–September 1992, p. 4.

33. Ibid.

34. Quoted in ibid.

35. R. W. Apple, Jr., "Bush Campaign Shows Fire, Then Lands in It," *The New York Times*, August 4, 1992, p. A12.

36. Michael Kramer, "Reading Between the Lines," *Time*, August 24, 1992, p. 25.

37. Dan Goodgame, "What's Wrong with Bush?," *Time*, August 10, 1992, p. 25.

38. "NBC Nightly News," October 21, 1992.

39. Jeffrey Katz, "Tilt? Did the Media Favor Bill Clinton, or Did George Bush Earn His Media Coverage?," *Washington Journalism Review*, January–February 1993, p. 35.

40. "Bad Press, Good Press," *Media Monitor* (Center for Media and Public Affairs, Washington, D.C.), June–July 1992, p. 5.

41. Bob Woodward and John Mintz, "Perot Launched Investigations of Bush," Washington *Post*, June 21, 1992, p. A1.

42. "NBC Nightly News," May 6, 1992.

43. Quoted in D. D. Guttenplan, "Tracking the Campaign," *Columbia Journalism Review*, November–December 1992, p. 30.

44. See David Von Drehle, "Perot Attacks GOP 'Assault' on Character," Washington *Post*, June 25, 1992, p. A1.

45. Tom Morgenthau, "The Quitter: Why Perot Bowed Out," *Newsweek*, July 27, 1992, p. 28.

46. "The Quitter," *Newsweek*, July 27, 1992, cover.

47. "Ego Trip," *Newsweek*, October 12, 1992, cover.

48. "CBS Evening News," October 22, 1992.

49. "Clinton's the One," *Media Monitor* (Center for Media and Public Affairs, Washington, D.C.), November 1992, p. 4.

50. Ibid.

51. Quoted in Stephen Budiansky, "The President in the Eye of the Storm," *US News & World Report*, September 14, 1992, p. 14.

52. Kurtz, "Bias in the Press," p. F12.

53. Edith Efron, *The News Twisters* (Los Angeles: Nash, 1971), p. 47.

54. Ibid.

55. S. Robert Lichter and Stanley Rothman, "Media and Business Elites," *Public Opinion*, October–November 1981, p. 42.

56. David H. Weaver and G. Cleveland Wilhoit, *The American Journalist*, 2nd ed. (Bloomington: Indiana University Press, 1986), p. 29; David H. Weaver and G. Cleveland Wilhoit, "The American Journalist in the 1990s," School of Journalism research paper, Indiana University (Bloomington: November 1992), p. 7.

57. Doris Graber, *Mass Media and Politics* (Washington, D.C.: Congressional Quarterly Press, 1980), pp. 167–68.

58. Robinson and Sheehan, *Over the Wire and on TV*, pp. 98–100.

59. C. Richard Hofstetter, *Bias in the News* (Columbus: Ohio State University Press, 1976).

60. Weaver, "Is Television News Biased?" p. 72.

61. "CBS Evening News," January 20, 1992.

62. E. J. Dionne, Jr., Richard Morin, Mary McGrory, and Christopher B. Daly, "Protest Vote Cuts Bush's N.H. Margin," Washington *Post*, February 19, 1992, p. A1.

63. See "The Parties Pick Their Candidates," *Media Monitor* (Center for Media and Public Affairs, Washington, D.C.), March 1992, p. 4.

64. "World News Tonight," ABC, August 17, 1992.

65. Joe Klein, "Fighting the Squish Factor," *Newsweek*, September 7, 1992, p. 39.

66. Kenneth T. Walsh, "All Things to All Voters," *US News & World Report*, September 14, 1992, p. 32.

67. "Clinton's the One," p. 4.

68. Weaver, "Is Television News Biased?," pp. 70–71.

69. "Clinton's the One," p. 2.

70. Knight-Ridder wire-service story, as reprinted in the Syracuse *Post-Standard*, October 3, 1992, p. A1.

71. "NBC Nightly News," August 17, 1992.

72. "World News Tonight," ABC, October 12, 1992.

73. Howard Fineman and Ann McDaniel, "Bush: What Bounce?," *Newsweek*, August 31, 1992, p. 28.

74. Quoted in Andrew Tyndall, *Tyndall Report* (ADT Research, New York), December 1992, p. 10.

75. "What Makes Teddy Run?," *Time*, April 21, 1980, p. 21.

76. "Jimmy Carter v. Inflation," *Time*, March 24, 1980, pp. 8–9.

77. "Foreign Policy as an Issue," *Time*, April 7, 1980, p. 25.

78. Edward Walsh, "Carter Strategy Aims to Plant Doubts about Reagan's Abilities," *Washington Post*, August 16, 1980, p. A10.

79. Caroline Atkinson, "Inflation Worsens in Final Statistics Before Election Day," *Washington Post*, October 25, 1980, p. A1.

80. Walter Isaacson, "A Vow to Zip His Lip," *Time*, October 20, 1980, p. 16.

81. Robinson and Sheehan, *Over the Wire and on TV*, p. 128.

82. Jonathan Alter, "Rooting for Reagan," *Washington Monthly*, January 1981, p. 12.

83. Kurtz, "Are Reporters Letting Clinton Off Easy?," p. 12.

84. David Broder, "Pollsters and Parliaments," *Washington Post National Weekly Edition*, July 13, 1987, p. 4.

85. Quoted in Thomas E. Patterson, "The Press and Candidate Images," *International Journal of Public Opinion Research* 1 (1989): 130.

86. Larry Martz, "Playing Hardball," *Newsweek*, October 3, 1988, pp. 22-23.

87. "The Smear Campaign," *Newsweek*, October 31, 1988, pp. 17, 19.

88. Jonathan Alter, "Getting Down and Dirty," *Newsweek*, September 12, 1988, p. 22.

89. ABC, October 17, 1988. Described in Kiku Adatto, *Sound Bite Democracy: Network Evening News Presidential Campaign Coverage, 1968 and 1988*, Joan Shorenstein Barone Center on the Press, Politics and Public Policy, Research Paper R-2, John F. Kennedy School of Government, Harvard University (Cambridge, Mass., June 1990), p. 13.

90. Stephen Ansolabehere, Roy Behr, and Shanto Iyengar, *The Media Game* (New York: Macmillan, 1992), p. 86.

91. Walter Shapiro, "Bush Scores a Warm Win," *Time*, October 24, 1988, p. 19.

92. Quoted in Patterson, "The Press and Candidate Images," p. 131.

93. Margaret Garrard Warner, "Fighting the Wimp Factor," *Newsweek*, October 19, 1987, pp. 28–30.

94. George Hackett, "George Bush's Made-for-TV Makeover," *Newsweek*, September 12, 1988, p. 24.

95. Ibid.

96. "Clinton's the One," p. 3.

97. Ibid., p. 4.

98. Quoted in ibid., p. 3.

99. "CBS Evening News," September 18, 1991.

100. "The Boom in Gloom," *Media Monitor* (Center for Media and Public Affairs, Washington, D.C.), October 1992, p. 3.

101. Howard Kurtz, "Networks Stressed the Negative in Comments about Bush, Study Finds," Washington *Post*, November 15, 1992, p. A7.

102. "Battle of the Sound Bites," p. 5.

103. Quoted in *Tyndall Report*, December 1992, p. 11.

104. Thomas C. Palmer, Jr., "Reputation for Bias Seems Well Earned," Boston *Globe*, January 3, 1993, p. 65.

105. "The Boom in Gloom," p. 3.

106. Seymour Martin Lipset, "The Significance of the 1992 Election," *P.S. Political Science and Politics* 24 (1993): 7.

107. Quoted in Katz, "Tilt?," p. 25.

108. See Thomas E. Patterson and Robert D. McClure, *The Unseeing Eye: The Myth of Television Power in National Elections* (New York: Putnam, 1976), pp. 63–68.

109. Dan Nimmo and James Combs, *Nightly Horrors* (Knoxville: University of Tennessee Press, 1985), p. 16.

110. Weaver, "Is Television News Biased?," p. 70.

111. Charles Peters, "Tilting at Windmills," Washington *Post*, February 24, 1980, p. B2.

112. "NBC Nightly News," July 18, 1992.

113. "Is Television News Biased?," p. 70.

114. Susan Fraker, "Qualms About Carter," *Newsweek*, June 7, 1976, p. 20.

115. Howard Fineman, "Face to Face to Face," *Newsweek*, October 19, 1992, p. 20.

116. "Is Television News Biased?," p. 71.

117. Patterson, *Mass Media Election*, pp. 43–48.

118. See S. Robert Lichter, Daniel Amundson, and Richard Noyes, *The Video Campaign: Network Coverage of the 1988 Primaries* (Washington, D.C.: American Enterprise Institute, 1989), pp. 89–91.

119. "CBS Evening News," January 7, 1980.

120. See Ann N. Crigler, Marion R. Just, and Timothy E. Cook, "Local News, Network News and the 1992 Presidential Campaign"

(paper delivered at the annual meeting of the American Political Science Association, Chicago, September 3–6, 1992), pp. 30–31.

121. Maureen Dowd, "Despite Appeals to Intellect, Brown Touches the Emotions," *The New York Times*, April 5, 1992, p. A1.

122. Greenfield, *The Real Campaign*, p. 43.

123. Robinson and Sheehan, *Over the Wire and on TV*, p. 116.

124. Marshall McLuhan, *Understanding Media* (New York: McGraw-Hill, 1964), pp. 277–78.

125. Joe McGinniss, *The Selling of the President* (New York: Trident Press, 1969).

126. Quoted in Thomas E. Patterson, "More Style Than Substance," *Political Communication and Persuasion* 8 (1991): 155.

127. See Kurt Lang and Gladys Engel Lang, *Politics and Television* (Chicago: Quadrangle, 1968), pp. 11–35.

128. Fraker, "Qualms about Carter," p. 20.

129. Quoted in Patterson, *The Mass Media Election*, p. 44.

130. Ibid.

131. Ibid., p. 45.

132. Ibid., pp. 43-56, 95-106.

133. Larry Bartels, *Presidential Primaries and the Dynamics of Public Choice* (Princeton, N.J.: Princeton University Press, 1988), pp. 193–205.

134. Patterson, *The Mass Media Election*, pp. 107–46.

135. Weaver, "Is Television News Biased?," p. 73.

136. Ibid.

137. "NBC Nightly News," January 28, 1992.

138. Shanto Iyengar and Donald Kinder, *News That Matters* (Chicago: University of Chicago Press, 1987), p. 126.

139. Paul Weaver, "Newspaper News and Television News," in *Television as Social Force*, ed. Douglas Cater and R. Adler (New York: Praeger, 1975), p. 90.

140. See Steven Chaffee and Sun Yuel Chou, "Time of Decision and Media Use during the Ford-Carter Campaign," *Public Opinion Quarterly* 44 (Spring 1980): 55, and Bruce Campbell, *The American Electorate* (New York: Holt, Rinehart and Winston, 1979), p. 262.

141. Iyengar and Kinder, *News That Matters*, p. 129.

142. Bruce Buchanan, *Electing a President: The Markle Commission's Report on Campaign '88* (Austin: University of Texas Press, 1991), p. 44.

143. Patterson, *The Mass Media Election*, p. 128.
144. V. O. Key, Jr., *The Responsible Electorate* (Cambridge, Mass.: Belknap Press, 1966), p. vii.

CHAPTER FOUR

1. Walter Lippmann, *Public Opinion* (1922; reprint, New York: Free Press, 1965), p. 221.
2. "Six in GOP Say They Would Ban Control of Guns; But Anderson Backs Idea at New Hampshire Event," *The New York Times*, February 19, 1980, p. A16.
3. "Excerpts from Forum in Iowa of Six G.O.P. Presidential Candidates," *The New York Times*, January 7, 1980, p. B4.
4. Warren Weaver, Jr., "Anderson Campaign Gets a Lift on His Showing in Iowa Debate," *The New York Times*, January 12, 1980, p. 9.
5. Colin Seymour-Ure, *The Political Impact of Mass Media* (Beverly Hills, Calif.: Sage, 1974), p. 223.
6. Los Angeles *Times* wire-service story, May 20, 1992.
7. " 'Murphy Brown' Is Bad Role Model, Quayle Says," Knight-Ridder news-service story reprinted in Syracuse *Herald-Journal*, May 20, 1992, p. A3.
8. John E. Yang and Ann Devroy, "Quayle: 'Hollywood Doesn't Get It,' " Washington *Post*, May 21, 1992, p. A1.
9. Wire-service composite, rewritten in Syracuse *Post Standard*, May 21, 1992, p. A1.
10. I am indebted for this argument to a paper titled "The Depoliticization of Politics," that I reviewed for a professional journal. The author's identity was withheld as part of the blind-review process.
11. Ken Auletta, "Loathe the Media," *Esquire*, November 1992, p. 179.
12. Thomas DeFrank, "Exclusive Interview with President Ford," *Newsweek*, October 11, 1976, p. 29.
13. Each candidate's stump speech was printed once in *The New York Times* in late February 1984.
14. Thomas E. Patterson and Richard Davis, "The Media Cam-

paign: Struggle for the Agenda," in *The Elections of 1984*, ed. Michael Nelson (Washington, D.C.: Congressional Quarterly Press, 1985), p. 118.

15. William C. Adams, "Media Coverage of Campaign 1984," *Public Opinion*, April–May 1984, pp. 12–13.

16. Howard Kurtz, "Bush Angrily Denounces Report of Extramarital Affair as a 'Lie,' " Washington *Post*, August 12, 1992, p. A12.

17. Michael Robinson and Margaret Sheehan, *Over the Wire and on TV* (New York: Sage Foundation, 1983), p. 57.

18. Maura Clancy and Michael Robinson, "General Election Coverage: Part I," in *The Mass Media in Campaign '84*, ed. Michael J. Robinson and Austin Ranney (Washington, D.C.: American Enterprise Institute, 1985), p. 29.

19. S. Robert Lichter, Daniel Amundson, and Richard E. Noyes, "Election '88: Media Coverage," *Public Opinion*, January–February 1989, p. 180.

20. "The Boom in Gloom," *Media Monitor* (Center for Media and Public Affairs, Washington, D.C.), October 1992, p. 5; "Clinton's the One," *Media Monitor* (Center for Media and Public Affairs, Washington, D.C.), November 1992, p. 1.

21. Seymour-Ure, *The Political Impact of Mass Media*, p. 219.

22. Kathleen Hall Jamieson, *Dirty Politics: Deception, Distraction, Democracy* (New York: Oxford University Press, 1992), pp. 184–85; see also Jane Blankenship, "The Search for the 1972 Democratic Nomination: A Metaphoric Perspective," in *Rhetoric and Communication*, ed. Jane Blankenship and Hermann G. Stelzner (Urbana: University of Illinois Press, 1976), and Jane Blankenship and Jong Guen Kang, "The 1984 Presidential and Vice-Presidential Debates: The Printed Press and 'Construction' by Metaphor," *Presidential Studies Quarterly* 21 (1991): 307–18.

23. Gwen Ifill, "Clinton, Out of Limelight, Ponders Attack on Perot," *The New York Times*, June 7, 1992, p. 24.

24. David E. Butler and Michael Pinto-Duschinskey, *The British General Election of 1970* (London: Macmillan, 1971), p. 137.

25. Bernard Berelson, Paul Lazarsfeld, and William McPhee, *Voting* (Chicago: University of Chicago Press, 1954), p. 236.

26. Benjamin I. Page, *Choices and Echoes in Presidential Elections* (Chicago: University of Chicago Press, 1978), pp. 152-191.

27. D. Roderick Kiewiet, *Macro-Economics and Micro-Politics* (Chicago: University of Chicago Press, 1983), pp. 154–58.

28. Quoted in Henry Louis Gates, Jr., "A Pretty Good Society," *Time*, November 16, 1992, p. 85.

29. Gerald Pomper, with Susan Lederman, *Elections in America* (New York: Longman, 1980), p. 169.

30. Jerry Hagstrom, "Political Consulting," Freedom Forum Media Studies Center report, Columbia University (New York, 1992), p. 16.

31. Quoted in a Los Angeles *Times* wire-service story, May 20, 1992.

32. Nelson Polsby, *The Consequences of Party Reform* (New York: Oxford University Press, 1983), p. 147.

33. Butler and Pinto-Duschinskey, *The British General Election of 1970*, p. 137.

34. Seymour-Ure, *The Political Impact of Mass Media*, p. 219.

35. Jane Bryant Quinn, "The Illusion of Tax Relief: Why Bush's Plan Misleads the Middle Class," *Newsweek*, February 10, 1992, p. 25.

36. "World News Tonight," ABC, September 10, 1992.

37. Quoted in D. D. Guttenplan, "Covering a Runaway Campaign," *Columbia Journalism Review*, November–December 1992, p. 33.

38. "Quayle Hunt: TV News Coverage of the Quayle Nomination," *Media Monitor* (Center for Media and Public Affairs, Washington, D.C.), September 1988, pp. 1–4.

39. Seymour-Ure, *The Political Impact of Mass Media*, p. 220.

40. James Reston, "Two Cheers for the Reporters," *The New York Times*, November 3, 1976, p. 43.

41. Quoted in Harvey Shapiro, "A Conversation with Jimmy Carter," *The New York Times Book Review*, Sunday, June 19, 1977, p. 34, sec. 7.

42. Dan Balz, "Clinton Hits Both GOP, Democrats on Economy," *Washington Post*, November 21, 1991, p. A4.

43. I could find no mention of the speech, for example, in the *Television News Index and Abstract* (Vanderbilt Television News Archive, Nashville, Tenn.), 1991.

44. Thomas E. Patterson, *The Mass Media Election* (New York: Praeger, 1980), p. 34.

45. Quoted in Thomas E. Patterson, "The Press and Candidate Images," *International Journal of Public Opinion* 1 (1989): 127.

46. Quoted in Donald R. Matthews, "The News Media and the 1976 Presidential Nominations," in *Race for the Presidency*, ed. James David Barber (Englewood Cliffs, N.J.: Prentice-Hall, 1978), p. 69.

47. Quoted in Patterson, *The Mass Media Election*, pp. 40–41.

48. See James B. Lemert, William R. Elliot, James M. Bernstein, and William L. Rosenberg, *News Verdicts, the Debates, and Presidential Campaigns* (Westport, Conn.: Praeger, 1991).

49. Quoted in Goodwin F. Berquist and James L. Golden, "Media Rhetoric, Criticism, and the Public Perception of the 1980 Presidential Debates," *Quarterly Journal of Speech* 67 (1981): 128–29.

50. John Tierney, "Longer Debate Shows Issues and Personalities," *The New York Times*, February 2, 1992, p. A24.

51. See, for example, Marion Just, Ann Crigler, and Lori Wallach, "Thirty Seconds or Thirty Minutes," *Journal of Communication* 51 (1990): 120–32.

52. V. O. Key, *The Responsible Electorate* (Cambridge, Mass.: Belknap Press, 1966), p. vii; Samuel L. Popkin, *The Reasoning Voter: Communication and Persuasion in Presidential Campaigns* (Chicago: University of Chicago Press, 1991), p. 7.

53. Bruce Buchanan, *Electing a President: The Markle Commission's Report on Campaign '88* (Austin: University of Texas Press, 1991), p. 135.

54. Quoted in Jeff Greenfield, *The Real Campaign: How the Media Missed the Story of the 1980 Campaign* (New York: Summit Books, 1982), p. 31.

55. Michael Kelly, "Clinton Uses Farm Speech to Begin New Offensive," *The New York Times*, September 28, 1992, p. A1.

56. "Rx for Health Care," *Newsweek*, September 28, 1992, p. 20.

57. Mary Earhart Dillon, *Wendell Willkie* (New York: Lippincott, 1952), p. 202.

58. Quoted in David R. Runkel, ed., *Campaign for President: The Managers Look at '88* (Dover, Mass.: Auburn House, 1989), p. 136.

59. Quoted in Kiku Adatto, *Sound Bite Democracy: Network Evening News Presidential Campaign Coverage, 1968 and 1988*, Joan Shorenstein Barone Center on the Press, Politics and Public Policy, Research Paper R-2, John F. Kennedy School of Government, Harvard University (Cambridge, Mass., June 1990), p. 120.

60. *Campaign Lessons for '92*, Joan Shorenstein Barone Center paper, John F. Kennedy School of Government, Harvard University (Cambridge, Mass., November 1991), p. 78.

61. Christopher F. Arterton, "The Media Politics of Presidential Campaigns," in *Race for the Presidency*, pp. 48–51.

62. Evelyn Nieves, "Error by Quayle Studiously Avoided," *The New York Times*, June 17, 1992, p. A23.

63. Patterson, *The Mass Media Election*, pp. 36–37.

64. Larry Sabato, *Feeding Frenzy: How Attack Journalism Has Transformed American Politics* (New York: Free Press, 1991), p. 1.

65. Arterton, "The Media Politics of Presidential Campaigns," pp. 48–51.

66. "Why Carter Wins the Black Vote," *Time*, April 5, 1976, p. 27.

67. Matthews, "The News Media and the 1976 Presidential Nominations," p. 70.

68. Stephen Ansolabehere, Roy Behr, and Shanto Iyengar, *The Media Game* (New York: Macmillan, 1992), p. 178.

69. Seymour-Ure, *The Political Impact of Mass Media*, pp. 202–39.

70. Kathleen Hall Jamieson, *Dirty Politics* (New York: Oxford University Press, 1992), p. 215.

71. *Campaign Lessons for '92*, p. 54.

72. "Public Figures and Private Lives," conference transcript, Joan Shorenstein Barone Center, John F. Kennedy School of Government, Harvard University (Cambridge, Mass., June 10, 1988), p. 141.

73. George Will, "Trickle Down Tawdriness," *Newsweek*, November 7, 1988, p. 132.

74. Quoted in Runkel, *Campaign for President*, pp. 135–36.

75. Howell Raines, "Stage Is Set for Tough Presidential Race," *The New York Times*, July 26, 1984, p. A20.

76. Francis X. Clines, "President Denies Plan to Increase Tax in Next Year," *The New York Times*, July 25, 1984, p. A1.

77. Francis X. Clines, "Reagan Ridicules Mondale 'Realism,' " *The New York Times*, July 26,1984, p. A21.

78. "President Denies Plan to Increase Tax in Next Year," *The New York Times*, July 25, 1984, p. A1.

79. "Reagan Ridicules Mondale 'Realism,' " *The New York Times*, July 26, 1984, p. A21.

80. Steven R. Weisman, "Presidential Aide Scoffs at Mondale Tax Pledge," *The New York Times*, July 21, 1984, p. 12.

81. Edwin L. Dale, Jr., "McGovern Income Plans Ridiculed by a Nixon Aide," *The New York Times*, June 18, 1972, p. 1.

82. "What McGovern Would Mean to the Country," *Time*, June 26, 1972, p. 15.

83. Michael Robinson, "TV's Newest Program," *Public Opinion*, May/June 1978, p. 44.

84. *Campaign Lessons for '92*, p. 54.

85. Quoted in Dan Hallin, "Covering the Campaign," *Wilson Quarterly*, Spring 1992, p. 35.

86. Adatto, *Sound Bite Democracy*, p. 40.

87. "Clinton's the One," p. 2.

88. See Guido H. Stempel III and John W. Windhauser, *The Media in the 1984 and 1988 Campaigns* (Westport, Conn.: Greenwood, 1991).

89. *The Campaign and the Press at Halftime* (Report of the Times Mirror Center for the People and the Press), supplement to *Columbia Journalism Review*, July–August 1992, p. 4.

90. "Clinton's the One," p. 2.

91. "The Press and the Presidential Campaign, 1988" (Seminar proceedings of the American Press Institute, Reston, Va., December 6, 1988), p. 16.

92. Quoted in Gil Troy, *See How They Ran* (New York: Free Press, 1991), p. 257.

93. "The Press and the Presidential Campaign, 1988," p. 4.

94. Fox Butterfield, "Dukakis Says Race Was Harmed by TV," *The New York Times*, Sunday, April 22, 1990, p. 23, sec. 1. Quoted in Philip Wander and David McNeil, "The Coming Crisis in American Politics," *Political Communication Review* 16 (1991): 38.

95. Howard Fineman, "Kerrey Reflects: 'The Tunnel of Unlove,' " *Newsweek*, February 10, 1992, p. 29.

96. Quoted in *Campaign Lessons for '92*, p. 1.

97. Paul Taylor, *See How They Run* (New York: Knopf, 1991), p. 6.

98. "Willie Horton," *Media Monitor* (Center for Media and Public Affairs, Washington, D.C.), September 1988.

99. Jamieson, *Dirty Politics*, p. 253.

100. Martin Shram, "The Making of Willie Horton," *The New Republic*, May 28, 1990, pp. 17–19.

101. Taylor, *See How They Run*, pp. 191, 214.

102. William Boot, "Campaign '88: TV Overdoses on the Inside Dope," *Columbia Journalism Review*, January–February 1989, p. 24.

103. Troy, *See How They Ran*, p. 257.

104. E. J. Dionne, Jr., "New Polls Show Attacks by Bush Are Building Lead," *The New York Times*, October 26, 1988, p. A22.

105. Buchanan, *Electing a President*, p. 17.

106. *Covering the Presidential Primaries*, Freedom Forum Media Studies Center report, Columbia University (New York, June 1992), p. 27.

107. See *Campaign Lessons for '92*, pp. 103–25.

108. "Campaign '92: Early Returns," *Media Monitor* (Center for Media and Public Affairs, Washington, D.C.), February 1992, p. 2.

109. "The Parties Pick Their Candidates," *Media Monitor* (Center for Media and Public Affairs, Washington, D.C.), March 1992, p. 2.

110. *Covering the Presidential Primaries*, p. 31.

111. Auletta, "Loathe the Media," p. 177.

112. *Covering the Presidential Primaries*, p. 23.

113. Lawrence N. Hanson, "Reflections: The Press Looks at Itself, Politicians, and the Public," Joyce Foundation report (Washington, D.C., 1992), p. 8.

114. Eleanor Clift, "Character Questions," *Newsweek*, February 10, 1992, p. 26.

115. Christopher Hitchens, "Voting in the Passive Voice," *Harper's*, April 1992, p. 49.

116. "Campaign '92: Early Returns," p. 3.

117. *The Campaign and the Press at Halftime*, p. 1.

118. CNN survey, January 30, 1992. The other responses were "right amount" (12 percent) and "don't know" (3 percent).

119. Quoted in Marvin Kalb, "Too Much Talk and Not Enough Action," *Washington Journalism Review*, September 1992, p. 33.

120. Auletta, "Loathe the Media," p. 179.

121. Ibid., p. 181.

122. Matthew R. Kerbel, "Cable and Television Coverage of the 1992 Primaries" (paper presented at the annual meeting of the American Political Science Association, Chicago, September 3–6, 1992).

123. "Clinton's the One," p. 2.

124. "Battle of the Sound Bites," *Media Monitor* (Center for Media and Public Affairs, Washington, D.C.), August–September 1992, p. 4.

125. Thomas Oliphant, "The Media 'Filter' Was a Sieve for Sleaze," Boston *Globe*, November 11, 1992, p. 13.

126. Renee Loth, "Studies Find Tilt in TV Coverage of Campaign," Boston *Globe*, September 2, 1992, p. 10.

127. Ken Auletta, untitled paper (Twentieth Century Fund, New York, September 3, 1992), p. 16.

128. Elizabeth Kolbert, "Talk Shows Wrangling to Book the Candidates," *The New York Times*, July 6, 1992, p. A10.

129. Oliphant, "The Media 'Filter,' " p. 13.

130. Editorial, Corpus Christi (Texas) *Caller-Times*, June 19, 1992.

131. Quoted in Elizabeth Kolbert, "Turning to Talk Shows to Boost a Campaign," *The New York Times*, June 5, 1992, p. A14.

132. *The Homestretch*, Freedom Forum Media Studies Center report, Columbia University (New York, 1992), p. 52.

133. "Meet the Press," NBC, May 3, 1992.

134. Howard Kurtz, "Backlash," *Washington Post Magazine*, July 12, 1992, p. 22.

135. Robert J. Donovan and Ray Scherer, "Politics Transformed," *Wilson Quarterly*, Spring 1992, p. 280.

136. "Reagan's Rhodesian Expeditionary Force," *Time*, June 14, 1976, p. 15.

137. John H. Kessel, *Presidential Campaign Politics* (Chicago: Dorsey Press, 1988), pp. 196–97.

138. Quoted in Jeffrey Schmalz, "Perot Petition Embraced as Manifesto of Change," *The New York Times*, Sunday, May 31, 1992, sec. 1, p. 20.

139. "Media Power," *Syracuse University Magazine*, September 1992, p. 14.

140. Gus Tyler, "The Power of Ross Perot," *New Leader*, May 4, 1992, p. 12.

141. "The No-Party System," editorial, *The New York Times*, June 3, 1992, p. A20.

142. Andrew Tyndall, *Tyndall Report* (ADT Research, New York), September 1992, p. 3.

143. "World News Tonight," ABC, October 14, 1976.

CHAPTER FIVE

1. Walter Lippmann, *Public Opinion* (1922; reprint, New York: Free Press, 1965), p. 229.

2. The example that follows is from Thomas E. Patterson, *The Mass Media Election* (New York: Praeger, 1980), pp. 49–50.

3. Robin Toner, "The Bounce: Blunt Reminders That It's Not Over until Nov. 3," *The New York Times*, Sunday, July 19, 1992, p. 1, sec. 4.

4. See, for example, Gregory B. Markus, "The Impact of Personal and National Economic Conditions on the Presidential Vote: A Pooled

Cross-Sectional Analysis," *American Journal of Political Science* 32 (1988): 137–54.

5. See Craig Allen Smith, "The Iowa Caucuses and Super Tuesday Primaries Reconsidered," *Presidential Studies Quarterly* 23 (1992): 519–23.

6. Carl Bernstein, "It's Press vs. Bush: A Bruising Fight," Los Angeles *Times*, October 25, 1992, p. M1.

7. See Gaye Tuchman, "Objectivity as Strategic Ritual," *American Journal of Sociology* 77 (1972): 671.

8. Patterson, *The Mass Media Election*, p. 51.

9. Lippmann, *Public Opinion*, p. 19.

10. Michael J. Robinson and Karen McPherson, "Television News Coverage Before the 1976 New Hampshire Primary," *Journal of Broadcasting* 21 (1977): 177–86.

11. Michael Robinson and Margaret Sheehan, *Over the Wire and on TV* (New York: Russell Sage Foundation, 1983), pp. 175–77.

12. William C. Adams, "As New Hampshire Goes," in *Media and Momentum: The New Hampshire Primary and Nomination Politics*, ed. Gary R. Orren and Nelson W. Polsby (Chatham, N.J.: Chatham House, 1987), p. 45.

13. "Covering the Primary States," *Media Monitor* (Center for Media and Public Affairs, Washington, D.C.), March 1988, p. 3.

14. See Patterson, *The Mass Media Election*, p. 45.

15. Quoted in Christopher F. Arterton, "Campaign Organizations Confront the Media-Political Environment," in *Race for the Presidency*, ed. James David Barber (Englewood Cliffs, N.J.: Prentice Hall, 1978), p. 11.

16. Ibid., p. 21.

17. See Paul-Henri Gurian, "Resource Allocation Strategies in Presidential Nomination Campaigns," *American Journal of Political Science* 30 (November 1986): 802–21.

18. Theodore H. White, *America in Search of Itself: The Making of the President 1956–1980* (New York: Harper and Row, 1982), p. 78.

19. Quoted in James David Barber, *The Pulse of Politics* (New York: Norton, 1980), p. 97.

20. Ibid.

21. Robinson and McPherson, "Television News Coverage Before the 1976 New Hampshire Primary," pp. 177–86.

22. Charles Brereton, *First in the Nation: New Hampshire and the*

Premier Presidential Primary (Portsmouth, N.H.: Peter E. Randall, 1987), pp. 181–82.

23. Quoted in Patterson, *The Mass Media Election*, p. 44.

24. R. W. Apple, Jr., "Carter Is Regarded as Getting Big Gain from Iowa Results," *The New York Times*, January 21, 1976, p. A1.

25. Alan Ehrenhalt, *The United States of Ambition* (New York: Times Books, 1991), p. 265.

26. "Bush Breaks Out of Pack," *Newsweek*, February 4, 1976, pp. 30–38.

27. See Patterson, *The Mass Media Election*, pp. 107–17, and David Moore, "Myths of the New Hampshire Voter" (paper presented at the annual meeting of the American Political Science Association, Washington, D.C., August 29, 1984), p. 13.

28. See Larry M. Bartels, *Presidential Primaries and the Dynamics of Public Choice* (Princeton, N.J.: Princeton University Press, 1988), pp. 137–71; and Robert M. Entman, "How the Media Affect What People Think," *Journal of Politics* 51 (1989): 347–70.

29. Quoted in William C. Adams, "Media Coverage of Campaign '84," *Public Opinion* 7 (1984): 13.

30. See Larry M. Bartels, "Candidate Choice and the Dynamics of the Presidential Nominating Process," *American Journal of Political Science* 31 (1987): 1–30; Alan Abramowitz, "Candidate Choice Before the Convention: The Democrats in 1984," *Political Behavior* 9 (1987): 49–61; Alan Abramowitz, "Viability, Electability, and Candidate Choice in a Presidential Primary Election," *Journal of Politics* 51 (1989): 977–92.

31. Doris Graber, *Processing the News* (New York: Longman, 1988), p. 203.

32. Adam Clymer "Missing Republican in Iowa," *The New York Times*, January 7, 1980, p. A1.

33. "Campaign '92: Early Returns," *Media Monitor* (Center for Media and Public Affairs, Washington, D.C.), February 1992, p. 3.

34. Howard Fineman, "Kerrey Reflects: 'The Tunnel of Unlove,' " *Newsweek*, February 10, 1992, p. 29.

35. Orren and Polsby, *Media and Momentum*, p. 17.

36. See Scott Keeter and Cliff Zukin, *Uninformed Choice* (New York: Praeger, 1983), and William C. Adams, "Media Coverage of Campaign '84: A Preliminary Report," *Public Opinion*, April–May 1984, p. 13.

37. Quoted in Christopher Hitchens, "Voting in the Passive Voice," *Harper's*, April 1992, p. 50.

38. Bartels, "Candidate Choice," pp. 1–30.

39. Larry M. Bartels, "Expectations and Preferences in Presidential Nominating Campaigns," *American Political Science Review* 79 (1985): 804–15.

40. See Keeter and Zukin, *Uninformed Choice*.

41. Thomas E. Patterson, "Voter Control of Information," in *Political Persuasion in Presidential Campaigns*, ed. L. Patrick Devlin (New Brunswick, N.J.: Transaction Books, 1987), pp. 175–84.

42. CBS/New York Times exit polls March 13, 1984; see also Kathleen Hall Jamieson, *Dirty Politics* (New York: Oxford University Press, 1992), p. 50.

43. Henry E. Brady, "Media and Momentum," unpublished paper, undated and with no address, pp. 29–30; see also Henry E. Brady and Richard Johnston, "What's the Primary Message?" in *Media and Momentum*, ed. Orren and Polsby, p. 184.

44. See Sig Mickelson, *The Electronic Mirror* (New York: Dodd, Mead, 1972).

45. Lippmann, *Public Opinion*, pp. 215, 221, 226.

46. W. Lance Bennett, *The Politics of Illusion*, 2nd ed. (New York: Longman, 1988), pp. 7–13.

47. *Covering the Presidential Primaries*, Freedom Forum Media Studies Center report, Columbia University (New York, June 1992), p. 32.

48. Philip Wander and David McNeil, "The Coming Crisis in American Politics," *Political Communication Review* 16 (1991): 41.

49. Cited in Thomas E. Patterson, *The American Democracy* (New York: McGraw-Hill, 1990), p. 340.

50. "Diagnosing the Health Care Crisis," *Media Monitor* (Center for Media and Public Affairs, Washington, D.C.), May 1992, p. 6.

51. Robert Leigh, *A Free and Responsible Press* (Chicago: University of Chicago Press, 1947), pp. 90–96.

52. Lippmann, *Public Opinion*, p. 222.

53. See *Covering the Presidential Primaries*, p. 79.

54. Ibid.

55. *School for Scandal*, Joan Shorenstein Barone Center conference transcript, John F. Kennedy School of Government, Harvard University (Cambridge, Mass., 1989), pp. 167–68.

56. Cited on "NBC Nightly News," October 5, 1992.

57. James David Barber, *The Presidential Character*, rev. ed. (Englewood Cliffs, N.J.: Prentice-Hall, 1978).

58. *Covering the Presidential Primaries*, pp. 79–80.

59. "The Parties Pick Their Candidates," *Media Monitor* (Center for Media and Public Affairs, Washington, D.C.), March 1992, pp. 4–5.

60. Ibid., p. 2.

61. Elizabeth Roth, "Networks Adjust Election Coverage," *Christian Science Monitor*, September 25, 1992, p. 12.

62. S. Robert Lichter, Daniel Amundson, and Richard Noyes, *The Video Campaign* (Washington, D.C.: American Enterprise Institute, 1988), pp. 69–101.

63. Stephen Ansolabehere, Roy Behr, and Shanto Iyengar, *The Media Game* (New York: Macmillan, 1992), p. 148.

64. Shanto Iyengar and Donald R. Kinder, *News That Matters* (Chicago: University of Chicago Press, 1987), p. 5.

65. *Covering the Presidential Primaries*, p. 30.

66. Judith Lichtenberg, *The Politics of Character and the Character of Politics*, Joan Shorenstein Barone Center on the Press, Politics and Public Policy paper, John F. Kennedy School of Government, Harvard University (Cambridge, Mass., 1989).

67. Tom Wicker, "The Issue Is Not Morality, It's Candor," *The New York Times*, May 6, 1987, p. A35.

68. Quoted in Ken Auletta, "Loathe the Media," *Esquire*, November 1992, p. 181.

69. Ibid.

70. Quoted in Jeffrey L. Katz, "Tilt?," *Washington Journalism Review*, January–February 1993, p. 24.

71. Paul Taylor, *See How They Run* (New York: Knopf, 1990), p. 63.

72. Alexander Heard, with Scarlett G. Graham and Kay L. Hancock, *Made in America* (New York: HarperCollins, 1991), p. 83.

73. Patterson, *The Mass Media Election*, pp. 77–91.

74. Pamela Johnston Conover and Stanley Feldman, "Candidate Perception in an Ambiguous World: Campaigns, Cues, and Inference Processes," *American Journal of Political Science* 33 (1989): 912–40.

75. Patterson, *The Mass Media Election*, p. 166.

76. Jay Rosen, "Forming and Informing the Public," *Kettering Review*, Winter 1992, p. 69.

77. Bernstein, "It's Press vs. Bush," p. M1.

78. W. Lance Bennett, "Assessing Presidential Character: Degradation Rituals in Political Campaigns," *Quarterly Journal of Speech* 67 (1981): 311–13.

79. News release, Center for Media and Public Affairs, November 28, 1992.

80. George Will, "We're Electing a Lame Duck," *Newsweek*, October 24, 1988, p. 84.

81. Meg Greenfield, "The Real Winners and Losers," *Newsweek*, November 12, 1984, p. 120.

82. Donald L. Battle, "None of the Above," *U.S. News & World Report*, September 29, 1980, p. 20.

83. James Comer, "Fence Sitters Beware," Washington *Post*, October 27, 1976, p. A13.

84. Harry Reasoner, "ABC Evening News," November 2, 1972.

85. Gary R. Orren and William G. Mayer, "The Press, Political Parties, and the Public-Private Balance in Elections," in *The Parties Respond*, ed. L. Sandy Maisel (Boulder, Col.: Westview Press, 1990), p. 204

86. *Lessons for Campaign '92*, Joan Shorenstein Barone Center paper, John F. Kennedy School of Government, Harvard University (Cambridge, Mass., 1991), pp. 30-31.

87. Taylor, *See How They Run*, p. 255.

88. Paul Weaver, "Is Television News Biased?," *Public Interest* 27 (1972): 69.

89. Dan Hallin, "Sound Bite News," in *Blurring the Lines: Media and Elections in America*, ed. Gary Orren (New York: Free Press, forthcoming).

90. V. O. Key, Jr., *Southern Politics* (New York: Knopf, 1949), p. 303.

91. Ibid., pp. 302–10.

92. Ibid.

93. Ibid.

94. Ibid., p. 16.

CHAPTER SIX

1. Walter Lippmann, *Public Opinion* (1922; reprint, New York: Free Press, 1965), p. 229.
2. See Paul Weaver, "Is Television News Biased?," *Public Interest* 27 (1972): 57–74.
3. Cited in *Problems of Governance*, Ford Foundation report, Maxwell School of Citizenship, Syracuse University (Syracuse, N.Y., 1992), p. 28.
4. Lawrence N. Hanson, *Reflections: The Press Looks at Itself, Politicians, and the Public*, Joyce Foundation report (Washington, D.C., 1992), p. 3.
5. See William Crotty, *Political Reform and the American Experiment* (New York: Thomas Y. Crowell, 1977), p. x.
6. Everett Carll Ladd, "Party Reform and the Public Interest," *Political Science Quarterly* 102 (Fall 1987): 355–70.
7. Jeane J. Kirkpatrick, Michael J. Malbin, Thomas E. Mann, Howard R. Penniman, and Austin Ranney, *The Presidential Nominating Process: Can It Be Improved?* (Washington, D.C.: American Enterprise Institute, 1980), p. 1.
8. Ibid., p. 2.
9. Ibid.
10. Louis Harris, "Dump the Primaries: An Agenda for Real Change," *New York Newsday*, July 15, 1992, p. 95.
11. Quoted in "Can We Make It a Better Race Next Time?," *New York Newsday*, November 3, 1992, p. 73.
12. Samuel J. Eldersveld, *Political Parties in American Society* (New York: Basic Books, 1982), p. 408.
13. *Problems of Governance*, p. 11.
14. Thomas Mann, "Should the Presidential Nominating System Be Changed?," in *Before Nomination: Our Primary Problems*, ed. George Grassmuck (Washington, D.C.: American Enterprise Institute, 1985), p. 35.
15. Michael Robinson and Margaret Sheehan, *Over the Wire and on TV* (New York: Russell Sage Foundation, 1983), p. 80.
16. Paul Taylor, *See How They Run* (New York: Knopf, 1990), p. 115.
17. "Grouchy Voters Knock System," *USA Today*, February 5–7, 1988, p. 1.

18. Michael Nelson, "The Case for the Current Presidential Nominating Process," in Grassmuck, *Before Nomination*, pp. 32–34.

19. Alan Ehrenhalt, *The United States of Ambition* (New York: Times Books, 1991), p. 268.

20. William C. Adams, "As New Hampshire Goes . . . ," in *Media and Momentum*, ed. Gary Orren and Nelson Polsby (Chatham, N.J.: Chatham House Publishers, 1987), p. 52.

21. Ibid., p. 51.

22. Ibid., p. 52.

23. Larry M. Bartels, *Presidential Primaries and the Dynamics of Public Choice* (Princeton, N.J.: Princeton University Press, 1988), p. 277.

24. Austin Ranney, *Channels of Power* (New York: Basic Books, 1983), p. 97.

25. Author's calculation based on 1976 turnout data.

26. See Thomas E. Patterson, *The Mass Media Election* (New York: Praeger, 1980), pp. 67–69.

27. James S. Fishkin, "Reforming the Invisible Primary: Thoughts on Presidential Selection and Media Coverage" (paper delivered at Mass Media and the Electoral Process conference, Princeton University, Princeton, N.J., April 30–May 1, 1992), p. 4.

28. Fishkin, "Reforming the Invisible Primary," p. 9.

29. Ibid., pp. 9–10.

30. Barbara Kellerman, "Introversion in the Oval Office," *Presidential Studies Quarterly* 18 (1983): 397.

31. See, for example, James L. Gibson, Cornelius P. Cotter, John F. Bibby, and Robert J. Huckshorn, "Assessing Party Organizational Strength," *American Journal of Political Science* 27 (1983): 200.

32. See, for example, Martin P. Wattenberg, *The Decline of American Political Parties* (Cambridge, Mass.: Harvard University Press, 1984).

33. Richard Moran and E. J. Dionne, Jr., "Majority of Voters Say Parties Have Lost Touch," Washington *Post*, July 8, 1992, p. A1.

34. Eldersveld, *Political Parties in American Society*, p. 417.

35. Michael J. Robinson, "Media Coverage in the Primary Campaign of 1976," in *The Party Symbol*, ed. William Crotty (San Francisco: W. J. Freeman, 1980), p. 187.

36. Ibid.

37. Arthur H. Miller, Edie N. Goldenberg, and Lutz Erbring, "Type-Set Politics: Impact of Newspapers on Public Confidence," *American Political Science Review* 73 (1979): 67–84.

38. E. E. Schattschneider, *Party Government* (New York: Holt, Rinehart and Winston, 1943), p. 60.

39. U.S. Senate Letter, Office of Senator Robert Packwood, Washington, D.C., February 1, 1991.

40. Gerald L. Baliles, letter to author, August 11, 1992.

41. Thomas E. Patterson, "Television and Presidential Politics," in *Presidential Selection*, ed. Alexander Heard and Michael Nelson (Durham, N.C.: Duke University Press, 1987), pp. 302–29.

42. John Ellis, *Nine Sundays: A Proposal for Better Presidential Campaign Coverage*," Joan Shorenstein Barone Center on the Press, Politics and Public Policy paper, John F. Kennedy School of Government, Harvard University (Cambridge, Mass., 1991).

43. Jay G. Blumler, Michael Gurevitch, and Julian Ives, "The Challenge of Election Broadcasting" (unpublished paper prepared for BBC, July 25, 1977), p. 10.

44. Taylor, *See How They Run*, pp. 267-83.

45. See *Campaign Lessons for 1992*, Joan Shorenstein Barone Center on the Press, Politics and Public Policy paper, John F. Kennedy School of Government, Harvard University (Cambridge, Mass., 1991), pp. 132–45.

46. James Bryce, *The American Commonwealth* (New York: Macmillan, 1893), p. 78.

BIBLIOGRAPHY

Abramson, Paul R. *Change and Continuity in the 1988 Elections.* Rev. ed. Congressional Quarterly Press, 1991.

———, John H. Aldrich, and David W. Rohde. *Chance and Continuity in the 1984 Elections.* Rev. ed. Congressional Quarterly Press, 1987.

Adatto, Kiku. *Sound Bite Democracy: Network Evening News Presidential Campaign Coverage, 1968 and 1988.* Joan Shorenstein Barone Center on the Press, Politics and Public Policy, Research Paper R-2, John F. Kennedy School of Government, Harvard University, Cambridge, Mass., June 1990.

Aldrich, John H. *Before the Convention: Strategies and Choices in Presidential Nomination Campaigns.* University of Chicago Press, 1980.

Altheide, David L. *Creating Reality: How TV News Distorts Events.* Sage, 1976.

———, and Robert P. Snow. *Media Logic.* Sage, 1979.

Ansolabehere, Stephen, Roy Behr, and Shanto Iyengar. *The Media Game: American Politics in the Television Age.* Macmillan, 1992.

Arterton, Christopher. *Media Politics: The News Strategies of Presidential Campaigns.* D. C. Heath, 1985.

Bagdikian, Ben H. *The Media Monopoly.* Beacon Press, 1983.

Barber, James David. *The Presidential Character: Predicting Performance in the White House.* Rev. ed. Prentice-Hall, 1977.

———. *The Pulse of Politics.* Norton, 1980.

———, ed. *Race for the Presidency: The Media and the Nominating Process.* Prentice-Hall, 1978.

Bartels, Larry M. *Presidential Primaries and the Dynamics of Public Choice.* Princeton University Press, 1988.

Bennett, W. Lance. *News: The Politics of Illusion.* 2nd ed. Longman, 1988.

Berelson, Bernard, Paul Lazarsfeld, and William McPhee. *Voting: A Study of Opinion Formation in a Presidential Campaign.* University of Chicago Press, 1954.

Black, Christine M., and Thomas Oliphant. *All by Myself: The Unmaking of a Presidential Campaign.* Globe Pequot, 1989.

Blume, Keith. *The Presidential Election Show: Campaign '84 and Beyond on the Nightly News.* Bergin and Garvey, 1985.

Blumler, Jay G., and Denis McQuail. *Television in Politics.* University of Chicago Press, 1969.

Broder, David S. *Behind the Front Page.* Simon and Schuster, 1987.

———. *The Party's Over: The Failure of Politics in America.* Harper Magazine Press, 1972.

Brody, Richard. *Assessing the President: The Media, Elite Opinion, and Public Support.* Stanford University Press, 1991.

Buchanan, Bruce. *Electing a President: The Markle Commission Report on Campaign '88.* University of Texas Press, 1991.

Campbell, Angus, Philip E. Converse, Warren E. Miller, and Donald E. Stokes. *The American Voter.* Wiley, 1960.

Ceaser, James W. *Reforming the Reforms.* Ballinger, 1982.

Chester, Lewis, Godfrey Hodgson, and Bruce Page. *An American Melodrama: The Presidential Campaign of 1968.* Dell, 1969.

Cohen, Bernard. *The Press, the Public and Foreign Policy.* Princeton University Press, 1963.

Commission on Party Structure and Delegate Selection. *Mandate for Reform.* Democratic National Committee, 1970.

Cook, Timothy. *Making Laws and Making News: Media Strategies in the U.S. House of Representatives.* Brookings Institution, 1989.

Crotty, William, and John S. Jackson III. *Presidential Primaries and Nominations.* American Enterprise Institute, 1977.

Crouse, Timothy. *The Boys on the Bus: Riding with the Campaign Press Corps.* Ballantine, 1974.

Davis, James W. *Presidential Primaries: Road to the White House.* Greenwood Press, 1980.

Diamond, Edwin, and Stephen Bates. *The Spot: The Rise of Political Advertising on Television.* MIT Press, 1988.

Dionne, E. J., Jr. *Why Americans Hate Politics.* Simon and Schuster, 1991.

Duncan, Dayton. *Grass Roots: One Year in the Life of the New Hampshire Presidential Primary.* Viking, 1991.

Edelman, Murray. *Constructing the Political Spectacle.* University of Chicago Press, 1988.

———. *The Symbolic Uses of Politics.* University of Illinois Press, 1974.

Edsall, Thomas Byrne, and Mary D. Edsall. *Chain Reaction: The Impact of Race, Rights, and Taxes on American Politics.* Norton, 1991.

Efron, Edith. *The News Twisters*. Nash, 1971.

Ehrenhalt, Alan. *The United States of Ambition*. Times Books, 1991.

Eldersveld, Samuel J. *Political Parties in American Society*. Basic Books, 1982.

Entman, Robert M. *Democracy without Citizens: Media and the Decay of American Politics*. Oxford University Press, 1989.

Epstein, Edward Jay. *News from Nowhere: Television and the News*. Random House, 1973.

Fishel, Jeff. *Presidents and Promises*. Congressional Quarterly Press, 1985.

Fowler, Linda L., and Robert D. McClure. *Political Ambition: Who Decides to Run for Congress*. Yale University Press, 1989.

Gans, Herbert J. *Deciding What's News: A Study of CBS Evening News, NBC Nightly News, Newsweek and Time*. Vintage, 1980.

Geer, John Gray. *Nominating Presidents: An Evaluation of Voters and Primaries*. Greenwood Press, 1989.

Germond, Jack. *Whose Broad Stripes and Bright Stars? The Trivial Pursuit of the Presidency, 1988*. Warner, 1989.

———, and Jules Witcover. *Blue Smoke and Mirrors: How Reagan Won and Why Carter Lost the Election of 1980*. Viking, 1981.

———, and Jules Witcover. *Wake Us When It's Over: Presidential Politics of 1984*. Macmillan, 1985.

Gitlin, Todd. *The Whole World Is Watching: Mass Media in the Making and Unmaking of the New Left*. University of California Press, 1980.

Goldenberg, Edie N., and Michael W. Traugott. *Campaigning for Congress*. Congressional Quarterly Press, 1984.

Graber, Doris S. *Processing the News: How People Tame the Information Tide*. Longman, 1984.

Greenfield, Jeff. *The Real Campaign: How the Media Missed the Story of the 1980 Campaign*. Summit, 1982.

Grossman, Michael B., and Martha J. Kumar. *Portraying the President: The White House and the News Media*. Johns Hopkins University Press, 1981.

Hallin, Daniel. *Sound Bite News: Television Coverage of Elections, 1968–1988*. Media Studies Project Occasional Paper, Woodrow Wilson International Center for Scholars, 1990.

———. *The Uncensored War: The Media and Vietnam*. University of California Press, 1987.

Hart, Roderick. *The Sound of Leadership: Presidential Communication in the Modern Age.* University of Chicago Press, 1987.

Heard, Alexander. *Made in America: Improving the Nomination and Election of Presidents.* HarperCollins, 1991.

———, and Michael Nelson, eds. *Presidential Selection.* Duke University Press, 1987.

Hess, Stephen. *The Presidential Campaign.* Rev. ed. Brookings Institution, 1978.

Hofstetter, C. Richard. *Bias in the News.* Ohio State University Press, 1976.

Horowitz, Donald L. *The Courts and Social Policy.* Brookings Institution, 1977.

Iyengar, Shanto. *Is Anyone Responsible? How Television Frames Political Issues.* University of Chicago Press, 1991.

———, and Donald Kinder. *News that Matters: Television and American Opinion.* University of Chicago Press, 1987.

Jamieson, Kathleen Hall. *Dirty Politics: Deception, Distraction, Democracy.* Oxford University Press, 1992.

———. *Packaging the Presidency: A History and Criticism of Presidential Campaign Advertising.* Oxford University Press, 1992.

———. *Presidential Debates: The Challenge of Creating an Informed Electorate.* Oxford University Press, 1988.

———, and Karlyn Kohrs Campbell. *The Interplay of Influence.* 2nd ed. Wadsworth, 1988.

Keech, William R., and Donald R. Matthews. *The Party's Choice.* Brookings Institution, 1976.

Keeter, Scott, and Cliff Zukin. *Uninformed Choice.* Praeger, 1984.

Kelley, Stanley, Jr. *Interpreting Elections.* Princeton University Press, 1983.

Kern, Montague. *Thirty-Second Politics: Political Advertising in the Eighties.* Praeger, 1989.

Kernell, Samuel. *Going Public: New Strategies of Presidential Leadership.* Congressional Quarterly Press, 1986.

Kessel, John H. *Presidential Campaign Politics: Coalition Strategies and Citizen Response.* Dorsey Press, 1988.

Key, V. O. *The Responsible Electorate: Rationality in Presidential Voting, 1936–1960.* Belknap Press, 1966.

Kirkpatrick, Jeane J., Michael J. Malbin, Thomas E. Mann, Howard R. Penniman, and Austin Ranney. *The Presidential Nominating*

Process: Can It Be Improved? American Enterprise Institute, 1980.

Kraus, Sidney. *Televised Presidential Debates and Public Policy*. Lawrence Erlbaum, 1988.

————, ed. *The Great Debates*. University of Indiana Press, 1962.

————, ed. *The Great Debates: Carter v. Ford, 1976*. Pennsylvania State University Press, 1979.

Krukones, Michael G. *Promises and Performance: Presidential Campaigns as Policy Predictors*. University Press of America, 1984.

Ladd, Everett Carll. *Where Have All the Voters Gone?* Norton, 1978.

Lang, Kurt, and Gladys Engel Lang. *Politics and Television*. Quadrangle, 1968.

Lanoue, David J. *The Joint Press Conference: The History, Impact, and Prospects of American Presidential Debates*. Greenwood Press, 1991.

Lavrakas, Paul J., and Jack K. Holley. *Polling and Presidential Election Coverage*. Sage, 1991.

Lazarsfeld, Paul, Bernard Berelson, and Hazel Gaudet. *The People's Choice*. Duell, Sloan, and Pearce, 1944. Reprint. Columbia University Press, 1968.

Lengle, James I. *Representation and Presidential Primaries: The Democratic Party in the Post-Reform Era*. Greenwood Press, 1981.

Lichtenberg, Judith, ed. *Democracy and the Mass Media*. Cambridge University Press, 1990.

Lichter, S. Robert. *The Video Campaign: Network Coverage of the 1988 Primaries*. American Enterprise Institute for Public Policy Research, 1988.

————, Stanley Rothman, and Linda S. Lichter. *The Media Elite*. Adler and Adler, 1986.

Lippmann, Walter. *Public Opinion*. 1922. Reprint. Free Press, 1965.

Luntz, Frank I. *Candidates, Parties, and Campaigns: Electoral Policies in America*. 2nd. ed. Congressional Quarterly Press, 1989.

Manheim, Jarol. *All the People, All the Time*. M. E. Sharper, 1991.

McCubbins, Mathew D., with John H. Aldrich, F. Christopher Arterton, Samuel L. Popkin, and Larry J. Sabato. *Under the Watchful Eye: Managing Presidential Campaigns in the Television Age*. Congressional Quarterly Press, 1992.

McGinniss, Joe. *The Selling of the President*. Trident Press, 1969.

McLuhan, Marshall. *Understanding Media*. McGraw-Hill, 1964.

Meyer, Phillip. *Precision Journalism*. University of Indiana Press, 1973.

Mickelson, Sig. *The Electric Mirror: Politics in an Age of Network Television.* Dodd, Mead, 1972.

Minow, Newton N. *For Great Debates: A New Plan for Future Presidential Television Debates.* Priority Press, 1987.

Navazio, Robert. "An Experimental Approach to Bandwagon Research." *Public Opinion Quarterly* 41 (1977): 217–25.

Nelson, Michael, ed. *The Elections of 1984.* Congressional Quarterly Press, 1985.

——. *The Elections of 1988.* Congressional Quarterly Press, 1989.

——. *The Elections of 1992.* Congressional Quarterly Press, 1993.

Neuman, W. Russell. *The Paradox of Mass Politics: Knowledge and Opinion in the American Electorate.* Harvard University Press, 1986.

Nie, Norman, Sidney Verba and John Petrocik. *The Changing American Voter.* Enl. ed. Harvard University Press, 1979.

Nimmo, Dan, and James E. Combs. *Mediated Political Realities.* Longman, 1983.

——, and Robert Savage. *Candidates and Their Images.* Goodyear, 1976.

Orren, Gary, and Nelson Polsby, eds. *Media and Momentum: The New Hampshire Primary and Nomination Politics.* Chatham House, 1987.

Owen, Diana Marie. *Media Messages in American Presidential Elections.* Greenwood Press, 1991.

Page, Benjamin. *Choices and Echoes in Presidential Elections.* University of Chicago Press, 1978.

Paletz, David L., and Robert M. Entman. *Media Power Politics.* Free Press, 1981.

Patterson, Thomas E. *The American Democracy.* McGraw-Hill, 1993.

——. *The Mass Media Election: How Americans Choose Their President.* Praeger, 1980.

——, and Robert D. McClure. *The Unseeing Eye: The Myth of Television Power in National Elections.* Putnam, 1976.

Polsby, Nelson W. *The Consequences of Party Reform.* Oxford University Press, 1983.

Pomper, Gerald, ed. *The Election of 1980: Reports and Interpretations.* Chatham House, 1981.

——, ed. *The Election of 1984: Reports and Interpretations.* Chatham House, 1985.

——, ed. *The Election of 1988: Reports and Interpretations.* Chatham House, 1988.

————, with Susan Lederman. *Elections in America*. Longman, 1980.

Popkin, Samuel. *The Reasoning Voter: Communication and Persuasion in Presidential Campaigns*. University of Chicago Press, 1991.

Ranney, Austin. *Channels of Power: The Impact of Television on American Politics*. Basic Books, 1983.

————. *Participation in American Presidential Nominations, 1976*. American Enterprise Institute, 1977.

Reinsch, J. Leonard. *Getting Elected: From Radio and Roosevelt to Television and Reagan*. Hippocrene, 1988.

Reiter, Howard. *Selecting the President*. University of Pennsylvania Press, 1985.

Robinson, Michael, and Margaret Sheehan. *Over the Wire and on TV*. Russell Sage Foundation, 1983.

Rubin, Richard. *Press, Party, and President*. Norton, 1980.

Runkel, David R. *Campaign for President: The Managers Look at '88*. Auburn House, 1989.

Sabato, Larry. *Feeding Frenzy: How Attack Journalism Has Transformed American Politics*. Free Press, 1991.

————. *The Rise of Political Consultants*. Basic Books, 1981.

Sanford, Terry. *A Danger of Democracy*. Westview Press, 1981.

Schattschneider, E. E. *Party Government*. Holt, Rinehart and Winston, 1942.

————. *The Semisovereign People: A Realist's View of Democracy in America*. Holt, Rinehart and Winston, 1960.

Schudson, Michael. *Discovering the News*. Basic Books, 1978.

Semetko, Holli, Jay G. Blumler, Michael Gurevitch, and David H. Weaver, with Steve Barkin and G. Cleveland Wilhoit. *The Formation of Campaign Agendas*. Lawrence Erlbaum, 1991.

Seymour-Ure, Colin. *The Political Impact of Mass Media*. Sage, 1974.

Shaw, Donald, and Maxwell McCombs. *The Emergence of American Political Issues: The Agenda-Setting Function of the Press*. West Publications, 1977.

Sigal, Leon V. *Reporters and Officials: The Organization and Politics of Newsmaking*. D. C. Heath, 1973.

Simon, Roger. *Road Show: In America, Anyone Can Become President. It's One of the Risks We Take*. Farrar, Straus and Giroux, 1990.

Sorauf, Frank. *Money in American Elections*. Little, Brown, 1988.

Stempel, Guido H., III, and John W. Windhauser, eds. *The Media in the 1984 and 1988 Presidential Campaigns*. Greenwood Press, 1991.

Swerdlow, Joel L. *Beyond Debate: A Paper on Televised Presidential Debates.* Twentieth Century Fund, 1984.

Taylor, Paul. *See How They Run: Electing the President in an Age of Mediacracy.* Knopf, 1990.

Thompson, Hunter S. *Fear and Loathing on the Campaign Trail '72.* Popular Library, 1973.

Troy, Gil. *See How They Ran.* Free Press, 1991.

Tuchman, Gaye. *Making News: A Study in the Construction of Reality.* Free Press, 1978.

Tulis, Jeffrey. *The Rhetorical Presidency.* Princeton University Press, 1987.

Wattenberg, Martin P. *The Decline of American Political Parties.* Harvard University Press, 1984.

———. *The Rise of Candidate-Centered Politics.* Harvard University Press, 1991.

White, Theodore. *America in Search of Itself: The Making of the President: 1956–1980.* Harper and Row, 1982.

———. *The Making of the President, 1960.* Atheneum, 1961.

———. *The Making of the President, 1964.* Atheneum, 1965.

———. *The Making of the President, 1968.* Atheneum, 1969.

———. *The Making of the President, 1972.* Atheneum, 1973.

Witcover, Jules. *Marathon: The Pursuit of the Presidency, 1972–1976.* New American Library, 1978.

Zaller, John. *The Origins and Nature of Mass Opinion.* Cambridge University Press, 1992.

INDEX

Ford, Gerald (*cont.*)
  in 1976 campaign, 56–7, 59,
    109, 138, 147, 149, 156, 176,
    178, 181, 189
  and press need for controversy,
    138
Fortune magazine, 33
Frank, Barney, 46
Frank, Reuven, 80
Friedman, Milton, 158
Friedman, Paul, 65
"frontrunner" candidates, 117,
    121–3, 124–5, 186, 220
Fulbright, J. William, 19

Gallup polls, 116
game schema, 57–65
  candidates as actors in, 58
  controversy in, 136–41
  dominance of, 66–9
  1980 example, 85–7
  oversimplification in, 87–8
  in primaries, 91–2, 183–4
  voters as audience in, 58, 89–90
  as weapon, 79–80
General Dynamics Corporation,
    78
Gephardt, Richard, 47, 216
Germond, Jack, 150
Gladstone, William, 38
Glenn, John, 40, 138
Goldberg, Bernard, 124
Goldenberg, Edie, 227
Goldwater, Barry, 22, 87, 120–1,
    124n, 177, 178
Gore, Al, 47, 49, 189
governing schema, 59, 60
Graber, Doris, 57, 90–1, 104, 187

"Great Communicator" (Reagan),
    98–9 and *n*
"Great Mentioner" (press), 35
Greenfield, Jeff, 125
Greenfield, Meg, 25
Gruenwald, Mandy, 166

Hagstrom, Jerry, 143
Hall, Arsenio, 170
Hallin, Dan, 77n, 159, 204
halo effect, 187
Hamilton, Alexander, 26, 38, 50,
    220
Hamilton, Bill, 171
Hannon, Tom, 78, 166
Harkin, Tom, 64, 165, 167, 187
Harris, Fred, 41
Hart, Gary
  in 1984 primaries, 40, 138, 139,
    188, 189
  and character issue, 196
  and Donna Rice, 154, 155, 166,
    195
  as "frontrunner" candidate, 186
  and Mondale's "Where's the
    beef?" comment, 40, 139
  withdraws from 1988 race, 156
Hattori, James, 65
health care issue, 64
Heard, Alexander, 198
Heclo, Hugh, 97
Hofferbert, Richard, 12
Hoffman, David, 27
Hofstetter, C. Richard, 7, 104, 115
Horowitz, Donald, 51–2
horse races, campaigns as, 62, 78,
    97, 168
  see also game schema

A NOTE ABOUT THE AUTHOR

Thomas Patterson is professor of political science at the Maxwell School of Citizenship and Public Affairs, Syracuse University. He has written extensively on the media's role in elections. His previous books include *The Unseeing Eye: The Myth of Television Power in National Elections; The Mass Media Election: How Americans Choose Their President;* and *The American Democracy.* In 1991–92 he was Lombard Visiting Professor of Press and Politics at Harvard University's John F. Kennedy School of Government. He has received grants for his work from the National Science Foundation, the Markle Foundation, the Mellon Foundation, and the Ford Foundation.

A NOTE ON THE TYPE

This book was set in Janson. The hot-metal version of Janson was a recutting made direct from type cast from matrices long thought to have been made by the Dutchman Anton Janson, who was a practicing type founder in Leipzig during the years 1668–1687. However, it has been conclusively demonstrated that these types are actually the work of Nicholas Kis (1650–1702), a Hungarian, who most probably learned his trade from the master Dutch type founder Dirk Voskens. The type is an excellent example of the influential and sturdy Dutch types that prevailed in England up to the time William Caslon (1692–1766) developed his own incomparable designs from them.

Composed by Dix Type, Syracuse, New York
Printed and bound by Haddon Craftsmen,
Scranton, Pennsylvania
Designed by Peter A. Andersen